Quicken® In Business

Steve Adams

Brady
New York London Toronto Sydney Tokyo Singapore

Brady

Simon & Schuster
15 Columbus Circle
New York, NY 10023

Distributed by Prentice Hall Trade

Manufactured in the United States of America

2 3 4 5 6 7 8 9 10

Library of Congress Cataloging-in-Publication Data

Adams, Steve, 1948-
Quicken in business / Steve Adams
p. cm.
1. Quicken (Computer program) 2. Small business--Finance--Data processing. 3. Accounting--Data processing. 4. Finance, Personal -Data processing. I. Title.
HG4027.7.A336 1989
658.15'028'55369--dc20 89-23969

ISBN 0-13-165440-3

Limits of Liability and Disclaimer of Warranty

Trademarks

Contents

For Dixie O'Connor

Thanks!

Introduction

Quicken is a fast, easy to use, inexpensive financial program that can help you manage your personal finances or small business without the fuss of a full-fledged accounting program. Even large companies use Quicken to manage petty cash.

As this was being written, Quicken had leapt to the top of the software charts, and it was getting rave reviews from national computer magazines. "Once in a great while, a software package comes along that lives up to its name," said *PC Computing*. "Happily, that's the case with Quicken. Much the same can be said about Intuit, the company that makes Quicken, because the program is...intuitive."

That is exactly what Scott Cook, Intuit's president, and Tom Proulx, vice president for engineering, had in mind when they formed the company in 1983 and created Quicken 1, the predecessor of the program you have now. Quicken 3 for IBM and compatible computers adds the sophistication to manage all of your personal or small business finances. More than half of Quicken's users, in fact, are small businesses. Quicken is the third-best-selling program in the world behind Lotus 1-2-3 and WordPerfect, and it outsells the competition in the financial software market by five-to-one, according to Intuit's founders.

Quicken efficiently allows you to write and record checks in a single step. It's a snap—simply a matter of filling out an onscreen display that looks just like your Quicken checks. The program even writes out the amount of the check automatically when you enter the amount numerically. To make check writing even easier, Quicken can "memorize" individual frequent transactions and groups of transactions that occur on a regular basis, like your monthly bills or a small business payroll. It even reminds you when to pay bills, so your money can earn interest as long as possible. And you can, of course, record checks you write by hand, deposits, and other transactions.

In short, Quicken functions very much like your paper check register, and it does your record keeping automatically. Reconciliation features make it easy to spot any discrepancies between your Quicken records and your bank or credit card statements. When you make an error, you can easily find and correct it.

However, Quicken is much more than an electronic check register. It not only keeps track of your bank account balance, but also allows you to assign each transaction to an Income or Expense category so you can keep track of where your money is going. The program's flexible reporting capability allows you to print detailed reports to assist you in your personal or business financial planning and tax preparation.

Above all, Quicken is easy to use. If you already keep a check register, you already understand how Quicken works; it requires no knowledge of double-entry bookkeeping. Cook and Proulx recently took the time to explain how they developed the program.

Cook: We have principles in the company that we hold dear, that every employee tries to follow at every juncture. One is intuitive design, to make our software obvious. Another is that our job is to steadfastly eliminate time and hassle. Another principle is customer service, and that's why we give free telephone support.

I programmed computers as a kid back in the '60s, and I have always been interested in how you could apply computers, this wonderful technology, to help millions of people instead of just making something that guys in white coats know how to use. My wife and I used to talk about that when we'd drive to her house. She grew up in Wisconsin, and we'd drive up there and bounce our views back and forth about how could you use computers to help people? One of the things that got me started to thinking about financial work was her complaining about how much time it took. I said, "Wait a minute, this is something computers could do really well. It's numbers and data, which is what computers are great at. It's also recurring work. Computers are great when they can automatically do recurring things." It was her complaining about how long the process took that got us started.

Proulx: Scott and I got together in March of 1983, and Quicken 1 shipped in October of 1984. We really targeted Version 1 to be a home product. That was our whole focus in the product itself, the packaging, the documentation, and the advertising. But the main focus of Quicken has never wavered.

We did a lot of research with households to find out what do they do with their finances. There were four things that people do, and they do them fairly frequently. They write checks, because they've got to pay bills, and maintain a check register because they've got to keep track of how much money they have. Occasionally they will reconcile their checkbook with their bank account. The fourth thing they do is that they want to track spending to some to degree. And that's about it. There are a lot of other things you can do with your finances. You can graph them and do budgets and so on, but we found that people by and large don't do those things.

The other thing we learned was that the attitude people had towards their finances was dislike. If we could invent a product that would completely eliminate the need to do anything with your finances, we'd sell a ton, but there's no way to do that. People have got to pay bills, so Quicken is the next best thing. We found that people hate doing this, and what they want is to save time, just like with any other household chore.

Cook: We asked ourselves, "Is there a problem that people who do financial work have that we can solve?" It turned out that, sure enough, there is a problem, and the problem is, "Do you like paying bills?" Of course not, and neither does anybody you know. The problem is that people hate doing this work; its a chore. Our goal, the mission for our company and our product, is to automate and provide insight into the financial work that everyone has to do. We want to eliminate the chore. We want to take a whole class of work and make it disappear.

We design things for our users, and that is really the theme throughout our company. They go out and apostletize their friends. We're not a big, well-funded corporation. We're a bootstrap operation of a bunch of guys who had a dream. Even before there was a program, there was a dream that Tom and I had that the broadest potential use of a computer should be in financial work, because its the only computerizable task that every household in America must do, and that every small business has to do, every month.

Proulx: (Quicken 3 is) a bigger program, but if you've seenVersion 2, you'll see a lot of similarities between the two. A lot of the code can be used from the existing program, so it didn't have to be rewritten from scratch. That took about a year, maybe a little more.

Quicken Version 3 was really just improving the product even more. We found that Quicken 2 was great for handling checkbooks, but that people wanted to get more of the total financial picture. They wanted to get credit cards in there, and Quicken 2 didn't specifically provide for credit cards. We also greatly improved the way reports work. Version 2 had a lot of same the reports, but it was a lot more complicated. Basically, Quicken 3's reports are more powerful and more flexible. Plus, we've added all of the preset reports. Most people don't have to understand all of the things on the report. They can just pick one from the list, and they get what they want.

Another thing people really wanted was transferring money between accounts. In Quicken 2, you had to load another account to show the other side of the transfer, and people wanted be able do that in one step. They wanted also to be able to get a report on all of their accounts, not just one at a time.

Cook: Three things: First, it's even easier. It works all kinds of accounts, such as credit cards, cash, assets, and liabilities. To do categorization, you had to learn about the @ sign (the old method of categorizing Quicken transactions). It used to be that to do a report, you had to fill out a report request; now you can pick most of the common reports right off a list. Also, the help index wasn't there before. Second, it's even faster. Our beta (prerelease) users called it a thousand percent faster. It's been much more effectively automated. The reports are faster as well. Finally, the class system (of classifying transactions) much improved its reporting power for businesses, so the program will handle much larger businesses.

(Quicken 3) shipped June 21 (1989). Its first availability in stores was the first of July. (Sales) are tremendous. One chain reported sales have more than doubled since the new version came out.

Proulx: (Other products) are competitors in the sense that people go into a software store looking for a piece of financial software—sometimes they'll come out with one of those products instead of Quicken—but they're really different in what they're trying to do. In a perfect world, a customer would walk in a store and say, "I want a piece financial software. What do you recommend?" and the salesman would say, "Do you want save time doing basic things you've got to do with your finances, or do you not care about saving time?" Some people don't mind spending time on their finances. We call them financial hobbyists.

There are really two different market segments. Managing Your Money does not save you time. Quicken does. Managing Your Money actually takes you longer than doing (your finances) by hand. When we started doing research in the early days, there were 42 products on the market. We specifically tested those products with people who were experts at using them. We actually timed how long it took people to do their routine monthly finances, writing x number of checks, reconciling their checkbook, and stuff like that. We found those three products took 22 to 39 percent longer than doing the same tasks by hand, because they were not designed to save time.

Cook: The difference between Quicken and all the others is that Quicken was designed from the ground up to eliminate hassle, and that's what it does. It slashes the time it takes to do your finances dramatically; the others don't. Dollars and Sense and Managing Your Money are slower than doing the same work by hand. We did our research in advance, and we found out that the single thing most people and most small businesses want far more than anything else is to eliminate the time and hassle it takes.

There are dozens of ways Quicken saves time. It memorizes recurring transactions, so you don't have to write out the same transactions month after month. Another way is learning time. (Other products) redefine keystrokes on every screen. We don't; we have the same keystrokes throughout. Another difference is that Quicken keeps all of your data on line, ready to use, at all times. Other products archive their data. We have automatic check alignment, and they don't.

Proulx: We had a single-minded focus on saving time. The other products were focused on doing a lot of more esoteric things, and they threw in check writing and some other things to make it complete. There were a lot of keystrokes you have to go through with those products you don't have to do with Quicken. For that segment of the market, (other products) are O.K. They're for people who are not looking to save time. These people don't mind tinkering with their finances. They enjoy it; they like accounting for every penny. Of course, you can do that with Quicken, but you don't have to. It really operates like your checkbook.

Cook: Quicken today is the third-best-selling applications software in the world, behind Lotus 1-2-3 and WordPerfect. What made us succeed was our single-minded focus on eliminating time and hassle from the financial work everybody has to do. Now we outsell (the competition) five-to-one, so you ask yourself why a little pipsqueak company with no big investors went from last place to outselling the established software five-to-one. The answer is that we save time and hassle and they don't.

Proulx: We've always been very research-oriented. After the first six months or so we did a survey of our users to find out how they were using Quicken and how they liked it. To our surprise, in spite of all of our efforts to target this product on the home, half of our customers were using Quicken for their small businesses. We shouldn't have been surprised, because the way small businesses do their books is not much different from the way you or I do our personal books. They get a bill in the mail, and they pay it. They don't know about accounting or double-entry ledgers or debits and credits, and they don't need to. That's why they have an accountant, and once a quarter or once a year, they take their check register and all of these receipts they've been keeping—probably in a shoe box—to the accountant, and he does some magic with it and gives them reports and helps them do their taxes.

Once we learned that, we realized as we designed Quicken 2 that we needed to pay a little more attention to the needs of small businesses. We learned about that from the calls and letters we were getting from customers saying, "I love the product. I use it for my small business, but it would really be great if it would do thus and such."

Cook: It boggles the mind how many different kinds of businesses (use Quicken). There's really not a trend: doctors, dentists, lawyers, accountants, consultants, real estate property managers, designers, artists and art firms, real estate agents. Branch offices of growing corporations use Quicken for petty cash and travel expenses. Each has a checking account, and this turns out be the perfect tool.

Proulx: We have a lot of real estate investment companies, little corner delis, and everything up to the Hawaii Department of Welfare. At one time, they had two people on IBM ATs, 40 hours a week, doing nothing but cutting checks with Quicken. We haven't heard from them in a while. They've probably got that on the mainframe now. (For small businesses) instead of a shoebox full of receipts, they're getting nice, organized reports, and they can spend their time on other activities. Most of them use Quicken for their bookkeeping, and then they have an accountant, who deals with the accounting stuff.

Cook: Even when a mainframe computer does the main accounting and the main checking account at headquarters, it turns out that checking accounts are one of the most ubiquitous features of American financial life everywhere. A corporation will have hundreds of checking accounts; the largest of those, the main payroll and the main payables account, will be on a mainframe. But they'll also have hundreds of other accounts in their branch offices, because sometimes it takes a week to get a check out of the mainframe, and the branch offices can't wait a week.

Proulx: I don't do a lot of actual hands-on programming these days, although I still have heavy involvement in the design of the products. When I get involved in a program, it's just all-consuming. Basically, on Quicken 2 that's what we did. It took us about five or six months from start to finish. We were working like crazy. There was about a six-week stretch towards the end when Eric Dunn and I were averaging about 120 hours a week. We never went home except to change clothes. We felt it was critical to the company's success that we ship the product in time for the 1987 Christmas season, which meant September, so we were willing, basically, to do or die, and we made it.

We will always spend a lot of time doing our homework up front to understand exactly what our customers need, and we're going to deliver a product that exactly suits their needs. Our giant competitor has been doing finances by hand. We've got to make sure Quicken is easier and faster.

Cook: We're going to make sure that Quicken stays the fastest, easiest way to do finances in the world.

1

Setting Up Quicken 3

It takes only a few minutes to get Quicken ready to run on your computer. If you have a hard disk, you will install the program on your computer. If you have floppy drives, you will make a working copy of the program disk and a data disk. Quicken's built-in Install program makes this task simple.

Unlike most programs, Quicken automatically adapts itself to most computers and printers. However, you may need to set up the program for your printer if you have a laser printer or a serial printer. Quicken's printer set-up feature also allows you to take advantage of advanced features of many popular printers, such as near-letter-quality type (especially useful for printing checks) and compressed type (for printing wide reports). With most printers, you need not adjust printer settings now; you can always do it later, as the need arises.

Hardware and Software Requirements

Quicken 3 is substantially expanded from Quicken 2. This means that the program now requires more internal memory (RAM) and disk storage capacity than earlier versions. To use Quicken 3, you need the following:

- Your Quicken program package. It should include two versions of the program—one on a 3.5-inch disk and another on two 5.25-inch disks.
- IBM PC/XT, PC AT, PS/2, or 100% compatible computer.
- At least 320K internal memory (RAM).
- At least one disk drive. Two floppy drives or a hard disk are highly recommended.
- A monochrome or color 80-column monitor.
- DOS 2.0 or higher.
- Two blank disks (3.5-inch or 5.25-inch) or a hard disk.
- Almost any printer. (Required only for printing checks and reports.) Thermal printers will not print Quicken checks, but they are fine for printing reports.
- Quicken checks (necessary only for printing checks).

INSTALLING QUICKEN

Quicken's built-in Install program recognizes what kind of disk drives you have and most types of monitors. Simple instructions on the screen lead you through the installation procedure. If you have a hard disk, the installation procedure will not damage any previously recorded Quicken data, even if you have used Quicken 3 before.

To get ready to install Quicken on a hard disk, all you have to do is to turn on your computer. The DOS C> prompt should be displayed. (If you have a menu program such as Microsoft Windows, see that program's manual for instructions on how to include Quicken in your menu of programs.)

To install Quicken on a two-floppy-drive system, you will need two blank, formatted disks. One will be your working copy of the Quicken program disk, the other your data disk.

You can install DOS on one of these two disks. This will allow you to start your computer with one of your Quicken disks, rather than your DOS disk. Alternatively, you can format both disks without DOS and use your DOS disk to start your computer. (If you have only one floppy drive and do not have a hard disk, read Using Quicken with a Single Drive, below, before continuing.)

With 3.5 -inch or 5.25-inch high-density disks, you can put DOS on your working copy of the Quicken program disk. With 360K 5.25-inch disks, there will not be enough room for DOS on your program disk; in fact, some Quicken program files will be copied onto your data disk. However, you can install DOS on your data disk and use that to start your computer. This will somewhat reduce the space available for storing information, but in most cases that will not be a problem.

To format disks with a two-drive computer, place your DOS disk in drive A and a blank disk in drive B. To format a disk without DOS, at the A> prompt type:

```
format b:
```

and press Enter. To format a bootable disk, with DOS, type:

```
format b:/s.
```

In either case, the on-screen prompts will lead you through the rest of the procedure.

Installation is simple and almost automatic, but the procedure varies slightly depending on the type of disks your computer uses. On-screen prompts will guide you through the variations.

To install Quicken, start your computer. (Place your DOS disk in drive A if you have a floppy drive system.) Then place the Quicken Help Disk (or the Program Disk if you use 3.5-inch disks) in drive A and type:

```
a:install
```

When you start the Install program, a window explaining the installation procedure appears (Figure 1.1). The second and third paragraphs are fairly technical. The information here may be useful to experienced computer users, but you can safely ignore anything unfamiliar.

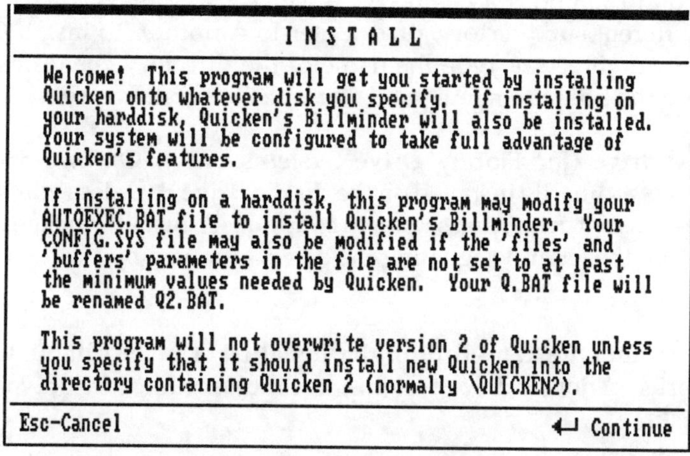

Figure 1.1. Beginning the installation procedure.

Instructions on the screen explain the rest of the procedure. They will provide all of the information you need. During installation—and in some cases the first time you use Quicken—you may see questions or messages about your system. These may include the following.

Do you have a color monitor? When you see this message, type 1 for Yes or 2 for No.

Quicken is being set up for a fast monitor: Some monitors can change displays faster than others. If you see this message, there is nothing you can do about it immediately. Press Enter to continue. However, if you see "snow" or if your screen breaks up when Quicken changes displays, you can later call up the Change Settings Menu to change the setting from fast to slow. Do this after you have completed installation.

Today's date: If you see this message, type the current date using this format: mm/dd/yy. June 10, 1989, for example, should be entered as 6/10/89. You can also adjust the date by pressing the + and - keys. The date will be adjusted one day forward or backward with each keystroke, or continuously if you hold the key down.

Specify drive/directory (for Hard Disk Systems only): Ordinarily, Quicken is installed in a subdirectory named C:\QUICKEN3. Unless you have a reason to use a different subdirectory, press Enter to continue. To install Quicken in a different subdirectory, type the name of the directory, then press Enter. You must use the full path name in this format: C:\subdirectory.

Specify drive (for Floppy Drive Systems only): On two-drive systems, Quicken is ordinarily installed on the disk in drive B. Unless you have a reason to use a different drive, press Enter to continue. To install Quicken on a different drive, type the letter designating the drive, followed by a colon (:), then press Enter.

Do you want Quicken's Billminder installed (Y/N?): Although Billminder also works on floppy drive systems, this message appears only if you have a hard disk.

To use Billminder, you will record bills as checks dated the day you intend to pay. You will never notice Billminder unless you record bills as postdated checks. If you enter Y(es) or press Enter to install Billminder on your hard disk, Quicken will remind you of bills that are almost due whenever you turn on your computer, even if you do not use Quicken during your current session. If you type: N(o) to bypass Billminder installation or if you have floppy drives, you will still see a reminder of due bills whenever you use Quicken, but not when you turn on your computer.

Your selection here does not limit your options. If you install Billminder but do not record bills as postdated checks, you will never notice Billminder. In addition, if you later decide not to use this feature, you can deactivate Billminder through the Change Settings Menu. If you decide not to install Billminder now, you can always do so later by running the Install program again. None of your records will be affected.

> **NOTE:** When you install Billminder, Quicken adds a line to your AUTOEXEC.BAT file, which tells your computer what to do when you turn it on. At the same time, your old AUTOEXEC.BAT file is renamed AUTOEXEC.B00. To restore the old file, use the DOS COPY command to copy AUTOEXEC.B00 to AUTOEXEC.BAT.

After you complete installation and begin using Quicken, you will not see most of these messages again. There is one exception: If your computer is not equipped with a calendar/clock, Quicken may ask you for the date when you load the program. It is important to enter the current date when you see this message, because the program will assume that it is correct. Quicken automatically enters the current date when you begin recording transactions. In addition, Quicken reports usually exclude transactions after today's date, and the program's Billminder feature uses the same date to determine when to remind you of bills that are due.

Using Quicken with a Single Drive

Quicken will run quite well on a single 3.5-inch or high-density 5.25-inch drive; there will be enough room on your program disk to store your Quicken records. You can also run the program on a single 360K drive, but some disk swapping is required.

To get ready, format disks as described above. If you have a 3.5- inch or a high-density drive, you will need only one formatted disk, labeled "Quicken." You can maximize storage space for your Quicken records by electing not to install DOS on this disk. If you have a standard, 360K drive, you will need two formatted disks. Label one "Quicken Program"; during installation, this will be Target Disk 1. Label the other "Quicken Data"; this will be Target Disk 2.

To begin installation, boot up DOS. The A> prompt should be displayed. From this point forward, installation is exactly the same as for a two-drive system, except that the program will prompt you to switch disks more often. The only caution is that you must be careful to insert the correct disks when prompted—especially with a 360K drive, which requires you to juggle four disks.

Starting to Use Quicken

Once you have completed installation, running Quicken is very simple. If you have a hard disk, type q at the DOS prompt (C:\ on most computers with hard disks). On a computer with floppy disks, put the working copy of your Quicken program in drive A and your data disk in drive B, then type q at the A> prompt. (If you have only one drive, put the working copy of the program disk in drive A. The program will prompt you when to remove it and insert your data disk.)

The first time you use Quicken, several questions or messages may appear on the screen. In most cases, you will not see these messages again. If your computer does not have a built-in clock/calendar, however, you may be asked for the date each time you start the program.

After you have answered these questions, the Main Menu (Figure 1.2) appears. This is the starting point for all Quicken activities. You must set up at least one Quicken account before you can use most of the options on the Main Menu. Getting started is explained in the next chapter.

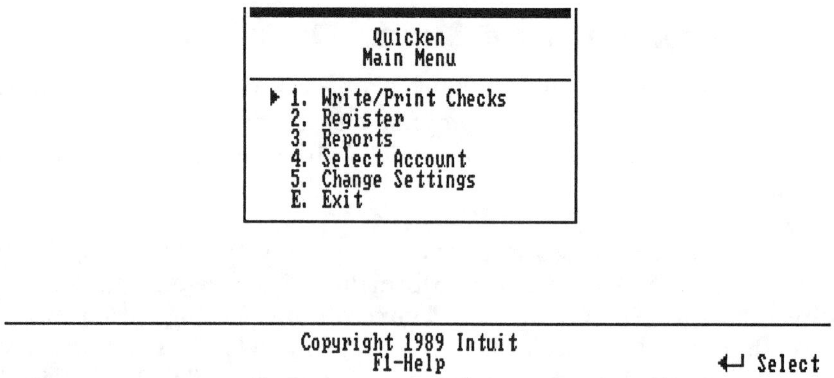

Figure 1.2. The Main Menu.

Customizing Quicken

Quicken automatically adapts to most computers and monitors. In addition, Quicken—out of the box—will run most parallel printers in their standard modes (typically 10-pitch "draft quality" for dot matrix printers). Nevertheless, you may want to adapt Quicken to your computer system, your printer, or personal needs. The Change Settings Menu (option 5 on the Main Menu) allows you to:

- Set screen colors.
- Set monitor speed (necessary only if "snow" appears when Quicken changes displays).
- Set up printers.
- Set up a password to protect your Quicken records.
- Customize certain aspects of the way Quicken works (Other Settings).

In most cases, you will not want to change any of these settings until you understand how Quicken works. However, you may want to set up Quicken for your printer now if you have a serial printer or use any printer port other than the standard parallel port (LPT1:).

The Printer Settings option (4 on the Change Settings Menu) allows you to set up as many as three different printers, or to set up one printer to operate in three different modes. You might, for example, want to print checks in near letter quality print, some reports in draft print, and some reports in compressed print.

Quicken offers predefined printer setups for the following printers: IBM compatibles, HP LaserJet I, HP LaserJet II, HP DeskJet, HP ThinkJet, IBM ProPrinter, IBM 4216, Epson, NEC 3530, NEC 8023A, Okidata (models 83, 92, 182, 192, 292, and 320), Panasonic laser, and Star. (In most cases, the program offers a choice between printing 10 characters per inch and 17 CPI.) Even if your printer is not listed, the Printer Settings option allows you to send control codes to your printer (you'll have to look them up in your printer manual) to govern the way it prints.

In addition, the Printer Settings option allows you to set these items for any printer: printer port, indentation, lines per page, characters per line, and pause between pages.

You can change printer settings—or any other options on the Change Settings Menu—at any time. Even if you want to set up Quicken for your printer, you will not need to do so until you have begun recording transactions. If you want to change settings now, refer to Chapter 13, Housekeeping.

Ordering Checks and Other Supplies

Your Quicken program comes with a catalogue, an order form for Quicken checks and other Intuit products, and sample Quicken checks. Once you have begun using Quicken, you can print another order form by selecting the Order Supplies option (3) from Quicken's Activities pull-down menu (F6). (This option won't be available until you set up at least one Quicken Account.) For more information, call Intuit at 1-800-624-8742 between 8:30 A.M. and 4:30 P.M. Pacific Time.

You can use Quicken without printing checks, but Quicken's ability to print checks and record transactions in a single step is one of the program's best time-saving features. All banks accept Quicken checks. You will probably want to continue using your regular bank checks for writing checks by hand.

Quicken checks come in three styles: regular checks, without stubs, pocket checks, with stubs to the left, and voucher checks, with detachable vouchers below each check. All three types are available in two-part forms, for carbonless copies (dot matrix and daisywheel printers only). For an additional fee, you can include your company logo on your checks. A black-and-white, camera-ready copy of your logo is required.

Checks come on continuous forms, for printers with tractor drives, or on 8-inch by 11-inch sheets, for laser printers and other printers with sheet feeders. In sheet form, regular and pocket checks come three to a page; voucher checks come one to a page.

All Quicken checks fit Intuit's window envelopes. Your return address will be printed at the top left, and the addresses on your Quicken checks will show through the window.

Intuit also offers "Check Savers," which feed your Quicken checks into printers that can't print the first check. You can use each Check Saver up to 50 times.

A final offering is the Quicken Transfer Utility. This inexpensive program transfers Quicken files to Lotus 1-2-3 and compatible programs. This allows you to create reports you can't produce with Quicken and to combine data from separate Account Groups (about which you will learn more in the next chapter). To use the Transfer Utility, you need Lotus 1-2-3 (Version 1A or higher), Lotus Symphony (Version 1.0 or higher), or compatible programs (Quattro, SuperCalc4, SuperCalc5, PFS Professional Plan, PFS First Choice Version 2 or 3, or VP Planner).

Conclusion

At this point, you should have installed Quicken on your hard disk or made working copies and reached the Main Menu. The next chapter gives an overview of the way Quicken works and explains the Main Menu. Succeeding chapters get down to the nuts and bolts of using Quicken to manage your business or personal finances.

2

Understanding Quicken

Place First Class
Postage Here
Post Office
Will Not Deliver
Without Postage

Brady Books
15 Columbus Circle
New York, NY 10023

ATT: J. Padlad

This chapter provides a brief survey of Quicken 3. You may want to set up a trial account to take the tour. (You will not have access to most of Quicken's features until you have set up at least one account.) The next chapter explains how to begin using Quicken and how to organize your business or personal finances.

Quicken 3 is simple yet very flexible. You can use the program just to print checks and maintain your checking account balance, to manage your personal finances, or to set up a full-fledged accounting system for a small business. You can use only the program's most basic features or stretch its limits. The choice is yours.

Quicken Features

With Quicken 3, you can keep track of Bank accounts, Cash accounts, Other Asset accounts, Credit Card accounts, and Other Liability accounts. This system allows you to manage all of your transactions, regardless of how they are executed. You can even include changes in your financial situation that do not involve cash, such as depreciation and increases or decreases in the value of your investments.

Quicken 3 provides a sophisticated system of sorting transactions so you can retrieve exactly the information you want with Quicken reports. You can use Quicken's preset Personal and Business Reports or define your own Custom Reports. Regardless of which you use, you can select exactly the information you want to include. These reports will give you a clear picture of where you've been, where you're going, and, perhaps most importantly, summarize income and expenses at tax time.

Quicken can also help you manage your cash flow. To maximize the interest earned on cash on hand you may want, as the saying goes, "to collect early and pay late." You record bills as postdated transactions when they arrive; the program's Billminder feature automatically reminds you when bills are due. Then, you can print checks for due bills with a few keystrokes. Similarly, you can record invoices and track aged receivables. Together, these features help you to maximize cash on hand.

Finally, Quicken 3's pop-up calculator allows you to make calculations on the screen—and insert the results directly into your Quicken records. In short, Quicken 3 is a powerful tool for printing checks, organizing your personal finances, and managing your business.

Quicken 3 versus Quicken 2

Quicken 3 is a significant advance over earlier versions of the program. If you've used Quicken 2, you'll recognize most of the new version's features for streamlining check writing and Bank account management. While retaining—or improving—most of the older version's features, however, Quicken 3 includes some important changes. Among the most significant are:

- Five types of accounts, mentioned earlier, compared with only one (Bank accounts) in the older version.

- Reports that summarize transactions from any or all of your accounts; Quicken 2 reports were limited to a single account.

- Preset personal and business reports, plus more flexibility in designating precisely what information to include in reports. (Quicken 2 users will find Quicken 3's reports generally familiar but considerably more sophisticated.)

- Automatic transfers from one account to another, with transfers included in Quicken reports.

- Improved methods of classifying income and expenses, along with the capability of flagging tax-related income and expenses.

- A pop-up calculator that can transfer results directly into your Quicken transactions.

Users of earlier versions and new users alike will find the basic features of Quicken 3 easy to learn and to use. From there, you can go on to the more elaborate uses described in the later chapters of this book.

How Quicken Organizes Information

Quicken organizes your financial records in several ways so that your Quicken reports can provide precisely the information you need to run your business, manage your personal finances, or prepare your taxes. If you want, you can record every quarter you spend for a newspaper. However, Quicken does not require you to record information you don't need.

Recording a transaction with Quicken is as easy as writing a check or recording a bank deposit in your paper check register. In fact, the simple procedure of writing a Quicken check with your computer automatically adds the transaction to your Quicken records. Most transactions are simple income or expenses, but a transaction can be anything that affects your financial picture. Examples include checks, credit card purchases, cash purchases, cash receipts, paycheck deposits, increases or decreases in the value of real estate or investments, new loans, and items payable or receivable.

The beauty of Quicken is that it will do *exactly* what you want. There is no need to record information that you won't need later, but you will use the program more effectively if you plan how you will use it in advance.

When you first use Quicken, the program automatically sets up an *account group* called QDATA. Initially at least, this group will include all of your Quicken accounts. An account group may consist of a single Bank account for writing checks and managing your checking account, or it can include any combination of Bank accounts, Cash accounts, Other Asset accounts, Credit Card accounts, and Other Liability accounts.

Quicken Bank accounts and Credit Card accounts correspond with your actual accounts at your bank, brokerage accounts at your securities dealer, and credit card accounts. Cash accounts are for recording cash transactions. They are ideal, for example, for keeping track of petty cash. Other Asset accounts and Other Liability accounts are a little different. You can use them, for example, to keep track of equity in real estate, the tax basis of your home, depreciable assets, outstanding principal on mortgages and other loans, or accounts receivable.

If you want to keep completely separate sets of records for different purposes, you can set up additional account groups. For example, you might want to set up separate account groups for personal and business records or for two or more businesses that operate independently. Bear in mind, however, that Quicken reports cannot gather information from more than one account group.

CLASSIFYING TRANSACTIONS

Quicken does much more than record the transactions in each account. Within each account group, you can classify transactions in two ways: by *Income* or *Expense Category* and by *Class*.

Income and expense categories are the equivalent of the income and expense accounts in an accountant's chart of accounts or the income and expense categories of your home budget. Examples might include Salary, Clothes, Groceries, Rent, Office Supplies, and so forth. Appropriate categories can be flagged as tax-related. If you already have a business accounting system or home budget, you can transfer the categories you already use to Quicken.

Quicken's classes offer an additional way to categorize transactions, and they work hand-in-hand with Quicken categories to classify income and expenses by purpose. You might, for example, use classes to distinguish similar business and personal expenses, to classify real estate investments by property, or to prepare reports sorted by client, vendor, or job.

When you record a transaction, the category and the class are separated by a slash (/). If you own rental properties on Elm and Spruce streets, for example, you might set up an expense category called Repairs and classes called Elm and Spruce. You would assign fix-up expenses to Repairs/Elm and Repairs/Spruce. By recording your rental income and expenses in this way, you can create reports showing your overall rental income expenses and reports that break down income and expenses by property.

If you need further refinement for your record keeping, you can group categories and classes into *subcategories* and *subclasses*. For example, you could set up a category for utilities with subcategories for electricity, gas, water, and telephone. Your Quicken reports would then include a total for utilities, plus subtotals for the subcategories.

Obviously, Quicken can accommodate quite an elaborate system of Accounts, Categories, Subcategories, Classes, and Subclasses. If your record keeping needs are relatively simple, however, one or two Accounts and a handful of Categories may be all you need. When in doubt, opt for simplicity. You can always add layers of complexity later.

Setting Up a First Quicken Account

Once you have made a working copy of Quicken or installed the program on your hard disk, you are ready to begin using the program. To run Quicken, type q at the DOS prompt (A> for floppy drives, C> for most hard disks). The Main Menu appears (see Figure 2.1).

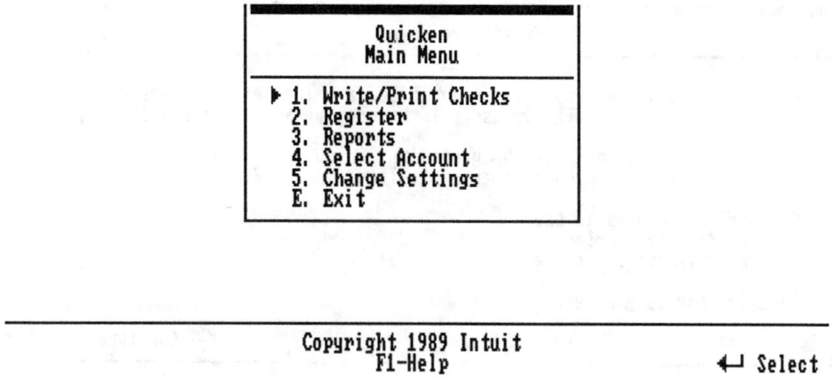

Figure 2.1. The Main Menu.

There are two ways to select an option on the Main Menu (or any Quicken menu):

- Use the up and down arrow keys to highlight an option and press Enter, or
- Type the number corresponding to the option you want to select.

Before you can explore Quicken you must set up set up at least one Quicken account. You may want to set up a practice account for now; you can easily delete it later.To set up your account:

1. Press 1 to choose Write/Print Checks from the Main Menu. (Actually, any of the first four options on the menu will do.) The First Time Setup window appears (Figure 2.2).

   NOTE: The First Time Setup window is a one-time opportunity. If you select Preset Categories, you will be able to add or delete categories as you want. Once you have made a selection, however, you will never see this window again unless you reinstall the program. There is no way to add Preset Categories to an existing Account Group. (The Preset Categories are listed in Tables 3.1 and 3.2 in the next chapter). If you want to experiment with Quicken before you actually begin using the program, you can later delete your experimental Account Group and create a new one with one or both of the Preset groups. This is quite easy to do, as explained in the next chapter.

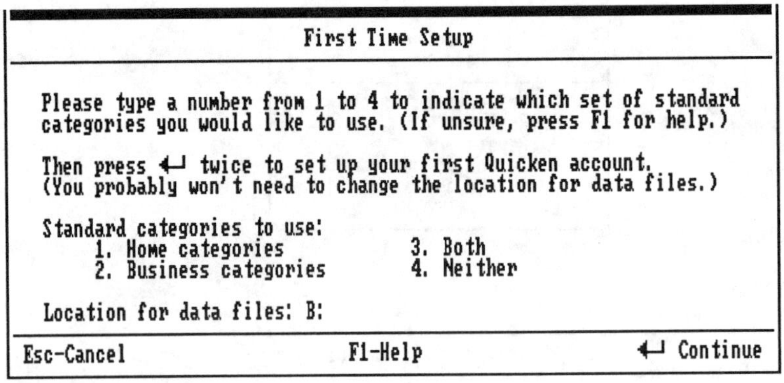

Figure 2.2. The First Time Setup window.

2. Type 1 to select the Preset Home Categories, 2 for Business Categories, 3 for both, or 4 for neither, then press Enter to confirm. The cursor jumps to the next blank on the screen. (To back up and change your preset categories selection, press Shift and Tab simultaneously.)

3. The cursor is now in the blank labeled: Location for data files. In most cases, Quicken automatically enters the correct location, normally drive B for a two-drive system or C:\QUICKEN3 for a hard disk. If you need to change the entry, the location must be in this format: B: (don't forget the colon) for a floppy drive or C:\subdirectory for a hard disk.

   Check your setup selections carefully before you leave the setup screen, then press Enter to confirm the location of your data files.

4. Next a window appears labeled Select Account to Use. After you have set up Quicken accounts, they will be listed on this screen. For now, press Enter to select <New Account>.

5. Fill out the Set Up New Account Window (Figure 2.3), pressing Enter after you complete each entry. The account name can be up to 15 characters. (We've named ours Checking.)

   For the purposes of following along with the next sections, press Enter to accept 1. Bank Account as the account Type. For Balance you can enter the current balance in one of your actual bank accounts. If you need to guess, you can always make a correction later. If you're just experimenting, make up a balance—you have to enter a number here.

   The current date should be displayed in the blank labeled: as of. Press Enter to accept, type over the date, or use the + or - key to advance or roll back the date a day at a time.

   The Description is optional and can be up to 21 characters long. You could enter, for example, the name of your bank or your account number.

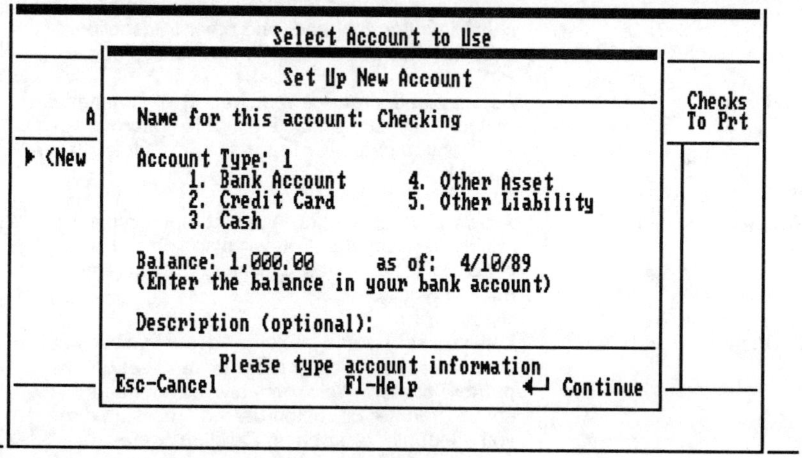

Figure 2.3. Setting Up a First Account.

6. When you complete the New Account window, the Select Account window reappears, with your new Account displayed. To select that Account, press the down arrow once to highlight the Account, then press Enter. A picture of a check appears on the screen. This is called the Write/Print Checks screen, and we'll return to it shortly. For now, however, press Esc to call up the Main Menu.

You're now ready to begin using Quicken, or to follow along with the next few sections to explore some of the program's main features.

Table 2.1 Main Menu Options.

1. Write/Print Checks	Allows you to write and print Quicken checks. This option always appears on the Main Menu, but you can use it only for Bank Accounts. In other types of accounts, all transactions are recorded on the Register.
2. Register	Displays the Register, where you can record deposits, automatic teller machine withdrawals, checks written by hand, and other transactions. You can also edit transactions recorded earlier.
3. Reports	Allows you to create a wide variety of summaries of your Quicken transactions. This feature is very flexible; you can tailor reports to your individual needs.
4. Select Account	Allows you to select an Account for recordingor editing transactions. You will also select this option to set up a new Quicken Account (any of the five types).
5. Change Settings	Lets you set up and back up Account Groups, customize the Quicken program, and set up one or more printers. You probably will not need to set up a printer or customize the program unless you encounter a problem. Quicken comes properly set up for most computers and printers.
6. Exit	Returns you to DOS. (If you have a hard disk, the program automatically takes you back to your root directory, usually designated C:\.)

The Main Menu

The Main Menu (Table 2.1) should now be displayed. It always appears when you begin a new session with Quicken, with the current Quicken account (the last one you used) displayed at the bottom left. The Main Menu is home base for all Quicken activities. You can reach the Main Menu from anywhere within the program by pressing Esc until it appears. The six options on the Main Menu are largely self-explanatory.

Getting Acquainted with Quicken Commands

Quicken uses the same simple keystrokes for certain purposes throughout the program. Once you understand these, you should be able to find your way around the program easily. No matter where you are in Quicken, you can always get help about your current activity by pressing F1. (Figure 2.4 shows the first screen of the help window for the Main Menu.) Use the Page Up and Page Down keys or the Up-Arrow and Down-Arrow keys to scroll through the information. To return to your activity, press Esc.

```
                        The Main Menu

   The Main Menu lists Quicken's main activities.  To
   select an activity from the menu, type its number.

   1. Write/Print Checks
      Select Write/Print Checks to write and print checks.

   2. Register
      Select Register to see the transactions in your
      account.  You can also enter and change transactions
      in the Register; usually these will be transactions
      not involving printed checks, such as handwritten
      checks, deposits, bank fees, electronic transfers,
      credit card charges, and so forth.

 Esc-Cancel              F1-Help Index          ↓,PgDn-More Help

Checking
```

Figure 2.4. The help screen for the Main Menu.

Several other keys function the same way throughout the program. These are shown in Table 2.2.

Table 2.2 Function Keys in Quicken.

Esc	Cancels what you are doing and returns you to the previous activity or screen.
Enter	On data screens, Enter accepts the information in the current blank and moves the cursor to the next. On menus, Enter selects the highlighted option.
Arrow keys	Move the cursor or highlight bar one space in the direction indicated. Used for selecting menu items and editing.
Ctrl —>, Ctrl <—	Move the cursor one word to the left or right, respectively.
Tab	Moves the cursor forward one blank on screens that have several blanks.
Shift-Tab	Moves the cursor backward one blank on screens with several blanks.
Ctrl-Enter	Confirms an entire screen containing several blanks.
F10	Same as Ctrl-Enter.
Ctrl-w	Calls up the Write/Print Checks screen from anywhere within Quicken when you are working with a Bank Account.
Ctrl-r	Calls up the Register for the current account from anywhere within Quicken.
+ and -	Whenever a date is displayed in the current blank, pressing + advances the date by one day, pressing - rolls the date back by a day. If you hold either key down, the days will scroll by continuously.

With these basic tools, you can perform most basic tasks in Quicken without a great deal of instruction. Recording transactions, for example, is just a matter of filling in the blanks.

Quicken Transactions

Most of the time you use Quicken, you will be writing checks and recording other transactions. You can get as fancy as you want, but the basics are very straightforward. Before continuing, you should have set up a Bank account, and the Main Menu should be displayed.

You can record transactions by writing Quicken checks (you can do this only in Bank accounts) or by entering them in the register. Although the Write/Print Checks screen and the Register look different, the procedure is almost the same for both—and quite similar to writing a check by hand or recording a check or deposit on a paper check register. This section provides enough information to get you started; for more details, see Chapter 4, Basic Transactions.

To call up the Write/Print Checks screen (Figure 2.5), select option 1 from the Main Menu or press Ctrl-w. To call up the Register (Figure 2.6), select option 2 or press Ctrl-r. The Registers for different types of Quicken accounts vary a little, but they all work basically the same way.

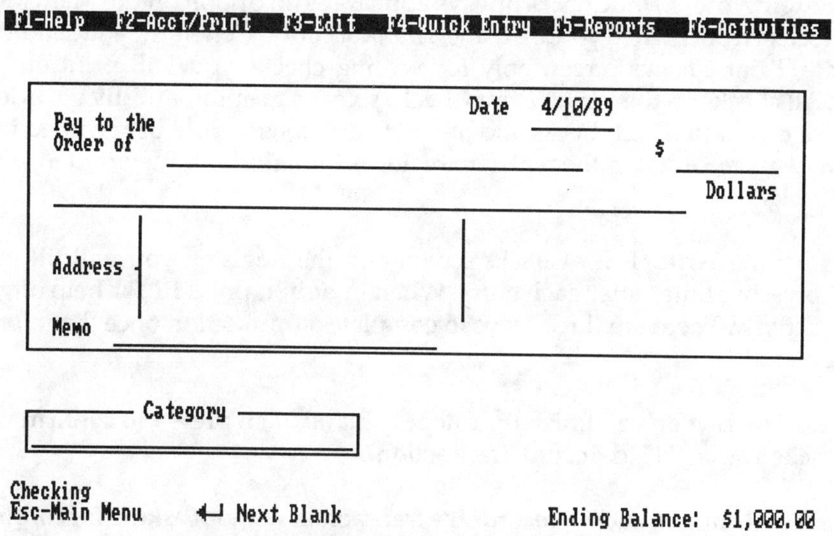

Figure 2.5. The Write/Print Checks screen.

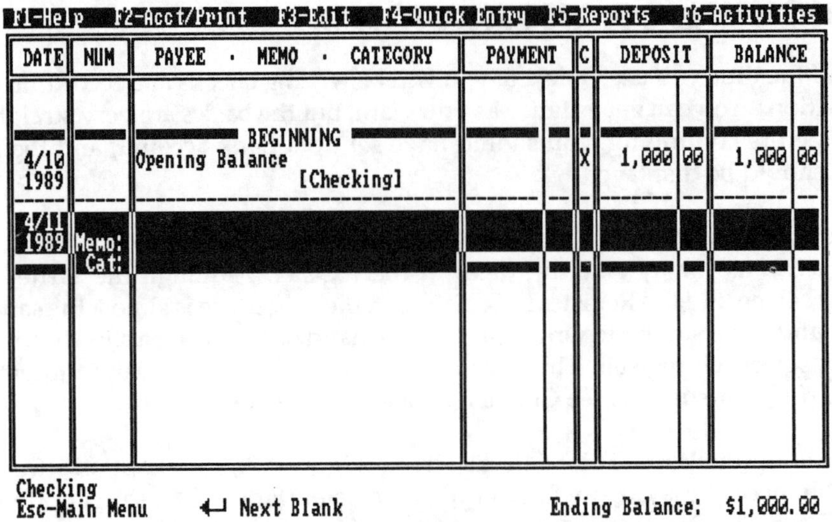

Figure 2.6. The Register for a Bank account.

Although Write/Print Checks always appears as an option on the Main Menu, you can select it only when you are using a Bank account. Generally, you should use the Write/Print Checks screen only for writing checks you will print on your printer. All checks on the Write/Print Checks screen are automatically recorded in the register. Handwritten checks and other transactions should be recorded in the register. Items recorded in the register are not automatically transferred to Write/Print Checks.

On both the Write/Print Checks screen and the Register, you will fill in the blanks, pressing Enter after each entry. When in doubt, press F1 for help on your current activity. There are three ways to complete a transaction once the information is entered:

1. Press Enter when you finish the category blank, then press 1 to confirm when Quicken asks, OK to Record Transaction?
2. Press Ctrl-Enter. Quicken records the transaction without asking for confirmation, even if the information is incomplete.
3. Press F10. This is the same as pressing Ctrl-Enter.

Quicken provides many features to help you record transactions. Quicken automatically enters the current date. To change the date, type over it or use the + or - key to advance or roll back the date a day at a time.

Quicken automatically calculates check numbers when you print checks, so there is no check number blank on the Write/Print Checks screen. For handwritten checks, you can type the check number in the NUM column of the Register.

When you enter a number in the $ blank of the Write/Print Checks screen, Quicken automatically writes out the amount on the next line.

To record a deposit on the Register, press Enter to bypass the PAYMENT column and type the amount under DEPOSIT.

To enter the payee's name as the first line of the address in Write/Print Checks, type a quotation mark (' or ") on the first line of the Address box. Quicken does the typing for you.

In the category blank, categories and classes are entered in this format: Category/Class or Category: Subcategory/Class:Subclass. If you type the name of a new Category or Class, you have the option of adding it to the category list or class list.

The category and class lists provide another way of selecting or setting up categories and classes. To make a selection, position the cursor in the category blank, then call up the appropriate list. (Select either from the Quick Entry pull-down menu, press Ctrl-c to call up the category list, or press Ctrl-l to call up the class list.) Now, use the arrow keys to highlight your selection and press Enter. Quicken automatically enters your choice in the category blank, adding appropriate punctuation. (To set up a new classification, select the first choice on either list (<New Category> or <New Class>), then fill out the setup window that appears next.)

Quicken's Billminder feature will remind you when bills are due. When you receive a bill, postdate a check for the day you want to mail the bill. If you have installed Billminder on a hard disk, Billminder will remind you of bills due soon whenever you turn on your computer. Otherwise, a reminder will appear at the bottom of the Main Menu whenever you begin a session with Quicken. Billminder is set up to remind you three days in advance, but you can change the interval through the Change Settings Menu.

Finally, when you are ready to print Quicken checks, get your printer ready and call up the Write/Print Checks screen in your Bank Account. Then press Ctrl-p or select Print Checks from the Acct/Print pull-down menu and fill out the Print Checks window.

All of these procedures are described in more detail, with specific examples, in Chapter 4, Basic Transactions, and the following chapters. These chapters also describe Quicken's more sophisticated transaction features, such as memorizing entire transactions or groups of transactions for paying your monthly bills.

Many of these advanced features are options on Quicken's pull-down menus, outlined briefly in the next section. For now, however, feel free to experiment. There is nothing you can do that can't be easily undone.

Pull-Down Menus

By now, you have undoubtedly noticed the options listed across the top of the Write/Print Checks screen and the Register. As you already know, you can get on screen help with your current activity by pressing F1.

The remaining five options are Quicken's five pull-down menus, which include dozens of options to help you use Quicken more effectively. With minor variations, the pull-down menus are basically the same for all five types of Quicken Accounts. This section gives a brief overview of the pull-down menus, using the Write Checks screen as a base. Individual options are explained in detail at appropriate places throughout this book.

To examine the pull-down menus, select Write/Print Checks from the Main Menu. Now you can pull down any of the menus by pressing the corresponding function key. When you press F2, for example, the Acct/Print menu appears (Figure 2.7). Once a pull-down menu is displayed, you can use the right and left-arrow keys to select the next menu to the right or left.

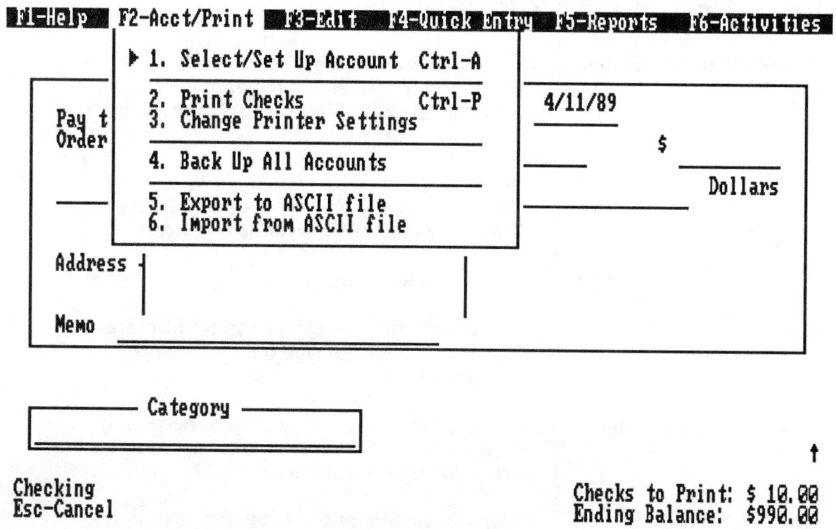

Figure 2.7. The Acct/Print pull-down menu.

As with the Main Menu, you can select an option from a pull-down menu by typing the corresponding number or by highlighting the option with the arrow keys, then pressing Enter. Many options can also be executed—without pulling down a menu—by pressing Ctrl and another key simultaneously. As already noted, for example, you can print checks either by choosing 2. Print Checks from the Acct/Print menu or by pressing Ctrl-p whenever the Write/Print Checks screen is displayed. Whenever a Ctrl command is available, it is indicated to the right of the selection of the pull-down menu. Some of these Ctrl commands will quickly become second nature, and they will save you time on frequently used options. On the other hand, the pull-down menus are always available for commands you use less often.

The next sections give a brief overview of Quicken's pull-down menus. To follow along, display the Write/Print Checks screen. Again, feel free to experiment.

The Acct/Print Menu

You will probably use the Acct/Print menu (F2) most often to switch Quicken accounts and to print checks, but it offers several other features as well.The five selections are shown in Table 2.3.

Table 2.3 Acct/Print Menu Selections.

1.Select/Set Up Account (Ctrl-a)	Displays the Select Account screen, which allows you to switch to a different account or to set up a new one. Identical to Select Account on the Main Menu.
2.Print...(Ctrl-p)	Prints Quicken checks when the Write/Print Checks screen is displayed, or a copy of your Register when the Register is displayed.
3.Change Printer Settings	Allows you to set up three different printers, or to set up one printer to print three different ways. Same as Printer Settings on the Change Settings Menu.
4.Back Up/All Accounts	Backs up the data in your current account group on a separate disk. Do this regularly to avoid the risk of losing valuable records.
5.Export to ASCII File	Stores the information in your Register in an ASCII file, using the Quicken import format.
6.Export to ASCII File	Retrieves data from an ASCII file. (Must be in the Quicken import format.)

The Edit Menu

With the options on the Edit menu (F3), you can record or delete transactions and find previously recorded transactions by date, by payee, etc. In addition, the Split Transaction feature allows you to assign a single transaction to several categories, classes, or purposes. For example, you might assign portions of a single mortgage payment to categories for principal, interest, taxes, and insurance. This allows you to keep records of such separate items even though, of course, you would never write separate checks. As you become familiar with Quicken, you will probably use the Ctrl commands to execute most of these options on the Edit menu.

Table 2.4 Edit Menu Selections.

1. Record Transaction (Ctrl-Enter)	Records the transaction on the current check screen or the highlighted transaction on a Register.
2. Delete Transaction (Ctrl-d)	Deletes the current transaction.
3. Split Transaction (Ctrl-s)	Assigns portions of a transaction to different categories, classes, or descriptions.
4. Find (Ctrl-f)	Finds the next transaction in the Register or in Write/Print Checks that matches specified information, such as payee, memo, or category.
5. Repeat Find (backwards) (Ctrl-b)	Finds the next previous transaction that meets specifications.
6. Repeat Find (next) (Ctrl-n)	Finds the next transaction that meets specifications.
7. Go to Date (Ctrl-g)	Finds a transaction on a given date. (Works both forward and backward.)
8. Go to Transfer (Ctrl-x)	When you make a transfer from one Quicken account to another—from savings to checking, for example—Quicken automatically enters transactions in both accounts. When the current transaction is a transfer, this option takes you automatically to the corresponding transaction in the second account.

THE QUICK ENTRY MENU

Quicken can memorize and recall frequently used transactions, whole groups of transactions (for paying monthly bills, for example), categories, and classes. The Quick Entry menu (F4) is the tool for all of these activities.

Table 2.5 Quick Entry Menu Selections.

1. Recall Transaction (Ctrl-t)	Recalls a previously memorized transaction.
2. Memorize Transaction (Ctrl-m)	Records information from the current transaction for future use.
3. Categorize/Transfer (Ctrl-c)	Calls up the Category List, which allows you to create or recall a category or to select a different account for a transfer.
4. Select/Set Up Class (Ctrl-l)	Calls up the Class List, which allows you to set up or recall a class.
5. Execute Transaction Group	Calls up a previously memorized group of transactions, such as monthly bills.
6. Set Up Transaction Group	Sets up or edits a regularly used group of transactions.

The Reports Menu

The Reports menu (F5) allows you to create any of Quicken's 16 types of reports. This pull-down menu is identical to the Reports selection on the Main Menu. The advantage is that you can bypass the Main Menu and go directly to Reports Menu directly from Write/Print Checks or the Register.

Quicken reports fall into three categories: Preset Personal Reports, Preset Business Reports, and Custom Reports. Custom Reports allow you to arrange or summarize your financial records in almost any way imaginable. The preset reports make certain assumptions about the information people generally need to manage their finances or to run a business. You can also tailor the preset reports to your own situation.

The options on the Reports Menu are shown in Table 2.6.

Table 2.6 Reports Menu Options.

1. Personal Reports	These include Cash Flow, Monthly Budget, itemized categories (groups transactions and subtotals by Category), Tax Summary, and Account Balances.
2. Business Reports	The choices are P&L Statement, Cash Flow, A/P by Vendor, A/R by Customer, Job/Project Report, Payroll Report, and Balance Sheet.
CUSTOM REPORTS:	
3. Transaction	Lists individual transactions, grouped and subtotaled in any of a variety of ways.
4. Summary	Lists subtotals, but not individual transactions.
5. Budget	Compares actual and budgeted income and expenses.
6. Account Balances	Lists balances for all accounts in the account group and calculates net worth. Same as a balance sheet or net worth statement.

You can't actually create any Quicken reports until you have begun entering transactions. Nevertheless, it is important to tailor your records to the types of reports you will need, so it's a good idea to experiment with Quicken reports before you become too committed to your record keeping system to change it. This is discussed in the next chapter, Setting Up a Cash Management System.

The Activities Menu

The Activities pull-down menu always includes five options, but the first two are different for the various types of Quicken accounts. These options are summarized in Table 2.7.

When the register of any account is displayed the first option on the menu is always Write Checks. In a Bank account, this allows you to go directly to the Write/Print Checks screen, bypassing the Main Menu. If you select this option in any other type of account, you will see a message that you must select a Bank account to use Write Checks. You can press Ctrl-w to go directly to Write/Print Checks from any part of the program, even when the Activities Menu is not displayed—when you are working with reports, for example.

When the Write/Print Checks screen is displayed in a bank account, the first menu option is Register, which allows you to go directly to the Register of the Bank account without using the Main Menu. And in any type of account, pressing Ctrl–r takes you directly to the Register from any other part of the program.

Table 2.7 Activities Menu Selections.

Write Checks (Ctrl-w)	Switches you to the Write/Print Checks screen when the Register is displayed in a bank account. In other types of accounts, you will have an opportunity to select a Bank account from the Select Account window. You can use the Ctrl-w command anywhere in Quicken, even when the Activities Menu isn't available.
Register (Ctrl-r)	Switches you from wherever you are to the Register of the current account. You can use the Ctrl-r command even when the Activities menu i sn't listed at the top of the screen.
Reconcile	Allows you to reconcile your Quicken records with your bank statement when using a Bank Account.
Pay Credit Card Bill	Allows you to record a payment and reconcile your records with your monthly statement in a Credit Card account.
Update Account Balance	Allows you to update the current balance in a Cash, Other Asset, or Other Liability account. The rest of the Activities menu options are the same, regardless of where you are in the program when you pull down the menu:
Order Supplies*	Prints a form for ordering checks, envelopes, and other supplies from Intuit, Quicken's publisher.
Calculator (Ctrl-o)*	Activates Quicken's pop-up calculator.
Use DOS*	Allows you to use DOS commands and continue using Quicken without reloading the program. When you have finished using DOS, type **exit** to leave DOS and return to Quicken.

*These options are the same, regardless of where you are in the program when you pull down the menu.

The second option on the Activities Menu also depends on the type of account you are using. In a Bank account, the second option is Reconcile, which allows you to reconcile your Quicken records with your bank statement. In a Credit Card account, the second option is Pay Credit Card Bill. This allows you to reconcile your records with your statement and to print a check automatically. In Cash, Other Asset, and Other Liabilities accounts, option 2 is Update Account Balance. All you have to do when you select it is to enter a new figure, and Quicken automatically records a transaction to bring the balance up to date.

In all types of account types, the remaining three options are the same (options 3 through 5 in Table 2.7). Order Supplies allows you to print a form for ordering checks and other supplies from Intuit; Calculator invokes the pop-up calculator; and Use DOS allows you to go temporarily to DOS without leaving Quicken.

> **NOTE:** If you have a floppy-drive system, the DOS file called COMMAND.COM must be on the disk in drive A when you select Use DOS. If you did not create a bootable copy of Quicken with DOS on it, as explained in the last chapter, insert your DOS disk in drive A before selecting Use DOS from the Activities menu. When you are ready to return to Quicken, replace your program disk in drive A before you type **exit**.

If you did make a bootable copy of Quicken, COMMAND.COM will be on your program diskette, and you can select Use DOS without swapping disks. You will be able to use such DOS commands as COPY and DIRECTORY. However, you must still insert your DOS diskette in drive A to execute certain commands, such as FORMAT and CHKDSK, which are not included in the COMMAND.COM file.

Using the Pop-Up Calculator

With Quicken's pop-up calculator, you can make simple calculations on the screen, then insert the result directly into a blank on the Write/Print Checks screen or on the Register. The calculator is particularly useful when you want to pay several bills or invoices with a single check, but don't need to itemize the particulars. However, the calculator is there, whenever you want to make a calculation, even one that has nothing to do with your Quicken records.

If you intend to transfer the result of a calculation directly into your Quicken records, the cursor should be in the appropriate blank before you call up the calculator. (Typical examples are the $ blank on the Write/Print Checks screen and the Payment or Deposit blanks of the Bank Account Register. However, you can insert the result in any blank where you want a number with two decimal places, e.g., 10.00.)

The calculator is option 4 on the Activities pull-down menu. When the Activities menu option is displayed at the top of the screen, you can call up the calculator by pressing F6 to pull down the menu, then 4 to display the calculator. You can also reach the calculator at any time (when the Main Menu is on the screen, for example) by pressing Ctrl-o. When you have completed your calculation, press Esc to return to where you were in Quicken.

When the calculator appears, Quicken automatically turns on the numeric keypad. Even if you usually use the keypad keys to move the cursor, you can use either the number keys there or the ones at the top of the keyboard to make your calculations.

The calculator works like any simple electronic calculator, with the results displayed on the screen as if they were printed on a paper tape. The +, -, * (multiplication), / (division), c (clear), = (total), and Enter (also total) keys work just as you would expect. The % key might require a little explanation.

To add 2+2, for example, type: **2**, then **+**, then = or Enter.

Figure 2.8 shows this calculation. The other math keys (-, *, and /) work the same way. To perform an additional calculation, press another math key. The result of your first calculation becomes the starting point for the next.

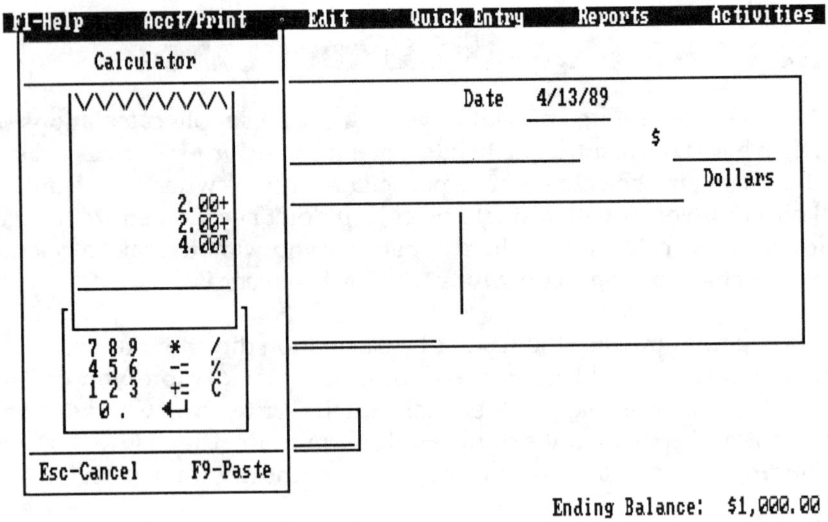

Figure 2.8. A Simple Calculation on the Pop-up Calculator.

The % key is a bit different. It converts an entry to a percentage, allowing you to add, subtract, multiply, or divide by a percentage instead of a number. For example, to compute 10% of 100, type 100*10%, then press = or Enter. The answer, of course, is 10.

To add 10% to 100, type 100+10%, then press = or Enter. The answer is 110. Or, to divide 100 by 10%, type 100/10%, then press = or Enter. The answer is 1,000.

In sum, the calculator will perform nearly all of the calculations you need to take full advantage of Quicken. While it does not include some of the more sophisticated functions found on some electronic calculators, it does offer the advantage of copying the results of your calculations directly into your records.

Conclusion

This chapter provided brief introduction to Quicken's basic features. If your record keeping needs are fairly simple, you can probably begin using the program right away, looking up an occasional bit of information in the manual or this book.

Quicken is easy to use, and your records don't have to be elaborate. Even if your needs are uncomplicated, however, you must use Quicken systematically to manage your personal finances or business. The next chapter explains how to set up a cash management system to help you use the program effectively.

3

Setting Up a Cash Management System

As you begin using Quicken, you should give some thought to exactly what information you will want to retrieve from your Quicken records. You can always modify your Quicken record keeping system as you go along, but effective financial record keeping requires consistency. Simplicity is the essence of Quicken; however, because the program is so flexible it is possible to set up an unnecessarily complicated system—and complexity can be the mother of confusion. Use Quicken to keep the records you need, but when in doubt, opt for simplicity. As Dizzy Dean—or maybe it was Yogi Berra—once said; "If you don't know where you're going, you'll probably end up someplace else."

How do you decide what records to keep with Quicken? You can use the program simply to print checks, to keep track of your checking account, to develop an extremely detailed accounting of your personal finances, or to set up a full-fledged business accounting system.

If your finances are uncomplicated, you may receive statements that provide all of the information you need to file your taxes—a W-2 from your employer and annual summaries from your mortgage lender and credit card companies, for example. You may not need to set up a sophisticated accounting system. Even if you use Quicken only to print checks, the program can save you enough time to be worth the modest investment, particularly if you take advantage of the program's ability to "memorize" frequent transactions and groups of transactions to streamline the process.

However, most Quicken users will want to keep track of at least their tax-related income and expenses. Businesses need to record all income and expenses, and perhaps all assets and liabilities as well. Quicken is easily adaptable to almost any personal record keeping system, and it will serve most small businesses quite well.

If you already have a home budget, Quicken will probably accommodate your current system of categorizing income and expenses quite easily. Similarly, if you already keep records for a business, you can easily adapt Quicken to your current accounting system. In either case, however, you may find that Quicken provides an opportunity to refine your bookkeeping. If you are keeping records for a business, you may want to consult with your accountant before revising your bookkeeping system or setting up a new one.

In the last chapter, you learned how Quicken organizes your financial information into account groups, accounts, categories, and classes. Remember that:

- Account groups are made up of accounts representing actual bank accounts, credit card accounts, cash, other assets, and other liabilities.

- Within account groups, you can assign income and expenses to particular categories, such as Salaries, Sales, Groceries, Clothing, Payroll, and Office Supplies. These categories are the equivalent of the familiar house hold budget accounts or a business's chart of accounts. If you like you can incorporate Quicken's preset Household Accounts (see Table 3.1 on page 60), preset Business Accounts (see Table 3.2 on page 61), or both when you set up an account group.

- Classes, working hand-in-hand with categories, offer a way of recording information about income and expenses, such as client names, accounting periods, or location.

- Quicken reports summarize transactions within an account group by category and/or class, or by several other variables, including payee, date, or a memo that can include any information you want.

These tools allow you to set up anything from a full-blown accounting system to a simple system for monitoring household income and expenses. Again, remember that you will have to keep records on the system you set up, and complexity may not be worth the price. The world is littered with unused personal and small business accounting programs, fallen in disuse because the people who used them set out to do too much.

The Basic Accounting Equation

The basic accounting equation, devised by monks in the Middle Ages, is very simple in principle, but it can become pretty unwieldy in execution. Fortunately, you don't have to understand the details to use Quicken. Nevertheless, it is worth the time to give it some thought as you set up your Quicken system. Quicken incorporates the equation in this form:

Net Worth (or Equity) Assets – Liabilities

This equation is the summation of every transaction you or your business has ever made. It always balances. Assets are cash and property, liabilities are amounts you owe. Income and expenses are the only transactions that change net worth. Transfers among assets and liabilities have no effect, regardless of whether they involve cash or property. To stay within the equation, in other words, you have to account for where everything *comes from*, as well as where it ends up.

This system is precisely accurate, and it is the system large businesses and the IRS use. The system works perfectly well for most individuals and small businesses as long as you are dealing with Bank accounts, Cash accounts, and Credit Card accounts. (Credit card purchases are generally treated as cash transactions in Quicken and by the IRS.)

Some examples will help make the point. When you deposit your paycheck, your bank account balance (an asset) increases.The paycheck is income, and your net worth increases. When you have dinner at a restaurant, you have incurred an expense—it doesn't matter how you pay. Your net worth decreases.

If your business buys a computer for $5,000, on the other hand, it has not technically incurred an expense, because you have paid $5,000 for a physical asset that is worth the same amount. The expense, which is tax deductible, occurs as you depreciate the property. When the computer is fully depreciated, its book value is zero. If you then sell it for, say, $2,000, the IRS will want the taxes on your $2,000 "profit." And in terms of the basic accounting formula, that will be treated as income.

These examples fit the equation without difficulty. Just set up the appropriate accounts and categories and enter the transactions.

However, when you begin dealing with noncash assets in Other Asset accounts and Other Liability accounts, you may have to "trick" Quicken into producing exactly the results you want. When you enter an item in accounts receivable, for example, you have techically generated income, because an asset—the balance in accounts receivable—has increased. If your business operates on a cash accounting basis, however, you do not want to count the income until cash is received.

Noncash assets and liabilities can also create accounting complications at home. If you buy a refrigerator for $700, for example, you probably think of this as a $700 expense, and you can record it as such in Quicken. But if you also want to record the refrigerator in a home inventory, you can't treat the same $700 transaction as both an expense and as a transfer to home inventory, so you have to find a way around the basic accounting equation.

By the same token, if your house appreciates by $15,000 over the course of a year, you will probably want to include the increase in your net worth when you fill out a financial statement for the bank. But you wouldn't want to count the appreciation as income. If you included it in your home budget, it might appear that you're ahead by $3,000 for the year when in fact you've been spending yourself into the hole at a rate of $1,000 a month.

Loans can also pose problems for home accounting. If you borrow $10,000 to buy a car, you have technically traded a liability (the loan) for an asset (the car), and each monthly payment will be part interest (cash expense) and part payment on principal (cash transfer). Meanwhile, the car is depreciating (noncash expense) at an unrelated rate. But you don't want to get into all of that. For home budgeting, you want to treat the car payment as a simple expense and use the bank's figures to calculate your interest payments. When you need a financial statement, you can update the balance of the loan and the value of the car, and you may or may not want either in your Quicken records at all.

All of these situations technically violate the accounting equation, even though they are examples of the way millions of people routinely manage their affairs. Quicken has a solution to many of them.

The solution is a Cash Flow Report, which recognizes inflows and outflows of cash, but not income and expenses as such. For example, a Cash Flow Report will reflect receivables when the money arrives, not when you send the bill. It will never notice appreciation on your house or depreciation on your car, or whether you enter the refrigerator in home inventory. It is indifferent to whether your car payment is an expense or a payment on principal.

But you still may have to juggle a little. For example, if you record receivables on a cash basis and claim depreciation as an expense, there is no simple way to summarize both on the same report. When you take out a loan for a major purchase, a Cash Flow Report may not show it the way you want for budgeting purposes. There are many other examples.

In many cases you can solve the problem by "filtering" your reports to exclude certain information. In others, you can get the results you want by recording transactions in certain—not necessarily obvious—ways. These are explained in various examples throughout this book.

The point is that there is no one "right" way to set up your Quicken records. In most cases you will find Quicken easy and straightforward. But as you begin setting up your Quicken system, particularly if you use Other Asset accounts and Other Liability accounts, you should look ahead to the types of reports you want to create.

This chapter gives a brief overview of Quicken reports, then explains how to set up account groups, accounts, categories, and classes.

Planning Ahead: Quicken Reports

Quicken's reporting capability is so flexible that it is impossible to suggest all of the possibilities here. You can create a report based on any of the information you record in your transactions, including categories, classes, payee, date, amount, or information on the Memo line provided for each transaction.

Quicken reports are flexible enough that you should be able to adapt the program to your situation—rather than vice-versa—but planning ahead can save frustration later. If you keep your Quicken records relatively simple, which is highly recommended, Quicken's reports will probably give you exactly the information you need. For example, you can set up categories that correspond to income and deductions on Form 1040 and Schedule A. (You may not need to worry about classes.) When April 15 rolls around, it will take only a few minutes to print a report that provides all of the information you need to file your taxes.

On the other hand, you can set up Quicken to meet the needs of most businesses that don't require a full-time accountant. In some instances, you will need to record transactions in particular ways in order to take full advantage of Quicken reports. You may want to review chapters on particular topics, such as Accounts Receivable, Accounts Payable, Job/Project Reports, and Payroll before you set up your system.

Pete Seeger once said of Woody Guthrie that any damn fool can get all complicated, but it takes a genius to stay simple. That's the general advice in setting up account groups, accounts, categories, and classes. The following sections provide tips about how your decisions about setting up Quicken will affect your reports. You may still want to review specific applications before you get started in earnest.

Setting Up Account Groups

When you begin using Quicken, the program automatically sets up an account group called QDATA. Within that account group you can set up Quicken accounts and record transactions within each account assigned to various categories and classes.

Many Quicken users will need only one account group; you will be able to retrieve the information you need by judicious use of categories and classes. However, you may want to set up more than one account group if you want to keep separate records for personal and business transactions, or if you keep records for two or more unrelated businesses. Freelance bookkeepers, for example, would set up separate account groups for each business they worked for.

The limiting feature of an account group is that it is the largest classification for which you can create a Quicken report. Within an account group, you can use Quicken reports to segregate your records in almost any way you want. For example, by account, category, and/or class. There is no routine way to integrate records from different account groups or to generate reports that integrate data from different groups. You can, however, transfer transactions from one group to another via the export and import options on the Acct/Print pull-down menu. See the section on Copying from One Account Group to Another in Chapter 13 for details.

The First Time Setup Screen

The First Time Setup screen (Figure 3.1) automatically appears the first time you select one of the first four options on Quicken's Main Menu. This screen is the easiest way to set up your first account group, which will be called QDATA. (You can change the name of the account group later, but you don't have a choice right now.)

NOTE: You can bypass the First Time Setup Screen by selecting 5. Change Settings the first time you use Quicken. Setting up account groups with this option is explained in the next section.

You have only two decisions to make to set up your first account group:

1. Do you want to use Quicken's preset categories listed in Table 3.1? Press 1 to select Home Categories, 2 for Business Categories, 3 for both, or 4 for neither.

2. Where will you keep your data files? Quicken automatically enters B: if you have a dual-floppy computer, or C:\QUICKEN3 if you have installed Quicken on a hard disk. There is usually no reason to change this. Just press Enter to complete the setup procedure. To change the data location, type a new entry, then press Enter to complete the procedure. When entering a new drive or subdirectory, capitalization doesn't matter, but letters designating drives must be followed by a colon (:), and subdirectories must be preceded by a backslash (\).

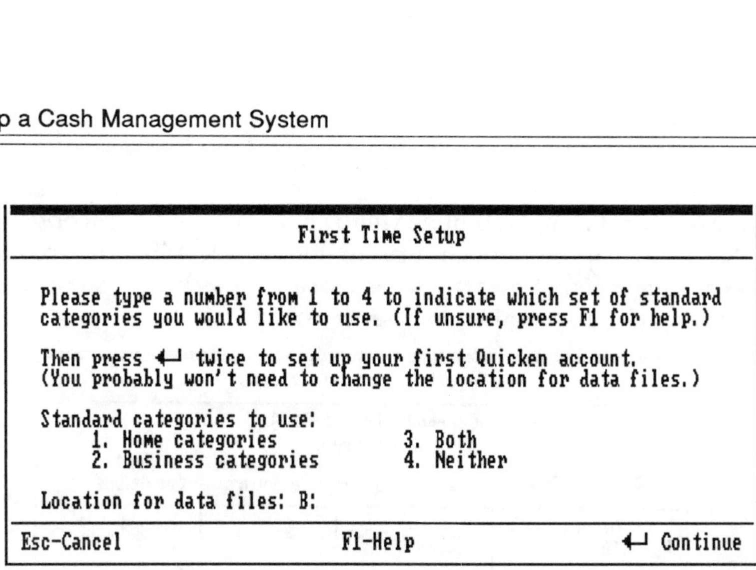

Figure 3.1. The First Time Setup screen.

When you complete First Time Setup, the Select Account window appears, and you are ready to begin setting up your Quicken accounts.

The First Time Setup window appears *only* the first time you use Quicken. You will never see it again unless you reinstall the program. However, the Change Settings Menu allows you to set up new Account Groups or revise old ones. This option requires a few more steps than First Time Setup, but the procedure is basically the same.

Setting Up an Account Group with Change Settings

Change Settings, the fifth selection on the Main Menu, provides a second way of setting up an account group. You can use this option to bypass First Time Setup, to create additional account groups, or to rename or change the location of your original account group (the one called QDATA). In addition, if you set up a trial account group to explore Quicken while you read the last chapter, you can use Change Settings to delete it.

To begin setting up a new account group or revising an old one, press 5 to select Change Settings from the Main Menu. The Change Settings Menu, which appears next, is Quicken's housekeeping department, and you don't have to worry about most of the options at this point. (See Chapter 13, Housekeeping: The Change Settings Menu, for details.) For now, press 1 to select Account Group Activities.

Next, the Account Group Activities Menu appears, with several options. Press 1 to choose Select/Set Up Account Group. Finally, the Select/Set Up Account Group screen appears. Figure 3.2 shows this screen for a floppy-drive system on which the QDATA Account Group has already been created.

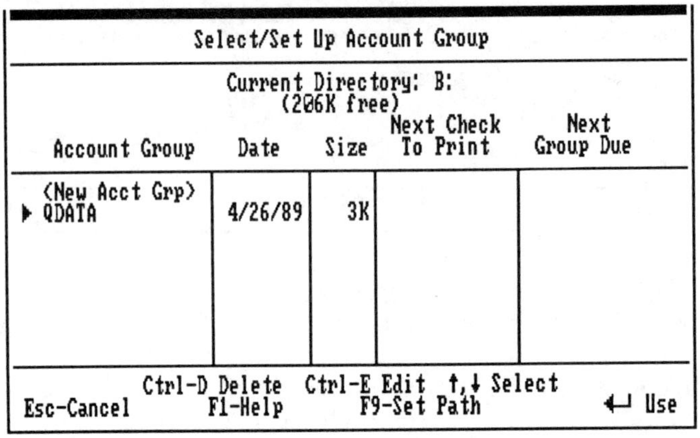

Checking

Figure 3.2. The Select/Set Up Account Group screen.

To create a new account group, select <New Acct Grp> from the Select/Set Up Account Group screen. The next window is labeled Create An Account Group (Figure 3.3). The only difference between it and First Time Setup is that here you must enter a name (up to eight characters) for the group. Again, you can select home categories, business categories, both, or neither.

On the last line of the window, Quicken enters your current data location (usually B: for floppy-drive systems or C:\QUICKEN3 for hard drives). In most cases, you will not need to change this. If you do want to change the location of your data files, remember to include a colon (:) after the drive letter and a backslash (\) before any subdirectory.

Finally, when the Select/Set up Account Group window reappears, select your new group. Now you can begin setting up accounts in your new group on the Select Account to Use window. See Chapter 13 for mfore information about selecting, editing, and deleting account groups.

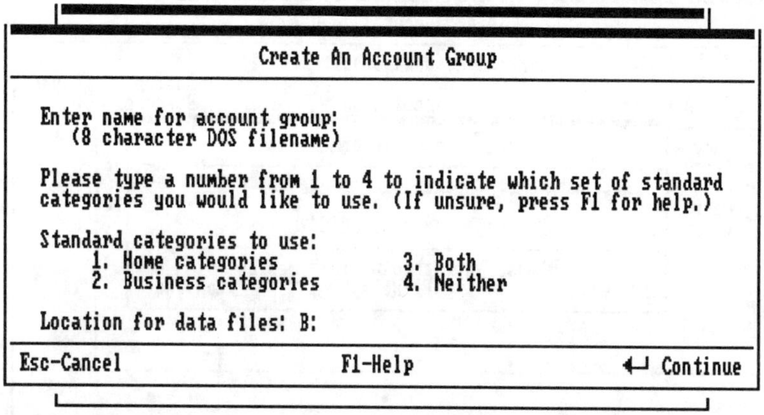

Checking

Figure 3.3. The Create an Account Group window.

If you set up more than one account group, you can also use the Set up/Select Account Group screen to switch between them. To change groups, call up the screen, highlight the group you want to use, then press Enter.

To delete an account, highlight the account on the Select Account screen (do not press Enter), then press Ctrl-d. You will see a window with this message:

```
Caution! permanently removing this account. Are you
sure?
```

To complete the deletion, type yes, then press Enter. You don't have to capitalize, and you don't use quotation marks, but you must type the full word; a y to designate 'yes' is not sufficient. The account and all of the transactions in it will be permanently erased. The Select Account screen reappears.

Editing an account name or description is far less risky; you can always change these items back. To edit an account , highlight the account on the Select Account screen (do not press Enter), then press Ctrl-e. You will see a window labeled Edit Account Information (Figure 3.4) This window also allows you to change the account name and description. In each blank, simply type the new information and press Enter, or press Enter to leave the information unchFigure 3.4. Editing an Account Definition.

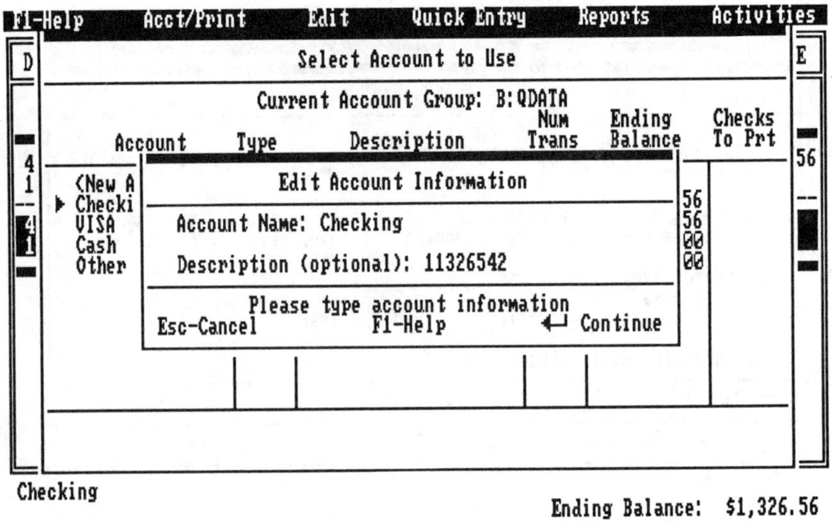

Figure 3.4. Editing an Account Definition

Unless you are editing a Credit Card account, the Select Account screen reappears, with the new account information displayed. For a Credit Card account, you will first see a window that allows you to modify your credit limit. Type the new limit, then press Enter, or press Enter to leave your credit limit unchanged.

Setting Up Accounts

Before you can record transactions, you must set up at least one Quicken account in your account group. Accounts represent actual assets and liabilities. These may be, for example, bank accounts, brokerage accounts, credit card accounts, loans, accounts payable, or accounts receivable. You can also set up accounts for noncash assets, such as real estate, stocks and bonds, or depreciable property. There are five types of Quicken accounts:

Bank accounts represent actual accounts where you keep money, including checking accounts, money market accounts, savings accounts, and brokerage accounts. A Bank account is the only type of account on which you can write Quicken checks.

Cash accounts allow you to keep track of cash transactions for which there is no other record. Most people don't need to record every cash transaction. However, if you regularly do business in cash, you may want to set up a Cash account to record your transactions. Many businesses use Cash accounts to keep track of petty cash.

Credit Card accounts, naturally, are for keeping track of credit card expenses and payments—particularly if you want to keep detailed records of credit card transactions.

Other Asset accounts track noncash assets. Examples might include accounts receivable, stocks and bonds, depreciable assets, real estate, home inventory, the tax basis of your home, or any asset other than cash.

Other Liability accounts can include accounts payable, accrued payroll taxes, outstanding principal on loans, or any other debt obligations.

Together, these five types of accounts allow you to tailor your Quicken records to your specific needs. You can use Quicken just to keep track of a checking account, to record everything that affects your financial situation, or something in between.

Again, keep it simple. If you will use Quicken simply to write checks and to keep straightforward records, you may need only Bank accounts that correspond to your actual accounts. You may not need the Cash or Credit Card accounts unless you want to keep records of individual purchases. (You can record cash withdrawals and credit card payments as miscellaneous expenses and forget them.) Other Asset and Other Liability accounts are more complicated to use and may require more advance planning.

Setting up Accounts in Midyear

As you start out, think about what you want to be the beginning date for your Quicken reports. Ideally, all of your opening balances will fall either on the same day or else on the days when you set up actual accounts at your bank, brokerage house, or elsewhere. Otherwise, your initial Quicken reports will be incomplete—and could be extremely misleading. In other words, you should start your Quicken records at a particular point in time and keep them up to date thereafter.

Suppose, for example, that you set up your first Quicken bank account in May, but don't get around to your credit card accounts—on which you owe several thousand dollars—until July. When you begin consolidating information from both types of accounts in midsummer, it may appear that your finances have taken a nose dive, when nothing of the sort has actually happened. On the other hand, your balance sheet may show an unrealistic rosy upturn if you start recording investment assets six months after you begin recording income and expenses.

If you are keeping books for a business or for filing personal income taxes, Quicken reports will be most useful if you set up accounts at the beginning of the fiscal year—or at least at the beginning of a quarter or month.

This doesn't mean that you have to record every transaction since the beginning of the year or other accounting period. If you have been keeping records by another method, you can use Quicken to record monthly, quarterly, or year-to-date summaries as if they were individual transactions. You will be able to create accurate reports. And if the IRS auditor wants to see you, you can present your old records along with your Quicken records.

Alternatively, you can simply start keeping records now, starting with your most recent statements from banks and other financial institutions; or you can begin with your next statement from each. At the point you are recording all of the information you want to track with Quicken, at least your monthly reports and balance sheets will be accurate.

Bank, Cash, and Credit Card Accounts

The different types of accounts work very similarly—and much as you would expect. Bank accounts, Cash accounts, and Credit Card accounts function exactly like your actual accounts.

When you receive income, for example, you record it as a deposit in a Bank account and assign the amount to an income category. The totals in both the account and the Income category increase. When you assign a purchase to an Expense category, the total for the category increases, but your bank balance decreases. Cash accounts function the same way.

A Credit Card account, on the other hand, works just like an actual credit card statement. When you record a purchase, the balance in the account *increases*, along with the total in an Expense category. When you write a check to pay your bill, the balances *decrease* in both your Bank account and your Credit Card account, but no expense is recorded. In other words, credit card purchases are recorded as expenses when they are made, not when you pay the bill.

Other Asset and Other Liability Accounts

Other Asset and Other Liability accounts are similar to the other types of accounts, but they are specifically designed to help you time your income and expenses correctly and still keep an accurate record of cash flow.

If your affairs are relatively simple—particularly if you are just managing a home budget—you may not need to worry about these accounts at all. If you do plan to use these accounts, however, it is critical that you plan ahead to make sure that you will be able retrieve precisely the information you need from your Quicken records.

The uses for Other Asset and Other Liability accounts are many and various, but they all involve keeping track of assets and liabilities other than cash. You may want to look ahead to specific examples later in this book. Meanwhile, understanding Quicken reports, particularly Cash Flow Reports, is the key to using these accounts correctly. Table 3.2 summarizes the way Quicken reports handle various transactions.

Table 3.2. Cash Flow Reports reflect flows in and out of Quicken's "money" accounts.

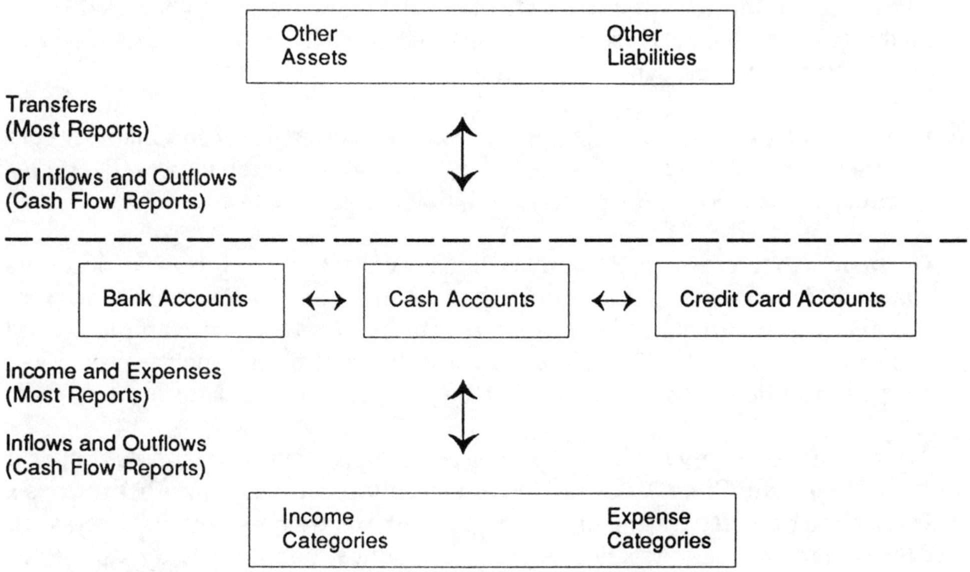

Transactions assigned to Income and Expense Categories are treated as income and expenses in most Quicken reports, as inflows and outflows in Cash Flow Reports. All transfers between Accounts are treated as transfers in most reports. But when money "crosses the line" between the cash Accounts and Other Assets and Liabilities, Cash Flow Reports treat the transaction as an inflow or an outflow.

Most Quicken reports treat income and expenses as occurring on the date transactions are recorded; shifts from one account to another are either ignored or treated as transfers. For example, you wouldn't want a transfer from checking to savings to appear as either an expense or an outflow of cash. Similarly, if you write a check for $10,000 to buy a business computer system and assign the transaction to an Other Asset account, the expense should not appear until you depreciate the computer.

Quicken Cash Flow Reports, on the other hand, reflect any transactions that change the net balance in your Bank, Cash, and Credit Card accounts—regardless of whether any income or expense has occurred in a technical accounting sense. An imaginary line divides these accounts from the Other Asset and Other Liability accounts, and transfers that "cross" this line are treated as inflows and outflows. Some examples will make this clearer:

- Income and expenses in the "regular" accounts appear as inflows and outflows on a Cash Flow Report, but transfers between these accounts do not. For example, an outflow appears when you write a check, spend cash, or make a purchase with a credit card.

- Paying a credit card bill is a transfer, because the decrease in your credit card liability offsets the decrease in your Bank account. (Otherwise you would have two outflows for the same expenditure.)

- Income and expenses recorded in the Other accounts (Asset and Liability) are omitted, because they do not affect your "money" account balances. Examples include unrealized capital gains and depreciation.

- Transfers that "cross" the imaginary line between the two groups of accounts *are* included in a Cash Flow Report, because they change your money account balances. The purchase of a computer mentioned earlier, for example, would be recorded as a $10,000 outflow. Similarly, sales of assets, such as securities, appear as inflows when you deposit the proceeds in a Bank account.

If you need to do any form of accrual accounting, as many businesses do, or if you need to use the Other Asset and Other Liability accounts for another purpose, it is worth the time to plan ahead now. Figure out exactly how you will keep your records, and refer ahead to sections on specific applications in the latter part of this book. A little effort now can save the frustration of discovering later that you have spent hours and hours recording transactions in ways that make it difficult to get the Quicken reports you need.

Creating the Accounts

Once you have decided what Quicken accounts you need, the procedure for creating accounts is the same for all five types. If you have just set up an Account Group or completed the First Time Setup screen, a screen labeled Select Account to Use (Figure 3.5) should be on your screen. If it is not, go to the main menu and choose 4. Select Account.

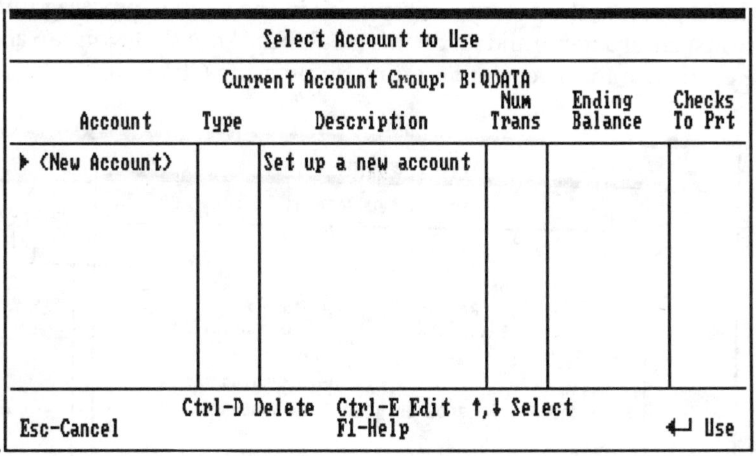

Checking

Figure 3.5. The Select Account screen.

If you have already set up accounts, they will be displayed. If you are starting a new account group, however, the only entry will be <New Account>. Once you have set up accounts, the other columns of the window will summarize information about each Account.

Type Specifies the type of account (Bank, CCard, Cash, OthA, or OthL).

Description Any descriptive information you include when you set up an account.

Num Trans The number of transactions recorded in the account (initially one, the opening balance).

Ending Balance The final balance of the account, after all transactions.

Checks to Prt Lets you know when you have previously recorded checks to print in a Bank account. (Not applicable to other account types.)

To create an account, highlight <New Account> on the Select Account screen and press Enter. The Set Up New Account window appears (Figure 3.6), with blanks for an account name, account type, an opening balance, the date, and an optional description of the account. Simply fill in the blanks, pressing Enter after each. You must enter a name and an opening balance. After that, you can accept the rest of the entries on the screen at any time by pressing Ctrl-Enter.

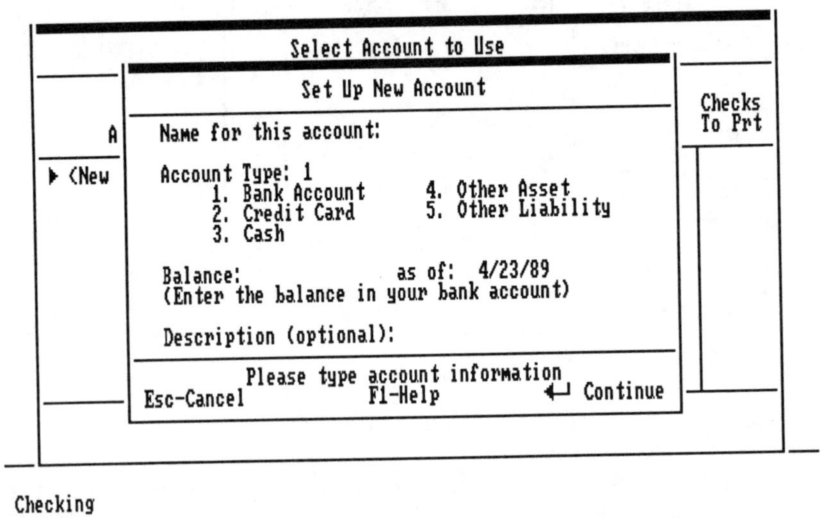

Figure 3.6. The Set Up New Account window.

NOTE: The account name can be up to 15 characters, including spaces. You can use any characters on the keyboard except colon (:), slash (/), ampersand (&), and brackets ([ ]).

Don't worry if you don't know the current balance in your actual account that corresponds to the Quicken account you are setting up. You can enter the balance on your last statement (even if it's out of date), make a guess, or enter 0. You can always correct the opening balance or record transactions since your last statement later.

Unless you are setting up a Credit Card account, the Select Account window again appears, with your new account displayed. To begin entering transactions, highlight the name of your new account and press Enter, or select <New Account> again to set up another new account.

When you are setting up a Credit Card account, a window for specifying your credit limit (Figure 3.7) precedes the return of the Select Account window. This is optional: enter a number and press Enter to record a limit, or simply press Enter to bypass the window without setting a limit. If you do record a credit limit, Quicken automatically calculates the amount of credit you have remaining at the bottom of the screen whenever you enter transactions in your Credit Card account.

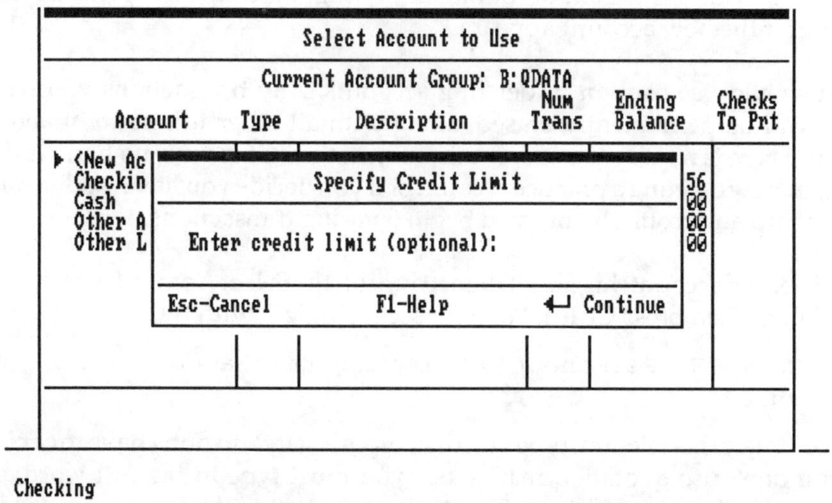

Figure 3.7. Specifying a credit limit in a Credit Card account.

Selecting, Editing, and Deleting Accounts

You can always return to the Select Account screen to set up new accounts by selecting <New Account>. This screen also allows you to work with a different account, rename accounts or change their descriptions, or delete accounts. Once you have set up an account, however, you cannot change its account type.

Once you begin recording transactions, there are three ways to call up the Select Account screen.

- You can choose 4. Select Account from the Main Menu.

- You can press F2 to pull down the Acct/Print menu anytime the Write/ Print Checks Screen or the Register for any Account is displayed. Then choose 1. Select/Set Up Account from the pull-down menu.

- You can press Ctrl-a to call up the window from anywhere within the program, regardless of what is on the screen at the moment.

To work with a different account, simply highlight it, then press Enter. The Register for the new account appears.

You should use caution in deleting accounts. Any transactions you have recorded will be permanently erased, along with all other information about the account. There is no way to recover this information. Of course, no harm is done if you are merely deleting a practice account or if you decide you have made a mistake in setting up an account before you begin entering transactions.

To delete an account, highlight the account on the Select Accounts screen (do not press Enter), then press Ctrl-d. You will see a window with this message:

```
CAUTION! Permanently removing this account. Are you
sure?
```

To complete the deletion, type yes, then press Enter. You don't have to capitalize, and you don't use quotation marks, but you must type in the full word; a y to designate 'YES' is not sufficient. The Account and all of the transactions in it will be permanently erased. The Select Account screen reappears.

Editing an Account name or description is far less risky; you can always change these items back. To edit an account, highlight the account on the Select Account screen (do not press Enter), then press Ctrl-e. You will see a window labeled Edit Account Information (Figure 3.7). This window allows you to change the account name and description. In each blank, simply type the new information and press Enter, or press Enter to leave the information unchanged.

Unless you are editing a Credit Card account, the Select Account screen reappears, with the new account information displayed. For a Credit Card account, you will first see a window that allows you to modify your credit limit. Type the new limit, then press Enter, or press Enter to leave your credit limit unchanged.

CATEGORIES AND CLASSES

Quicken would be little more than an electronic checkbook if it merely listed your transactions by account. Categories and classes allow you to sort your financial records with Quicken reports to provide precisely the information you need.

In contrast to accounts, categories and classes merely record your financial activity; they do not represent assets or debts. Categories and classes allow you to summarize income and expenses from any or all accounts in an account group. For example, if you sometimes pay for office supplies by check and sometimes by credit card, you can include all of your office supplies purchases in your Quicken reports, even though the purchases are recorded in different accounts.

Categories are the equivalent of the familiar items in your home budget or business chart of accounts: Salary, Clothes, Utilities, Groceries, and Entertainment, for example; or Sales, Office Supplies, Commissions, and so forth. When you set up a category, you designate it as an income or expense category. You can also flag categories as tax related for preparing tax reports.

Since some transactions are for more than one purpose, Quicken allows you to "split" transactions among two or more categories. For example, you can divide a mortgage payment into subtotals for principal, interest, insurance, and taxes. Similarly, you can record an entire payroll check transaction in a single step, even though the net amount of the check is less than the total transaction. Quicken will then provide accurate records of gross pay, state and federal withholding, F.I.C.A., and any other deductions included in the transaction. If you use Quicken voucher checks, the entire transaction will be summarized on the voucher.

You can set up your own categories from scratch, or you can choose to use Quicken's preset personal and business categories—or both. (See Tables 3.1 and 3.2). If you use the preset categories, you can always simplify your Quicken system by deleting the ones you don't need.

Table 3.1. Quicken's Predefined Home Categories.

Category	Description	Tax
Income Categories		
Bonus	Bonus Income	*
Canada Pen	Canadian Pension	*
Div Income	Dividend Income	*
Family Allow	Family Allowance	*
Inc Sal	Salary Income	*
Int Inc	Interest Income	*
Invest Inc	Investment Income	*
Oldage Pen	Old Age Pension	*
Other Inc	Other Income	*
Expense Categories		
Auto Fuel	Automobile Fuel	
Auto Other	Automobile Expense	
Bank Chrg	Bank Charge	
Canada Pension	Canadian Pension Plan	
Charity	Charitable Donations	*
Childcare	Childcare Expense	
Christmas	Christmas Expenses	
Clothing	Clothing	
Dining	Dining Out	
Dues	Dues	
Education	Education	
Enter.	Entertainment	
FICA	Social Security Tax	*
Gifts	Gift Expenses	
Groceries	Groceries	
Home Rpair	Home Repair & Maint.	
Household	Household Misc. Exp	
Housing	Housing	
Insurance	Insurance	
Int Exp	Interest Expense	*
Invest Exp	Investment Expense	*
Medical	Medical & Dental	*
Misc	Miscellaneous	
Mort Int	Mortgage Interest Exp	*
Mort Prin	Mortgage Principal	
Other Exp	Other Expenses	
Recreation	Recreation Expense	
RRSP	Reg Retirement Sav Plan	
Subscriptions	Subscriptions	
Tax Fed	Federal Tax Witholding	*
Tax Other	Misc. Taxes	*
Tax Prop	Property Tax	*
Tax State	State Tax Witholding	*
Telephone	Telephone Expense	
Utilities	Water, Gas, Electric	

Table 3.2. Quicken's Predefined Business Categories

Category	Description	Tax
Income Categories		
Gr Sales	Gross Sales	*
Other Inc	Other Income	*
Rent Income	Rent Income	*
Expense Categories		
Ads	Advertising	*
Bank Chrg	Bank Charge	*
Canada Pension	Canadian Pension Plan	
Car	Car & Truck	*
Commission	Commissions	*
Enter.	Entertainment	*
Freight	Freight	*
Insurance	Insurance	*
Int Paid	Interest Paid	*
L&P Fees	Legal & Prof. Fees	*
Late Fees	Late Payment Fees	*
Misc	Miscellaneous Expense	
Mort Int	Mortgage Interest	*
Office	Office Expenses	*
Other Exp	Other Expenses	*
Rent Paid	Rent Paid	*
Repairs	Repairs	*
Returns	Returns & Allowances	*
Supplies	Supplies	*
Taxes	Taxes	*
Travel	Travel Expenses	*
Utilities	Utilities & Phone	*
Wages	Wages & Job Credits	*

Classes work along with categories to further refine your record keeping. Classes allow you to sort similar income and expenses by purpose. While categories specify *what* a transaction is for, classes typically specify who, where, or when, although you can use them for any purpose. Examples might include separating business and personal transactions, classifying investment real estate income and expenses by property, sorting accounts receivable by client, or assigning income and expenses to a particular accounting period.

With Quicken reports, you can generate subtotals by category, by class, or both, giving you a great deal of flexibility in analyzing your finances. Again, classes lend themselves to a number of specialized business uses discussed later in this book. There are no preset classes.

If you need a more elaborate system, you can also assign transactions to subcategories and subclasses. It is possible, for example, to assign a single transaction to a category, subcategory, class, and subclass. The result could look like this: Utilities:Telephone/Business:Jones (where Jones might be a particular client). You could then generate a report grouping the transactions—in a variety of ways—with others that match any combination of those classifications.

The danger, however, is that your record keeping system may run amok if it becomes too complicated. Consistency is the key to using Quicken effectively. To create meaningful reports, you must always categorize and classify transactions the same way. Thus, it is important to think out your money management system in advance, so that it will provide exactly the information you need without being unnecessarily cumbersome.

Unless you use Quicken simply to manage a bank account, you will probably want to set up categories. It is important to be consistent in assigning transactions to categories throughout an account group. You should not, for example, sometimes assign similar purchases to Office Supplies and sometimes to Supplies. It is also important to make sure in advance that your categories match your reporting needs. For example, if you assign both mortgage and personal interest to the same category, it will be difficult to separate the two when you fill out Schedule A of Form 1040.

You may not want to use classes unless you have a specific need. If you do use classes, however, you should plan your system carefully in advance. You can use classes for broad purposes, such as separating business and personal transactions, or for more specialized applications. Later chapters suggest using classes to manage an investment portfolio and rental real estate properties, among other things.

You can use classes for several different purposes. If you use classes for both rental properties and securities investments, you can create custom reports on the different activities by restricting them to the relevant classes. In that case, however, a global report showing both the real estate and the investment classes probably wouldn't make much sense. Of course, you could still produce global reports showing subtotals by category, but not by class.

In some cases, multiple uses for classes are incompatible. It would be awkward, for example, to use classes for *both* a broad purpose, like separating business and personal transactions, *and* specialized purposes, like classifying stock transactions. You might (or might not, depending on the ways you use classes) be able to devise a system of using classes for the broader purpose and subclasses for the specialized ones, but such a solution would come at the price of a more complicated record keeping system.

You may also want to decide in advance whether you want to assign *all* of your Quicken transactions to categories. Quicken does not require you to do this; there is no need, for example, if you just want to keep your bank account balanced and to track tax-related items. Writing a check at the grocery store, after all, has no effect on your taxes. You can easily eliminate uncategorized transactions from your reports.

If, however, you want to keep comprehensive records, your Quicken reports will be incomplete if you neglect to assign some transactions to categories. The Change Settings option on the Main Menu allows you to reset the program to require categories for all new transactions.

You can always add categories and classifications as you work with your Quicken accounts. Again, however, it's important to think through your classification system before you begin recording transactions—and it's worth the effort to experiment with Quicken reports to make sure your system works as you intend before you have recorded a large number of transactions.

Setting Up Categories

As you begin setting up categories, think about how you want your reports to appear. Quicken reports list categories alphabetically (numbers and punctuation marks precede letters). You can take advantage of this feature to group related categories in your reports by assigning related categories similar names or by numbering your categories the way a business numbers its chart of accounts. For example, you can group your office expenses together by setting up office supplies, office rent, office telephone, and office utilities.

Assigning account numbers to categories gives you still more flexibility in determining the order in which categories appear in reports. You might, for example, want to set budget priorities by giving low numbers to the most important categories and higher numbers to categories for discretionary spending. For example, Quicken reports will list these accounts in order: 100 Mortgage, 110 Car Payment, 120 Utilities, 130 Groceries, and 140 Entertainment.

Account numbers are also useful for grouping categories by purpose. If you pay both personal and business expenses from the same account, for example, you could number your personal categories 100 to 199 and your business categories at 500 to 599. You will then be able to use matching criteria to create separate reports for each group.

NOTE: It is a good idea to space account numbers at intervals of 5 or 10, so you can insert new categories in the proper order later.

All categories are recorded on the Category List. You can add categories to the list anytime the Write/Print Checks screen or the Register is displayed—either in advance or while you are entering a transaction.

There are two ways to call up the Category List. Either press F4 to pull down the Quick Entry menu, then select 3. Categorize/Transfer from the menu; or press Ctrl–c.

When the Category List appears, any previously recorded categories and accounts are displayed. (The accounts are there for transferring money between accounts and are not relevant for the moment.) Figure 3.8 shows the category list for an account group in which only a Checking bank account has been established.

To set up a new category, highlight <New Category> on the Category List and press Enter. The Set Up Category window appears (Figure 3.9). This window allows you to name the category; designate it as an income category, expense category, or subcategory; record a description; and indicate whether the category is tax related. As usual, you simply fill in the blanks, pressing enter after each.

Type the category name exactly as you want it to appear, including capitalization, in your reports. It can be up to 16 characters long, including numbers and

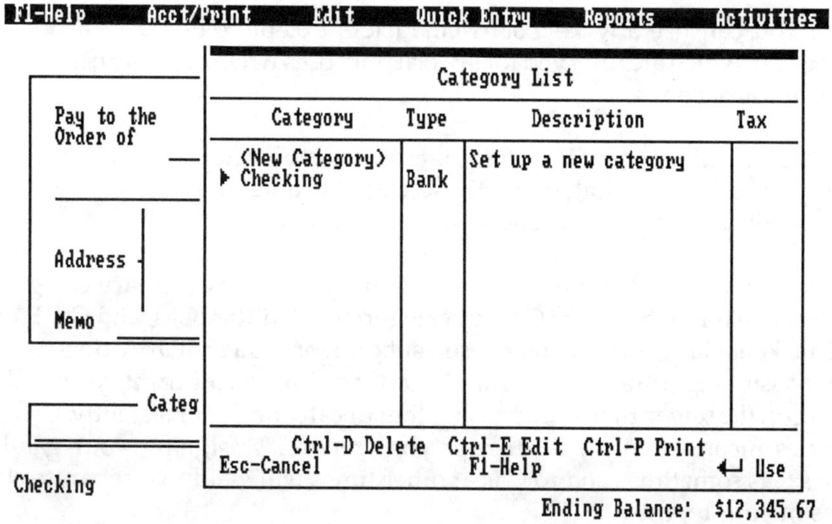

Figure 3.8. The Category List.

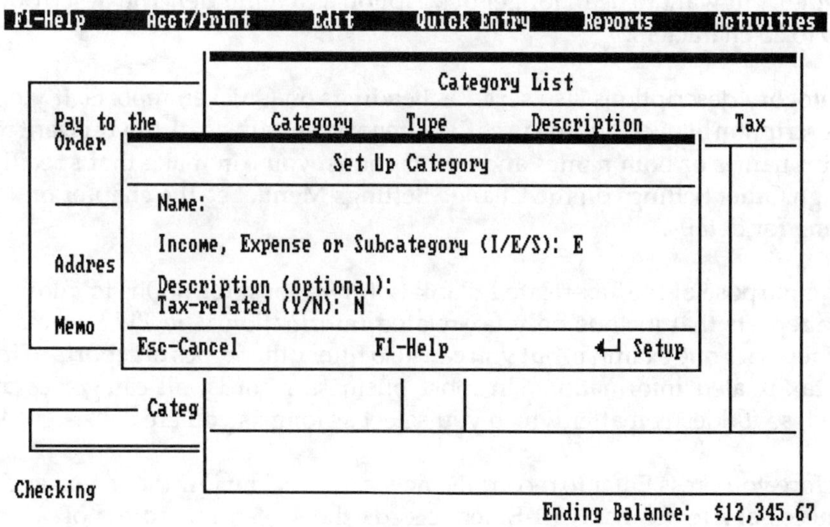

Figure 3.9. The Set Up Category window.

spaces. You can use any keyboard characters except colons (:), slashes (/), or brackets ([ ]), which are reserved for special purposes when entering categories and classes in transactions.

At the next line, enter i to designate an income category, e for an expense category, or s for a subcategory. These classifications determine how the new category will appear in your reports.

Once you set up a subcategory, you can use it with any primary category. For example, you might have two Gas subcategories— Utilities:Gas, and Car Expense: Gas. Quicken will also allow you to use a subcategory as a primary category (in this case by assigning a transaction simply to Gas), but if you try it, you will see a warning on the screen that you are using the subcategory inconsistently. Using subcategories inconsistently will disrupt your reports. Assigning your gas bill to Utilities:Gas sometimes and to Gas at other times will yield two separate classifications in your reports.

The description allows you to provide more information about the new category than appears in the name. You might, for example, enter a number or abbreviation for a category name (COS for Cost of Sales, or E&D for Entertainment & Dining, for example), but want to use a longer description as a reminder. The description can be up to 25 characters.

Category descriptions also serve as headings on Quicken reports. If you leave the description blank, Quicken uses the category name instead. (If you want reports to print names or both names and descriptions, you can make that specification through Other Settings on the Change Settings Menu. See the chapter on Housekeeping for details.)

The purpose of the Tax-related blank (y for yes or n for no) is to allow you to create reports that include only tax-related information. The Tax Summary personal report is one example, but you can also filter other types of reports to include only tax related information. (In most business records, all categories are tax related, so it doesn't matter which you select as long as you are consistent.)

Before you press Enter to record the new category, review the screen and make any necessary revisions. (Ctrl-Enter records the screen regardless of where the cursor is.) The Category List reappears when you record your new category. You can make another selection or press Esc to return to other work.

Setting Up Classes

Quicken, at your option, can organize reports by class as well as by category. While income and expense categories are a familiar idea to anyone who has ever kept a home budget or kept records for a business, classes are Quicken's own invention.

If categories identify *what* a transaction is for, classes are intended to specify who, where, or when—but you can use them for any purpose you want. Some examples include separating personal and business transactions; identifying transactions by vendor, client, or customer; identifying payroll records by employee; classifying rental income and expenses by property; specifying the tax form on which a category is reported; sorting income and expenses by family member; and identifying stocks and bonds by company.

All classes are recorded on the Class List. Setting up a class is similar to setting up a category, except that the only information you record is the name and description. There are no provisions for income and expenses, tax-related classes, or subclasses. (You can use subclasses when you record transactions, but there is no distinction between classes and subclasses on the Class List.)

Whenever the Write/Print Checks screen or an account Register is displayed, you can call up the Class List two ways. You can press F4 to pull down the Quicken Entry menu, then select 4. Select/Set Up Class or you can press Ctrl-l.

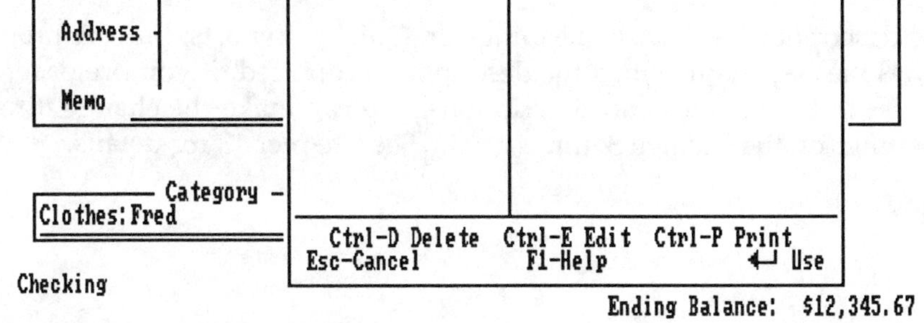

Figure 3.10. The Class List.

When the Class List appears, any Classes you have already recorded are listed. Figure 3.10 shows a brand-new Class List.

To set up a new class, highlight <New Class> on the Class List, then press Enter. The Set Up Class window appears (Figure 3.11). To complete the window, type the class name and, if you want, a description, pressing Enter after each.

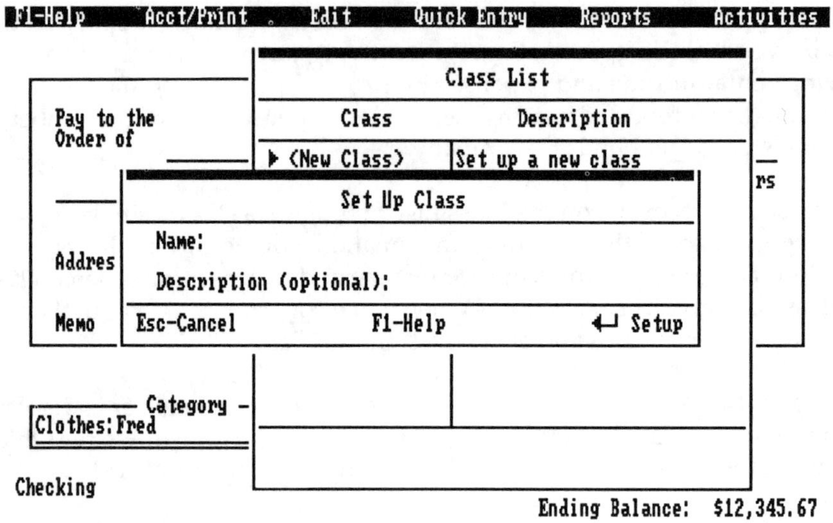

Figure 3.11. The Set Up Class window.

Class names and descriptions work just like category names and descriptions and follow the same conventions. The name can be up to 15 characters long and cannot include slashes (/), colons (:), or brackets ([ ]). Descriptions can be up to 25 characters long. To classify transactions by client, for example, you might name a class Jones, then enter Ronald Jones for a description.

Class descriptions appear as headings on Quicken reports, but the program substitutes the class name when the description is omitted. If you prefer reports with names or both names and descriptions, you can make the change through Other Settings on the Change Settings Menu. See Chapter 13 for details.

Recalling Categories and Classes

Every Quicken transaction, whether on the Write/Print Checks screen or the Register of any type of account, provides a blank labeled category for assigning the transaction to a category and/or class.

You can enter a simple category name, or set up a more elaborate classification by completing the blank in this format:

Category:Subcategory/Class:Subclass

You can use any or all of these classifications. You can even subcategorize subcategories and subclasses by adding a colon (:) and entering another subcategory or subclass like this (provided the line does not exceed 31 characters):

Category:Subcategory:Subcategory/Class:Subclass:Subclass

It bears repeating, however, that it is critical to classify your transactions consistently in order to produce meaningful reports; the more complicated you get, the more difficult it will be to maintain the necessary consistency over the course of a year.

There are two ways to complete the category line. The first is to type the entry and press Enter. If you include a category or class that does not yet exist, you will have a choice between adding the classification to the appropriate list or selecting a replacement from the list.

The second is to select categories or classes from their respective lists. You must still type the colon between classifications and subclassifications, but Quicken automatically inserts the slash between categories and classes. Specific examples are given in the next chapter.

Other Options: Deleting, Editing, and Printing

Options at the bottom of the Category and Class Lists allow you to delete, edit, or print the information contained in the window.You should think carefully before deleting or editing any category, subcategory, or class, because Quicken will automatically reclassify any transactions already assigned to the grouping you delete or edit. In many cases, the outcome will be exactly what you intended. In others however, the change could disrupt your records in a way that takes hours to repair.

Particularly when making deletions, you should back up your account group in advance. That way, you can easily recover and start over if the result of your deletions takes an unexpected turn. (To back up an Account Group, select Change Settings (option 5) from the Main Menu, then select 1. Account Group Activities, and then 2. Back Up Account Group. For more details, see Chapter 13.)

In addition, after making changes, you should create several trial reports before you begin recording new transactions. This will allow you to make corrections or restore your account group from the backup before any damage is done if your reports come out different than you expected.

The procedure for deleting and editing is essentially the same for categories, subcategories, and classes (subclasses aren't designated as such on the Class List).

> NOTE: Although your Quicken accounts appear on the Category List, you cannot delete or edit them on this screen. To work with accounts, press Ctrl-a to call up the Select Account screen.

Deleting

When you delete a category, subcategory, or class, Quicken removes it from the Category line of any transaction assigned to it. For example, if you have been assigning interest income to a category called Interest, your transactions become completely unclassified when you delete the Interest category. You can go back to the Register and add a new classification to each transaction individually, but this will be tedious if more than a few transactions are assigned to the classification you have deleted.

Anything to the right of the deleted classification is moved to the left. However, if you have been assigning income to Interest:Personal, the Personal subcategory moves over to the category spot. Similarly, classes and subclasses entered in those transactions remain intact. This is perhaps where you run the highest risk of unexpected results.

To delete a category, subcategory, or class, call up the Category List (Ctrl-c) or the Class List (Ctrl-l), then highlight the classification to be deleted and press Ctrl-d. You will see a message that you are about to permanently delete a category, or class. If you decide not to delete the category, press Esc to cancel. If you are certain you want to go ahead, press Enter to complete the deletion.

EDITING

Editing is far safer than deleting; there is not much you can do that can't be undone. When you edit a classification, Quicken automatically updates all of the transactions that have been assigned to it, and the result will be reflected in your reports.

To edit a category, subcategory, or class call up the Category List (Ctrl-c) or the Class List (Ctrl-l) and highlight the classification you want to edit. (Do not press Enter.) Next, press Ctrl-e to call up the Edit Category window (Figure 3.12) or the Edit Class window (Figure 3.13). These windows work exactly like the windows you use to set up categories and classes. Type over or add whatever information you want to change. To record the changes, press Enter when you complete the last blank or Ctrl-Enter whenever all of the information is on the screen.

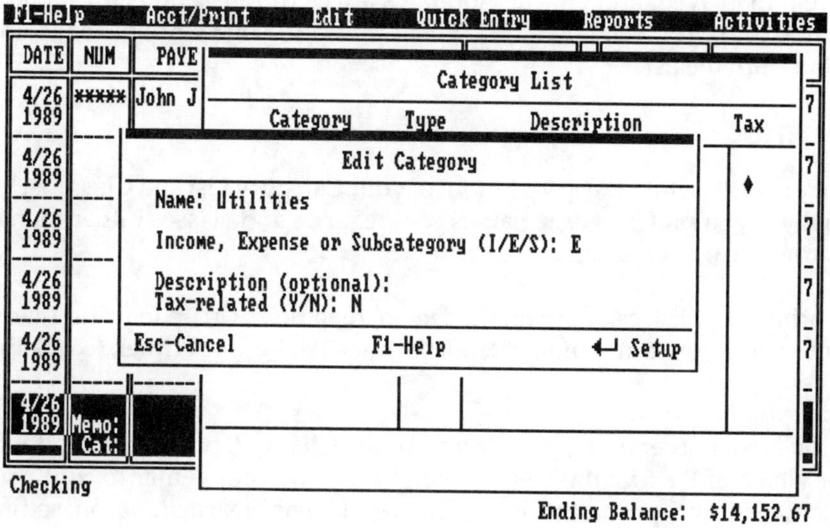

Figure 3.12. The Edit Category window.

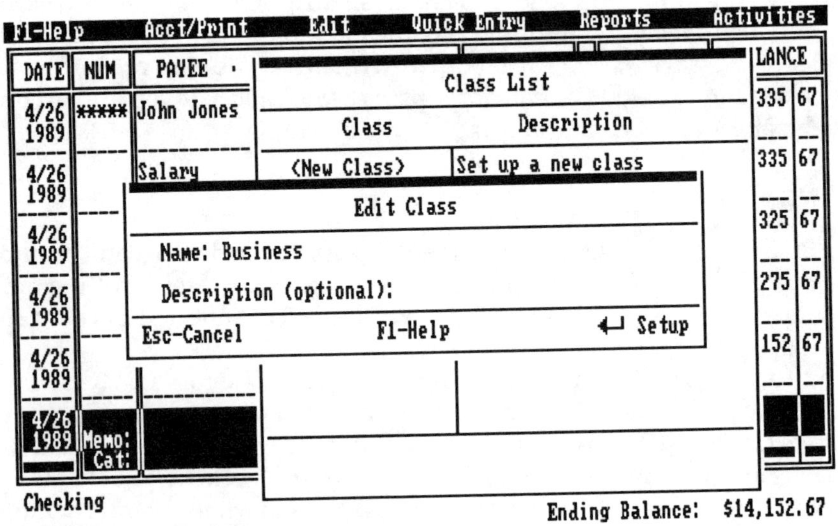

Figure 3.13. The Edit Class window.

When you have finished, the Category List or Class List appears with the new definition displayed, and Quicken updates affected transactions throughout the Account Group. You can now press Esc to return to your work or make another selection from the list.

Printing

You may find it useful to keep a printout of your Category List and Class List handy, especially if you prefer to type names of categories and classes rather than select them from the lists on screen.

To print either list, call it up on the screen, then press Ctrl-p to print. A window appears giving you four options: Report Printer, Alt Report Printer, Check Printer, and Disk.

If you have not set up a printer through the Change Settings Menu, it will not matter which of the first three you select. When you press Enter to confirm your selection, Quicken prints the list. (Chapter 13 has instructions on setting up printers.)

The fourth option prints your list to an ASCII file on disk. You will then be able to call the list up with your word processor. When you select this option, a Print to Disk window appears. You probably will not want to change the Lines per page or Width entries, but you must enter a file name or a full path name.

Unless you specify otherwise, Quicken will record the new file in the same directory as your Quicken program. This is usually C:\QUICKEN3 if you have a hard disk or drive A if you have two floppies.) If this is acceptable, enter any DOS file name, up to eight characters—LIST, for example. To choose another directory, enter the full path name, such as b:list for drive B or c:\subdirectory\list to select another subdirectory on your hard disk. When you complete your selections, press Ctrl-Enter to save the file.

CONCLUSION

This chapter explained the basic steps for setting up a cash management system with Quicken, including Account Groups, five types of accounts, categories and subcategories, and classes. While you can set any of these as you go along, planning in advance makes it easier to set up a consistent system that produces exactly the reports you need. You can always add to or modify your system at any time.

The next chapter gets down to the nuts and bolts of using Quicken to manage your finances or business: entering and classifying transactions and printing checks.

4

Basic Transactions

Entering transactions in Quicken is as easy as—actually easier than—writing a check and recording it in your checkbook register. Quicken can help you manage almost any aspect of your business or personal finances, but it will save you time even if you use it only to print checks and keep track of the balance in your checking account.

This chapter explains Quicken's most basic features:

- Writing and printing Quicken checks.
- Postdating checks and using Billminder to manage your bills.
- Recording deposits and other transactions in a Bank account.
- Reviewing your checks and deposits.
- Printing Quicken checks.
- Reconciling your Quicken records with your bank statement.

Once you understand these basics, the rest of the program will tend to come naturally, and it is tempting to plunge ahead. Unless your finances are very simple, however, it is strongly recommended that you plan your Quicken system in advance, so you will be able to create precisely the reports you need. Refer to the following chapters for information about Quicken's more sophisticated features and reporting capabilities.

Quicken's Transaction Screens

All transactions are recorded on either the Write/Print Checks screen on a Register, the first two options on the Main Menu. Figure 4.1 shows a check for a utilities bill on Write/Print Checks. Figure 4.2 shows the same transaction as it appears on the Register for a Bank account.

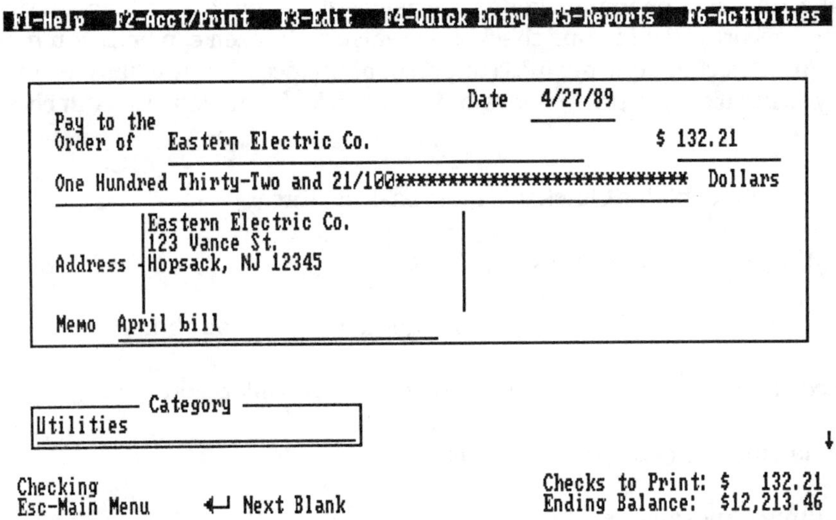

Figure 4.1. The Write/Print Checks screen.

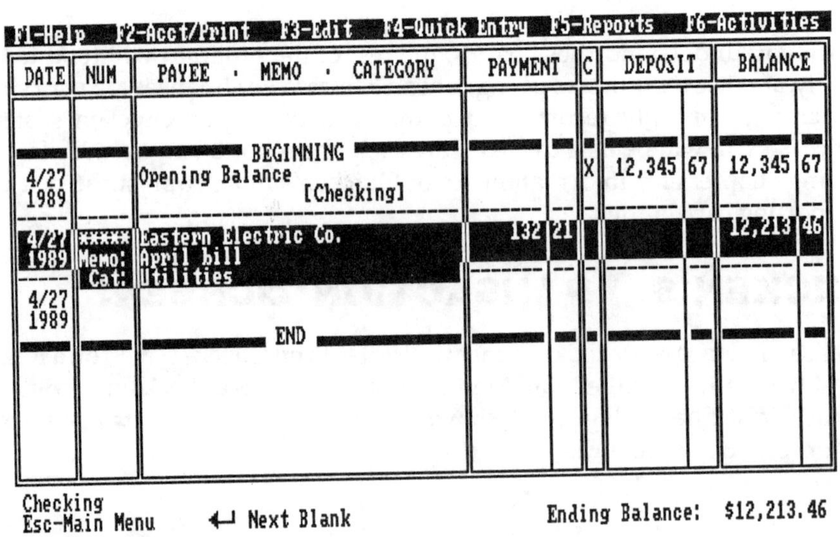

Figure 4.2. The Register for a Bank account.

Generally, you will enter the checks you print with Quicken—and only those transactions—on the Write/Print Checks screen. When you enter a check on Write/Print Checks, Quicken automatically adds it to the list of checks to be printed, and it remains there until you actually print the check. Quicken checks are also automatically recorded in your Bank account Register.

You can write Quicken checks only on Bank accounts. Thus, any account on which you write checks must be set up as a Bank account, even if it isn't actually at a bank. Examples of nonbank checking accounts include brokerage accounts and some money market funds. (The Write/Print Checks option appears on the Main Menu in other types of accounts, but the program will not allow you to select it.)

All other transactions are recorded on the Register of the appropriate account. Examples include handwritten checks, credit card purchases, cash purchases, deposits, account transfers, loans, or any other transaction besides a printed check. The Registers for different types of accounts differ slightly, but they all work pretty much the same way. Quicken does not transfer Register transactions to Write/Print Checks, because they will not often involve Quicken checks.

Despite their difference in appearance, Write/Print Checks and the Register are quite similar. For the most part, they contain the same information about each transaction: date, payee (or payer), amount, memo (for miscellaneous information), and a category line for entering categories and classes. The Write/Print Checks screen also provides a space for an address, which the Register does not. Both screens display your account balance at the bottom right, and both list the same pull-down menus across the top.

Recording a transaction on either screen is simply a matter of filling in the blanks. The two screens share the basic commands listed in Chapter 2.

Writing Checks

As you saw in Figure 4.1, the Write/Print Checks screen looks much like a paper check, and recording a check is much the same as filling out a regular check. Quicken does some of the work for you. When you enter the amount of the check next to the $ sign, for example, Quicken automatically spells it out on the next line. In addition, if you buy Quicken window envelopes, the address and return address on the check will appear in the windows. The address will also appear on your check voucher if you use two-part Quicken checks.

Notice that no check number appears on the screen. This is because your Quicken checks have numbers printed on them. When you print checks, you will enter the number of the next check, and Quicken will automatically record the correct numbers in the Register.

There are three ways to call up the Write/Print Checks screen:

- Select 1. Write/Print Checks from the Main Menu.
- Press Ctrl-w (for Write Checks) anytime you are using a Bank account. (This won't work in other types of accounts, because you can't write checks on them.)
- When you are using the Register, press F6 to pull down the Activities menu, then press 1 to select Write Checks.

When the Write/Print Checks screen appears, simply fill in each blank, pressing Enter after each entry. The check is automatically recorded after you press Enter to complete the category line. You can also record the transaction by pressing Ctrl-Enter when the cursor is anywhere.

Writing a check is quite straightforward, but Quicken does provide some handy tools to make the task even simpler. The following sections explain entering the date, the written amount, the first line of the address box, and the category line. For the payee and memo, simply type the entry and press Enter.

The Date

The current date is entered automatically in the date blank. To change it, press Shift-Tab (if necessary) to back up and type a new date. You can also use the + and - keys to scroll forward or backward through the days.

You don't have to write checks the day you send them. You can postdate checks and print them later. Quicken's Billminder feature automatically reminds you when postdated checks are due, and the program automatically adds them to the list of checks to print at the appropriate time.

The Amount

On handwritten checks, you have to spell out the amount of the check on the line below the one for the payee. Not with Quicken. The program automatically writes out the amount when you enter a number in the $ blank. For round amounts, you don't even have to fill in the cents. For a $159.00 check, for example, you can simply type 159 and press Enter. Quicken adds the decimal and zeros automatically.

The Address

Quicken can enter the payee's name as the first line of the address automatically. When the cursor reaches the address box, just type a single or double quote (' or "). (It doesn't matter whether you press the Shift key.) Quicken enters the payee's name, and the cursor jumps to the next line.

If you don't want to enter an address, press Enter when the cursor reaches the address box. The cursor skips directly to the memo line.

> NOTE: The address can include up to five lines of 31 characters each. The Change Settings Menu allows you to add an additional message to the right of the address on your Quicken checks. (This is option 4—Extra message line on check on the Other Settings Menu.) This message will appear on your Quicken checks, but nowhere else. It will not be saved in your Quicken records.

The Category Line

Categorizing transactions allows you to take advantage of Quicken reports to manage your finances. To assign a check to a category and/or class, you can simply type the entry on the category line and press Enter, or you can make selections from the Category and Class Lists, as explained below.

Building a Category/Class Entry

Usually the category entry will be a simple category (e.g., Telephone) or a category and a class separated by a slash (e.g. , Telephone/Business). However, you can build more elaborate classifications with entries in this format:

```
Category:Subcategory/Class:Subclass
```

You can even assign checks to sub-subcategories or sub-subclasses. The entry Office:Utilities:Telephone, for example, assigns a check to an Office category, a Utilities subcategory, and a Telephone sub-subcategory. The only limitation is that the maximum length of the entry is 31 characters. Table 4.1 gives several examples of combinations of categories and classes.

Table 4.1. Combining Categories and Classes.

Utilities:Telephone	Assigns the transaction to a Utilities category and a Telephone subcategory.
Telephone/Business	Assigns a class to separate business telephone expenses from personal telephone expenses.
Telephone/Business: Jones	Assigns a telephone expense to a particular client. You might do this, for example, to report expenses by job or to bill a client for expenses.
Utilities:Phone/Bus:Jones	Combines all of the above possibilities. (Names have been shortened to stay under the 31-character limit.)
/Personal	The occasion may seldom arise, but you can assign a transaction to a class without assigning it to a category. This entry assigns an uncategorized transaction to a Personal class.

Selecting From the Category and Class Lists

If you prefer, you can make selections from the category and class lists rather than typing the entry on the category line. Using the lists may take slightly longer, but it also helps to assure consistency.

You can call up the category list by pressing Ctrl-c or by pressing F4 to pull down the Quick Entry menu, then selecting 3. Categories/Transfer. Once the list is displayed, highlight a category. (If the list is long, type the first initial of the category name. Quicken highlights the first category with that initial.) When you press Enter to confirm, Quicken returns you to the Write/Print Checks screen and automatically enters your selection on the category line.

After you have entered a category, you can select a class from the class list exactly the same way. (To call up the class list, press Ctrl-l or select 4. Select/Set Up Class from the Quick Entry menu.) Quicken automatically supplies the slash (/) designating the entry as a class. To enter Telephone/Business, for example, you would first select Telephone from the category list, then call up the class list and select Business.

You can also select subcategories and subclasses from the lists, but you must type a colon (:) on the category line before making the selection. To enter Utilities:Telephone, for example, you would select Utilities from the list, type a colon, then select Telephone. You can use the same procedure to select subclasses from the class list.

ENSURING CONSISTENCY

If you prefer to type entries on the category line, Quicken warns you if it does not recognize a category or class. This helps you to classify transactions consistently and protects you against typographical errors. If you have an expense category called Utilities, for example, you would not to assign a check to Utility or Utlity.

When you type a category or class that does not appear on the lists, you will see a message like the one in Figure 4.3. (The message for an unrecognized class is similar.) When this message appears, you have two options: press 1 to add the category or class to the appropriate list, or press 2 to select from the appropriate list. If you elect to add to the list, Quicken takes you through the procedure automatically, just as if you were setting up a category or class from scratch.

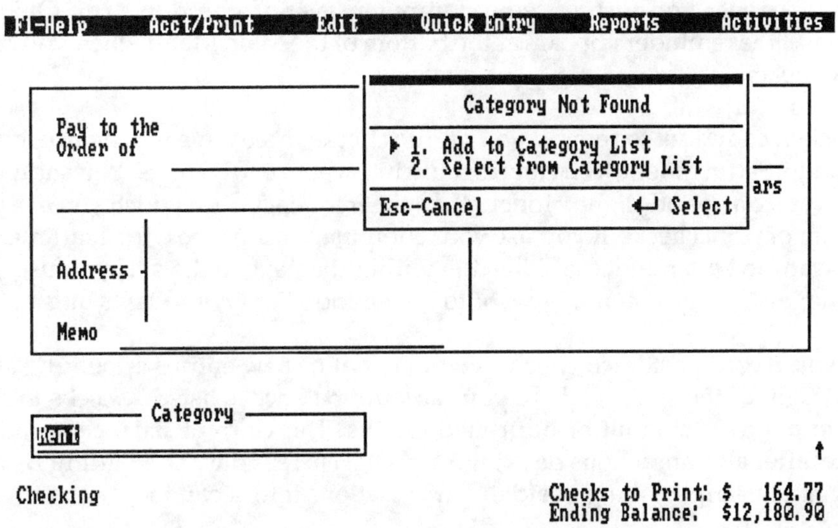

Figure 4.3. A warning appears if you enter a category or class that Quicken doesn't recognize.

NOTE: Sometimes you may write a check for several different purposes. For example, you might want to divide a mortgage payment into payments for principal, interest, insurance, and taxes. Or you might want to assign a check written at a department store to several different categories. You can "split" a transaction by pressing Ctrl-s any time while you are completing a transaction. A Split Transaction window appears, allowing you to assign subtotals to different categories and/or classes. Split transactions are explained at the beginning of the next chapter.

Postdating Checks

Quicken's Billminder feature provides a simple way to manage your cash by reminding you when bills are due. This allows you to leave your money in an interest-bearing account as long as possible and still pay your bills on time.

When a bill arrives, simply enter it in Quicken, dated the day you want to pay. When the bill comes due, Quicken reminds you that you have checks to print and automatically adds due checks to the list of checks to print.

If you have installed Billminder on your hard disk, Quicken reminds you of due checks whenever you turn on your computer, even if you don't run Quicken. Otherwise, the reminder appears at the bottom of the Main Menu when you begin using Quicken.

Quicken comes set to remind you of due checks three days in advance, but on the Change Setting Menu you can reset the interval to 0 to 30 days. You should set the interval to a period slightly longer than the frequency with which you use your computer or print checks. If you use your computer once a week, for example, you might want to be reminded of bills due within the next 10 days. If you use your computer every day, you might want to be reminded only of today's bills.

As you record postdated checks, you may notice new entries appearing at the bottom right of the screen, where your account balance is listed. Checks to Print refers to the total amount of unprinted checks. The Current Balance is today's balance, after all transactions dated through the current day. The Ending Balance is your final balance, taking postdated transactions into account.

NOTE: You can also postdate deposits and other types of transactions. If you do, these will be taken into account in the Current Balance and Ending Balance entries.

Printing Checks

Once you have recorded checks on the Write/Print Checks screen, Quicken is ready to print your checks on forms available from Intuit, the program's publisher. The procedure is quite straightforward.

The Write/Print Checks screen must be displayed before you begin printing. To begin, press Ctrl-p or select 2. Print Checks from the Acct/Print pull-down menu. The Print Checks window (Figure 4.4) appears.

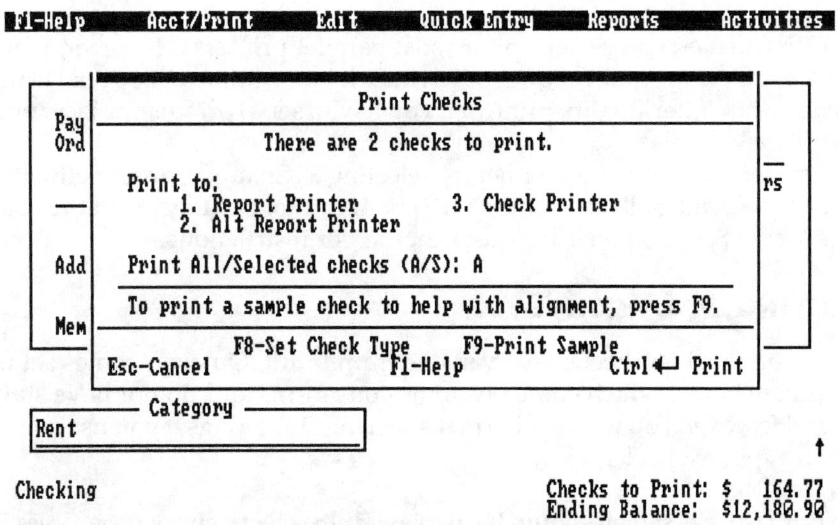

Figure 4.4 The Print Checks window.

At the top of the window, Quicken tells you how many unprinted checks are in the print queue. The options are mostly self-explanatory.

Print to allows you to select a printer if you have set up more than one or set up one printer to print several ways. If you have set up more than one printer—or have set up one printer to print more than one way—the selection is usually 3. Check printer. If you have not set up printers, any of the options should work.

Print All/Selected checks lets you decide whether to print all of the checks in the print queue or to select specific checks from the Select Checks to Print screen.

Print checks dated through appears only if you have postdated checks. Quicken will print only checks dated on or before the date indicated, but you can change the date to print postdated checks and mail them later.

The Print Checks window also allows you to select a check type (F8) from the five kinds of checks Intuit offers and to print a sample check (F9) to check the alignment of checks in your printer.

After you have begun printing checks with Quicken, you will breeze through this screen in a matter of seconds. The first time, however, you may need to select a check type and print a sample check.

> NOTE: Quicken comes set up for most parallel printers. However, you will need to tell the program about your printer if you want to use special features, such as near -letter-quality print, or if you have a serial printer or a laser printer.

You can set up your printer either by selecting 3. Change Printer Settings from the Acct/Print pull-down menu (F2) or 4. Printer Settings from the Change Settings Menu. See Chapter 13, Housekeeping, for instructions.

Selecting A Check Type

Five types of Quicken checks are available from Intuit. Quicken comes set up to print regular checks, which come on continuous forms and do not have stubs or vouchers. However, you will need to make a change in settings if you use one of the other four types of checks.

The Print Checks screen should be displayed. To select a check type, press F8. A window appears with the options shown in Table 4.2. When you have made a selection, press Ctrl-Enter to record the information. Quicken stores the settings until you change them.

Table 4.2. Quicken Check Selections.

1. Regular	Regular checks, 3 1/2 inches high.
2. Wallet	2 5/6-inches high with end stub on the left.
3. Voucher	3 1/2-inch checks with vouchers underneath.
4. Laser	3 1/2-inch checks printed on sheets to fit the paper tray of your printer.
5. Laser Voucher	3 1/2-inch voucher checks on sheets that fit your paper tray.
Number of additional copies (Laser only):	This setting is normally 0, but you can change it to 1, 2, or 3 if you have multipart checks for your laser printer

NOTE: If you have a laser printer, you can use the sample continuous form checks that came with your Quicken package. Tear them into groups of three and remove the tractor strips, then insert them in your printer as you would letterhead stationery. Make sure Quicken is properly configured for your printer. On the Choose Printer Settings window, Page-oriented (e.g., laser) printer should be set to Y(es). Printer setup is explained in Chapter 13.

Printing a Sample Check

The first time you print checks, you should print a sample to check your printer alignment. If the alignment is not correct, Quicken offers a simple system for adjusting vertical alignment automatically. You can usually solve problems with horizontal alignment by moving the checks in your printer by hand.

On-screen messages lead you through the test print procedure. Before you begin, note the position numbers in the margins of your Quicken checks. These will help you position your checks in your printer.

To print a sample check, load the checks in your printer as you would ordinary computer forms and make sure your printer is ready. If you have a laser printer, position the checks in the tray as you would letterhead stationery. The Print Checks window should be displayed, and you should already have selected a printer and check type.

To print the check press F9. You will see a message warning you not to adjust your printer after printing is complete. Quicken will do this for you automatically. Press Enter to print.

Examine the sample check carefully *without* moving the checks in the printer. Each line should be printed just above the correct line on the check. If the sample is printed correctly, press Enter to return to the Print Checks window.

If the entries are misaligned vertically, note the number indicated by the pointer line on the check and enter that number as the Position number on the screen. Quicken will print another sample check. At this point, the vertical alignment of the sample check should be almost perfect; you can make further adjustments by moving the check forms by hand.

You may also have problems with horizontal alignment. If the line length is too long or too short, you may need to adjust the pitch on your printer setup through Change Settings Menu, as explained in Chapter 13. The pitch (characters per inch) for printing checks should be 10. If the check is printed too far to the left or right, realign the checks in the printer manually or change your printer settings to adjust the Indent setting for your check printer.

When your sample check is correctly positioned, carefully note the alignment of the edges of the check and the position numbers with a part of your printer, such as tractor sprockets or the roller bar. This will help you align your checks correctly in future sessions.

Printing Your Checks

Before you print your checks, you should have aligned your checks in your printer and selected the style of checks you use. The Print Checks window should be displayed. (Press Ctrl-p or select 2. Print Checks from the Acct/Print pull-down menu.)

When the window appears, select a printer and choose A(ll) or S(elected) checks. If you want to print postdated checks, adjust the date on the line labeled: Print checks dated through.

If you are printing selected checks, the Select Checks to Print window appears (Figure 4.5). Initially, all checks are selected, as indicated by the word Print in the right column. To exclude a check from the print run, highlight it with the arrow keys, then press the space bar. To return a check to the print queue, highlight the check again, then press the space bar. Press Enter when your selections are complete.

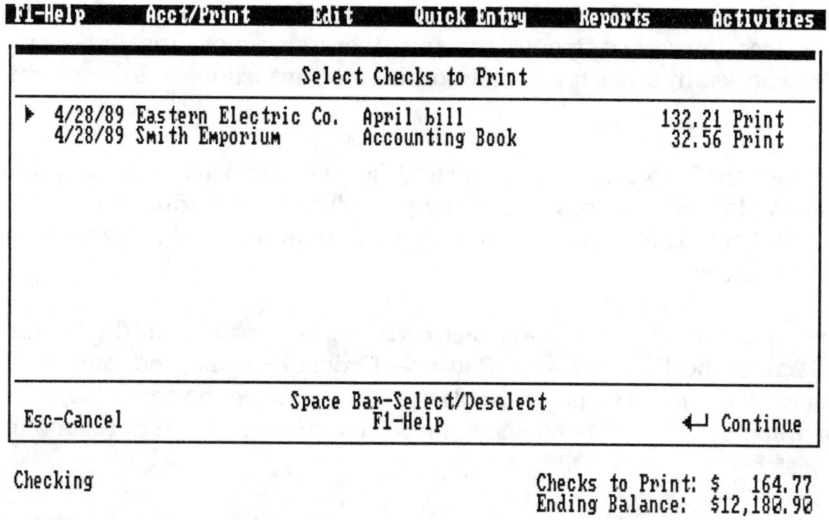

Figure 4.5. Selecting checks to print.

Next, Quicken asks for the number of your next Quicken check. Find the check number on the next check in your printer. If that number matches the number displayed, press Enter to confirm; otherwise, type the check number, then press Enter. Quicken prints your checks.

When printing is completed, Quicken asks: Did Checks print OK? Quicken removes printed checks from the list of checks to print, but this option gives you an opportunity to reprint checks that did not print correctly. If some checks are incorrectly printed, type the number of the first incorrectly printed check and press Enter. The Print Checks window reappears, and you can repeat the alignment test on a sample check. If your checks are correctly aligned, press Enter.

When printing is completed, the Write/Print Checks screen reappears, and Quicken removes the checks you have just printed from the print queue. If you later discover that a check is incorrectly printed, you can return it to the print queue by calling up the Register and entering an asterisk in the NUM column.

ENTERING TRANSACTIONS ON THE REGISTER

Many types of transactions are recorded in the Register rather than on the Write/Print Checks screen. In a Bank account, these include checks written by hand, deposits, fees, interest payments, and any other transactions that are not printed Quicken checks. In other types of accounts, all transactions are recorded in the Register.

Although the Bank account Register (see Figure 4.2) looks considerably different than the Write/Print Checks screen, the procedure for recording a transaction is almost identical. (The Registers of other types of accounts are slightly different, but work the same way.)

Most of the blanks on the Register correspond to blanks on the Write/Print Checks screen: the date, the payee (Pay to the Order of), memo, and category blanks are, in fact, the same. The payment blank corresponds to the check blank labeled with a dollar sign. There is no need to record addresses or spell out amounts on the Register.

The Register does, however, have several features absent from the Write/Print Checks screen. The most notable difference is the NUM column. Here, you enter the numbers of handwritten checks or identifying numbers for other types of transactions. If you split a transaction, Quicken also enters the word SPLIT here, rather than on the category line.

In addition, the Register includes a C(leared) column, for marking transactions that have cleared the bank; a deposit column for deposits and other transactions that increase the account balance; and the balance column, which shows the account balance after each transaction.

As on the Write/Print Checks screen, to record a transaction, you simply fill in the blanks, pressing Enter after each. You can press either Enter or Tab to skip a blank. To back up a blank, press Shift-Tab. To record a transaction, press Enter after completing the category line or Ctrl-Enter when the cursor is anywhere in the transaction.

Recording a Check

The procedure for recording a check in the Register is the same as for writing a check, with a few exceptions. If you have already written Quicken checks, you know the basics.

To record a check, correct the date (if necessary), enter a check number in the NUM column, and an amount in the payment column. Next, press Enter or Tab twice to skip the c(leared) column and the deposit column, then fill out the memo and category lines as usual. Finally, press Ctrl-Enter to record the transaction.

Quicken does not automatically transfer Register checks to the Write/Print Checks screen, but you make a transfer by typing an asterisk (*) in the NUM column of the Register. (Five will appear automatically.) If you want to include an address, you will have to switch to Write/Print Checks (press Ctrl-w) and enter it there. Once you make the transfer, Quicken treats the check just as if it were originally recorded on the Write/Print Checks screen.

Recording a Deposit

Recording a deposit on a Bank account Register is not much different from recording a check. The only differences are that you leave the NUM column blank, and you record the amount in the deposit column instead of the payment column.

To record a simple deposit, correct the date if necessary, press Enter to skip the NUM column, and record the source of the money in the payee blank. Next, press Enter twice to skip the payment and c(leared) columns, and record the amount in the deposit column. Now you can complete the memo and category lines just as you would for a check. Finally, press Ctrl-Enter to record the transaction.

Usually, you will want to assign a deposit to an income category. Some exceptions are discussed in the next chapter.

Reviewing Your Work

You can review and edit all transactions, including unprinted checks, on the Register. Only unprinted checks appear on the Write/Print Checks screen. Changes made on either screen are automatically transferred to the other. After checks are printed, Quicken removes them from Write/Print Checks, and you can review and edit them only on the Register.

Obviously, you should be careful in editing amounts or payees of checks you have already printed, since the edited transactions may not match the actual checks. However, it is perfectly safe to change the category and/or class for a check, which is of no concern to the recipient or the bank.

While reviewing your work, you have full use of all of the editing commands available when you record transactions. You can also delete transactions. In addition, several special commands can help you navigate through your transactions (see Table 4.3).

When you execute any of these commands after making a change in a transaction, this message appears: Leaving Transaction. Press 1 to select Record changes and leave; press 2 to select Cancel changes and leave.

Quicken then displays the transaction indicated by the cursor command.

Table 4.3. Cursor Commands for Reviewing Transactions.

Page Up	Displays the previous check or page
Page Down	Displays the next check or page
Ctrl-Page Up	Locates the first transaction of the previous month
Ctrl-Page Down	Locates the first transaction of the next month
Home	Moves the cursor to the beginning of the check list or Register
End	Moves the cursor to the end of the check list or Register
Up Arrow, Down Arrow	On the Register moves forward or back one transaction

Finding Specific Transactions

Often you will want to locate a specific transaction on the Register or the Write/Print Checks screen. Since both list transactions in chronological order, you can easily find most transactions by using cursor controls.

In addition, the Find options on the Edit pull-down menu (F3) can help you locate transactions that inclue specific information, such as a particular payee or category, or occurred that on a given date. You can also locate a check by its number. (See Table 4.4). Repeat Find (backwards) and Repeat Find (next) work in conjunction with Find. Go to Date operates independently.

Notice that control-key commands are available for all of these options. For example, you can execute Find by pressing Ctrl-f rather than selecting the option from the menu. Once you are familiar with these commands you may prefer to use them rather than menu selections.

Table 4.4. Search Options on the Edit Pull-down Menu.

Find (Ctrl-f)	Begins the search and allows you to specify search criteria, such as a particular payee.
Repeat Find (backwards) (Ctrl-b)	Finds the next earlier transaction that matches the criteria specified with Find.
Repeat Find (next) (Ctrl-n)	Finds the next later transaction that matches the criteria specified with Find.
Go to Date (Ctrl-g)	Searches forward or backward to the next transaction on a specified date.

Using Find

The Find command helps you locate transactions that meet specific criteria, such as payee, category, or any other information recorded in a transaction, except the address on an unprinted check.

Finding a transaction is a two-step procedure. First, you select Find (Ctrl-f) and specify the information for the transaction you want to locate. Then you choose Repeat Find (backwards) (Ctrl-b) to search backwards by date or Repeat Find (next) (Ctrl-n) to search future transactions.

The search begins at the current transaction. To include all transactions, go to the first or last transaction before beginning the search. To find the first transaction that meets your search criteria, press Home to go to the first transaction, then press Ctrl-n to search forward. To find the most recent, press End to go to the last transaction, then press Ctrl-b.

When you press Ctrl-f or select Find from the Edit menu, the Transaction to Find window appears (Figure 4.6). The window is laid out exactly like an individual transaction on the Register. You can search for transactions that match any (or all) of the blanks on the window. (If the window already includes information from an earlier search, you can clear it by pressing Ctrl-d.)

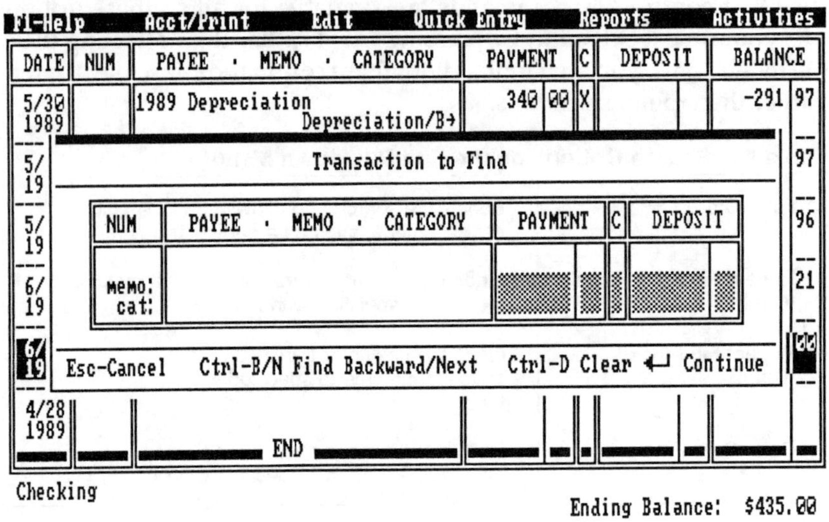

Figure 4.6. The Transaction to Find window.

Quicken will locate only transactions that match the search criteria *exactly* , except that Find does not distinguish between capital and lowercase letters. If you complete more than one blank, Quicken will find only transactions that meet *all* of the criteria specified. For example, if you enter Dr. John Smith in the payee blank, Quicken will ignore transactions made out to John Smith. If you enter Dr. John Smith as the payee and Medical as the category, Quicken will find transactions made out to Dr. John Smith and categorized as Medical, but not transactions to Dr. John Smith categorized as Dental.

You can use double periods (..) for wildcard searches if you are not sure exactly how your recorded the transaction you're looking for. For example:

`..smith..`	Finds Dr. Smith, Fred Smith, Smith & Wesson, Alias Smith & Jones, or Arrowsmith Booksellers.
`smith..`	Locates checks made out to Smith & Wesson, but not the other examples.

`..smith`	Locates checks made out to Dr. Smith and Fred Smith, but not to Smith & Wesson, Alias Smith & Jones, or Arrowsmith Booksellers.

Once you have completed the search criteria, the simplest way to complete the search is to press Ctrl-n to find the next transaction that matches or Ctrl-b to search backwards.

If you press Enter after completing the category line or Ctrl-Enter anytime the Find window is displayed, a window appears asking: Search Direction? At this point, you may select 1. Find backwards (or press Ctrl-b) to search backwards, or select 2. Find next (or press Ctrl-n) to search forwards. Esc returns you to the Transaction to Find window.

You don't have to repeat the Find (Ctrl-f) command to find another transaction that matches the same criteria. Just press Ctrl-b to search backwards or Ctrl-n to search forward. Quicken will find the next matching transaction.

With these techniques, including wildcard searches, you can easily locate any transaction, even if you have recorded hundreds on the Register. You can also locate transactions on a particular date, as explained in the next section.

Using Go to Date

The Go to Date (Ctrl-g) command on the Edit menu helps you find the next transaction on a particular date. When you execute the command, the Go to Date window (Figure 4.7) appears. As usual, you can type over the current date or press + or - to go forward or backward a day at a time.

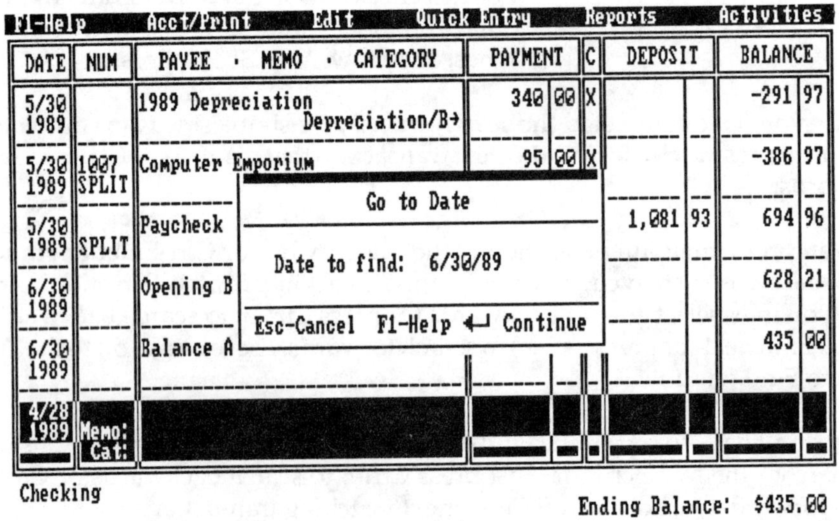

Figure 4.7. The Go to Date window.

When you press Enter to confirm the date, Quicken searches forward or backward to locate the next transaction on that date. If there are no transactions on the specified date, Quicken will find the next check *after* that date if it is later than the one currently displayed or the next check *before* the date if it is earlier.

Deleting and Voiding Transactions

When you record a transaction incorrectly, you can remove it from your Quicken records by deleting the transaction entirely or by voiding it. When you tear up a check, voiding the transaction may be preferable, since it provides a record of what happened to the check. Once a transaction is deleted, it is irretrievably lost. If you change your mind, you will simply have to enter the transaction again.

To delete a transaction:

1. Highlight it on the Register or display it on the Write/Print Checks screen.

2. Press Ctrl-d or select 2. Delete transaction from the Edit pull-down menu (F3). Quicken asks: OK to Delete Transaction?

3. Press 1 to select Delete transaction or press 2 to select Do not delete.

Voiding a transaction is safer than deleting it, because it leaves a record. However, the amount is permanently erased. If you want to keep a record of the amount, you can enter it on the memo line before you void the transaction.

You can void a transaction only on the Register: highlight the transaction, then press Ctrl-v or select 9. Void Transaction from the Edit menu.

Quicken enters the word VOID in the Payee blank, removes the amount, and marks the transaction cleared so it won't interfere with reconciliation. The rest of the information in the transaction remains intact. You can restore a voided transaction by deleting the word VOID from the payee blank and reentering the amount.

Table 4.5. Entries on the Print Register Window.

Print transactions from, to	Enter a beginning and ending date for the transactions you want to print.
Print to	Allows you to select a printer. If in doubt, choose 1. Report Printer. Selecting 4. Disk records an ASCII file on your data disk. You can call up this file in your word processor or other program.
Title (optional)	Type a report name if you want. If you leave this line blank, the report will be entitled "Register."
Print one transaction per line	Select Y(es) to condense transactions to one line each. To print transactions in full, select N(o).
Print transaction splits	If you select Y(es), Quicken prints transaction splits below the main line of each transaction. Choose N(o) for a compressed report.
Sort by check number	Choose Y(es) if you want transactions sorted first by check number, then by date. If you select N(o) transactions will be ordered by date.

PRINTING THE REGISTER

While you can print checks only in Bank accounts, you can print the Register of any type of account when the Register is displayed. To print, press Ctrl-p or select 2.

Print Register from the Acct/Print pull-down menu (F2). The Print Register window appears.

The unusual feature of this window is that it allows you to sort transactions by check number. This is the only place in Quicken you can do this. The rest of the options are explained in Table 4.5. When you have completed the window, press Ctrl-Enter to print. If the Register does not print correctly, you may need to change your printer settings. See Chapter 13 for instructions.

Bank Reconciliation

The Reconcile option on the Activities pull-down menu (F2) offers an easy and straightforward way of checking your records against your bank statement. You will simply mark your Quicken transactions as cleared as you check them against your bank statement; Quicken does all of the math.

If there is a discrepancy between your records and your statement, you can recheck and edit your work, add or delete transactions, or correct your opening balance. If the difference is small, have the program update your balance to match the statement.

To ensure the accuracy of your records, you should reconcile your Quicken Bank accounts each time you receive a statement. If necessary, however, you can process several statements at once, beginning with the oldest.

Your First Bank Reconciliation

When you begin using Quicken, your records and your bank statements are likely to be out of sync. You may have recorded transactions that cleared before the current statement, or the statement may include transactions that you have not recorded in Quicken. You will need to establish a point at which Quicken and the bank agree on the balance in your account, then make sure that all subsequent transactions are recorded.

Provided you are satisfied with the accuracy of the opening balance on the first statement you receive after you begin using Quicken, the reconciliation procedure solves all of these problems. During reconciliation you can mark old transactions as cleared before the current statement, add transactions, or update your opening balance to match the bank's at the beginning of the statement period.

Once you have completed your first reconciliation, your Quicken records should be accurate from then on, but you may not have any Quicken records for earlier periods or your records for those periods may be incomplete. Suppose, for example, that you begin using Quicken on June 1 and your next statement begins on June 15. Once you have reconciled your account, your Quicken records should be accurate from June 15 forward. This will probably mean that July is the first month for which you can create accurate Quicken reports.

The easiest solution is to rely on your paper records until the first period for which your Quicken records are complete. If need be, you can transfer old records from paper to Quicken as far back as you want, then begin reconciliation with the first period in which you recorded transactions.

Beginning Reconciliation

Before you begin reconciliation, the Write/Print Checks Screen or the Register of your Bank account should be displayed. To begin the procedure, press F6 to pull down the Activities menu, then choose 2. Reconcile. The Reconcile Register window (Figure 4.8) appears. As with other Quicken windows, you simply fill in the blanks, pressing Enter after each.

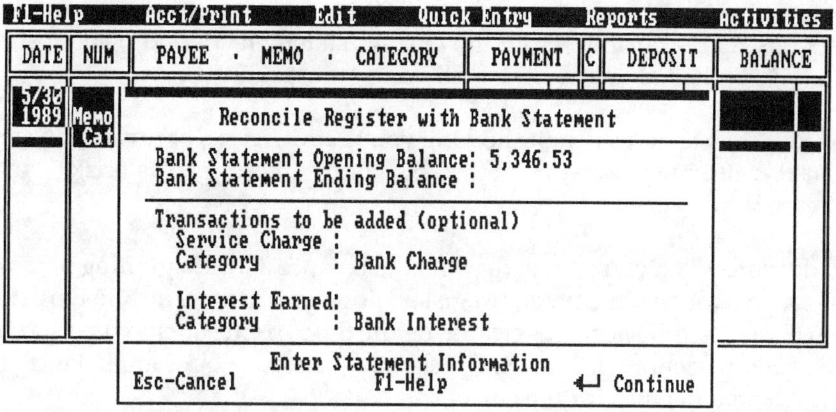

Figure 4.8. Recording information from your bank statement.

Quicken automatically enters your opening balance, according to your Quicken records, in the first blank. (This is the balance prior to any uncleared transactions, not necessarily the opening balance you established when you set up the account or the balance at the beginning of the statement period.) Compare the opening balance on the screen with the one on your bank statement. If they conflict, correct the entry to match the bank statement's opening balance.

In the next blank, Bank Statement Ending Balance, enter the closing balance shown on your bank statement. The remaining blanks allow you to record service charges and interest earned, as reported on your bank statement. Quicken automatically assigns these to categories called Bank Charge and Bank Interest, but you can change them if you want.

When you have finished, press Ctrl-Enter to record the window. What happens next depends on whether you have adjusted your opening balance. (Skip the following section if you have not.)

Correcting an Opening Balance

If you changed the opening balance on the Reconcile Register window, a window appears warning you: Opening Balance Does Not Match Bank. This means that you need to work with transactions that occurred before the beginning of the current statement period before you begin clearing current transactions. When you have read the window, press Enter to continue.

A special version of the Register appears, with a Reconciliation Summary at the bottom. For the moment, the objective is to bring the Opening Bal Difference at the top of the summary's right column to 0.00 by adding, correcting, or clearing transactions that occurred before the current statement period. (The rest of the summary is explained below under Clearing Transactions.)

The Register works as usual, allowing you to add, delete, or revise transactions. You can also clear a transaction on the Register by entering an asterisk (*) or a c in the C(leared) column.

In addition, when you correct the opening balance at the beginning of reconciliation—and only then—the special Register allows you to enter an X in the C(leared) column to mark a transaction as cleared before the current statement period. When you clear a transaction with an X, Quicken adjusts your opening balance, rather than the cleared balance for the current statement.

To locate the opening balance discrepancy, compare the transactions on the Register with past bank statements, beginning with the previous month. Look for uncleared transactions, errors in the amount of a transaction, omitted transactions, transactions recorded more than once, and bank fees or interest earned that you have not recorded.

Since uncleared transactions are the easiest to spot, you may want to begin there. Just look for transactions with blank C(leared) columns. If you find a transaction that cleared before your current statement but is not marked "cleared" in your Quicken records, enter an X—not an asterisk—in the C(leared) column. When you have corrected discrepancies between your previous bank statements and your Quicken records, the Opening Bal Difference in the Reconciliation Summary should be 0.00. If you prefer, however, you can have Quicken automatically enter an adjustment to bring your records and statement into agreement, as explained below.

When you are ready to begin working with transactions on the current statement, press F9 to shift to the Reconciliation Summary screen, described in the next section.

Clearing Transactions

After you have completed the Reconcile Register window—and, if necessary, resolved any discrepancy in opening balance—you can begin clearing transactions on the Reconciliation Summary screen (Figure 4.9). This screen appears automatically if you do not change your opening balance, or when you press F9 after reconciling your opening balance.

F1-Help　Acct/Print　Edit　Quick Entry　Reports　Activities

NUM	C	AMOUNT	DATE	PAYEE	MEMO
▸		400.50	5/ 3/89	Deposit	John Smith
		400.00	5/ 3/89	Deposit	John Smith
		-3,000.00	5/ 3/89	Transfer	
		-100.00	5/ 5/89	Computer Emporium	Withdrawal 5/5
		-100.00	5/ 7/89	ATM withdrawal	
		100.00	5/14/89	Cash Advance	
		-195.46	5/14/89	VISA	
	*	-3.25	5/30/89	Service Charge	
		-340.00	5/30/89	1989 Depreciation	
	*	13.26	5/30/89	Interest Earned	

▪ To Mark Cleared Items, press Space Bar　▪ To Add or Change Items, press F9

RECONCILIATION SUMMARY

Items You Have Marked Cleared (*)				
			Cleared (X,*) Balance	5,356.54
1	Checks, Debits	-3.25	Bank Statement Balance	546.16
1	Deposits, Credits	13.26	Difference	4,810.38

F1-Help　F8-Mark Range　F9-View as Register　Ctrl-End Done

Figure 4.9. The Reconciliation Summary screen.

The top part of the screen lists uncleared transactions. (If you entered a service charge or interest earned, note that it is automatically entered and marked as cleared with an asterisk.) Below, to the left, the Reconciliation Summary lists the number and total amount of checks or debits and of deposits or credits. To the right, the summary compares the balance in your account after all cleared transactions with the bank statement's ending balance.

At the outset, the summary will not balance, because you have not begun clearing transactions. As you proceed, the Cleared Balance will come closer to the Bank Statement Balance. If your records match the statement's, the Difference should be 0.00 when you are finished.

As you match a transaction on the screen with your bank statement, highlight the transaction and press the space bar or Enter to mark it as cleared. An asterisk (*) will appear in the C(leared) column. (To unclear a transaction, repeat the procedure. The asterisk will disappear.)

If all goes well, you may find that all of your recorded checks match the statement. In this case, you can take a shortcut by marking a range of checks as cleared at once. To do this, press F8. When the Mark Range window appears (Figure 4.10), type the beginning and ending check numbers of the range, pressing Enter

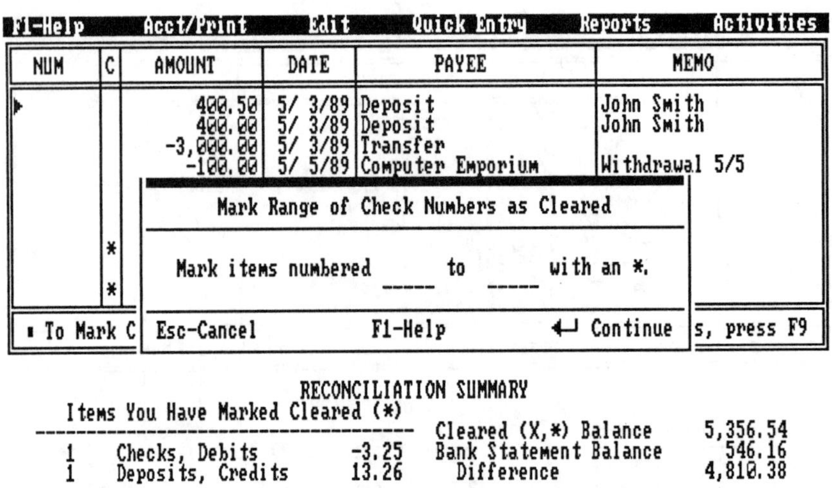

Figure 4.10. Clearing a range of checks.

after each. When the Reconciliation Summary screen reappears, the checks in the range will be marked with asterisks. You will still have to clear deposits and other transactions individually.

If your records balance with the bank statement when you have finished clearing transactions, press Ctrl-End (Ctrl-Enter doesn't work here) to complete the reconciliation procedure. Quicken offers a congratulatory note and asks whether you want to print a reconciliation report. See the last section of this chapter for printing instructions.

If your account still doesn't balance, Quicken offers help in finding the problem. Read on.

Making Corrections

As you check transactions on the Reconciliation Summary screen against your bank statement, you may find discrepancies in amounts, missing transactions, or transactions that cleared before the current statement period. The reconciliation procedure provides a special version of the Register to help resolve such conflicts.

To make a correction, press F9 to switch to the special Register. (This is the same Register you saw first if you changed your opening balance.) The Reconciliation Summary remains at the bottom of the screen to keep you up to date with your progress. (Press F9 again to return to the Reconciliation Summary Screen.)

The Register works as usual, allowing you to add, delete, or revise transactions. You can also clear a transaction on the Register by entering an asterisk or a c in the C(leared) column. (See the last section for information on clearing transactions before the current statement period.)

When you have finished clearing transactions and making corrections, the Cleared Balance should equal the Bank Statement Balance, and the Difference should be 0.00. Congratulations! Your Quicken records now balance. Press Ctrl-End (not Ctrl-Enter) to complete the procedure. (You can print a Reconciliation Report if you want, as explained in the last section below.)

If your account still doesn't balance, you can recheck your work. A good place to start is by comparing the number and amounts of cleared items on the Reconciliation Summary with those on your statement. If you find a difference, you can narrow your search. If you still have an Opening Balance discrepancy, at least part of the problem occurred before the beginning of the current statement.

If the difference between your records and your statement is small, you can have Quicken make a correction in either your Opening Balance or your Cleared Balance. This is explained below.

Having Quicken Adjust Your Balance

Your records may not always match the bank's. If your Reconciliation Summary does not balance after you complete the procedure, you have one of the following problems:

- Your Quicken opening balance does not match the bank's. This means that the discrepancy occurred before the opening date of your current statement.
- The transaction totals you have recorded since the opening date do not match those on your statement.
- The bank statement is incorrect.

The most accurate solution is to find any discrepancies and correct them. Nevertheless, if you press Ctrl-End to complete the Reconciliation Summary screen when there is still a discrepancy, Quicken gives you a chance to update your balance automatically.

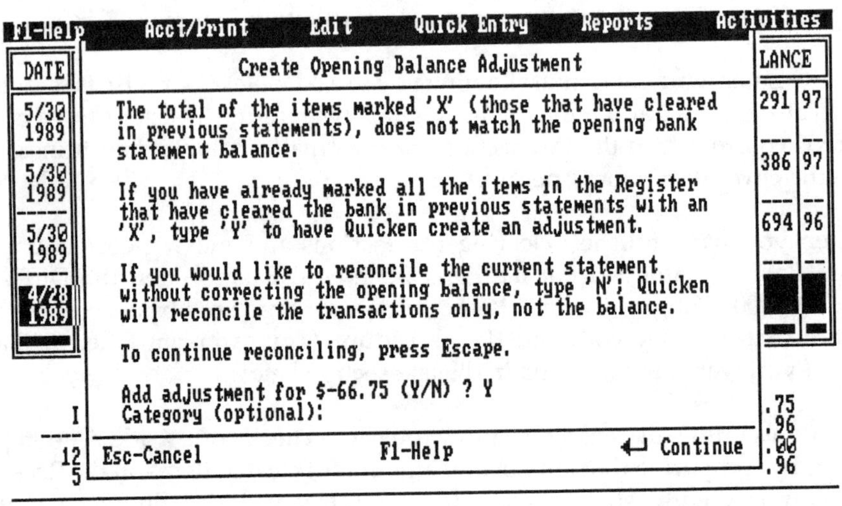

Figure 4.11. Creating an opening balance adjustment after reconciliation.

If your Opening Balance conflicts with the bank's you will see a screen labeled Create Opening Balance Adjustment (Figure 4.11). Enter Y(es) to have Quicken enter a transaction to adjust your balance or N(o) to complete reconciliation without updating. If you elect to accept the balance adjustment, you can assign it to a category if you want. The transaction will be dated on the current date, but you can go back and change the date after reconciliation.

If there is still a discrepancy between Quicken and your statement, you will see a new screen, labeled

```
Problem: Check Register does not balance with Bank
Statement.
```

(This window appears first if there is no discrepancy in opening balances.) At this point, you can press F9 to return to the Register and make additional adjustments or press Enter to update the account balance.

If you choose to make the adjustment, a window labeled Adding Balance Adjustment Entry appears (Figure 4.12). To accept, enter Y(es) to confirm, then enter a category if you want. (If you enter N for No, Quicken returns you to the reconciliation Register.) You cannot complete reconcilation without balancing your account.

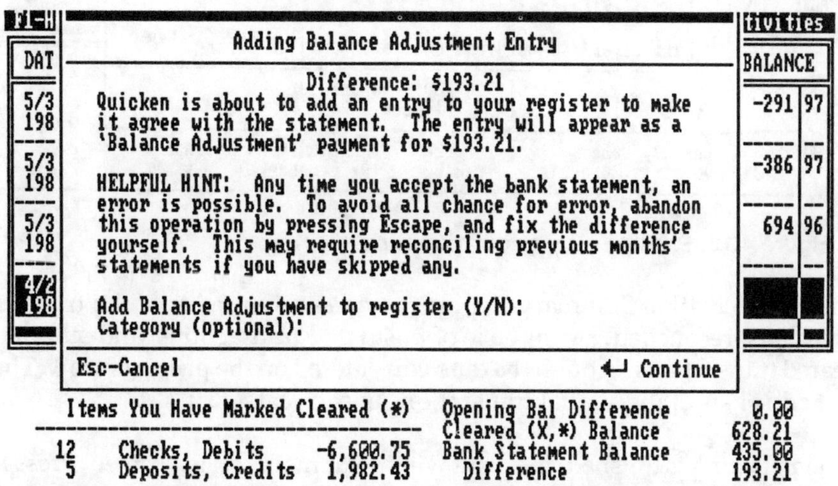

Figure 4.12. Adjusting an account balance to complete reconciliation.

When you complete the adjustment screen, Quicken notifies you that the Register has been adjusted to agree with your statement and offers you the option of printing a Reconciliation Report, as explained in the next section. Again, the adjustment transaction will be dated on the current date, but you can change it later.

Printing a Reconciliation Report

When you have completed reconciliation, Quicken asks: Print reconciliation report (Y/N). If you enter N(o) (or press Enter), the Main Menu reappears. To print a report, type Y(es) and press Enter. A window labeled Print Reconciliation Report appears (Figure 4.13). Fill out the blanks, then press Ctrl-Enter.

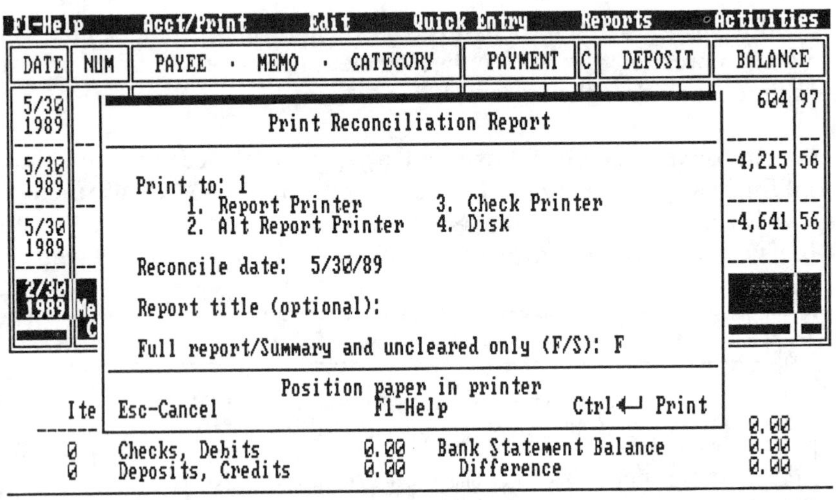

Figure 4.13. Printing a reconciliation report.

The Reconciliation Summary Report provides a summary of the transactions you have just reconciled, a summary of postdated transactions, and subtotals for uncleared transactions through the date you entered on the print window. The Full Report adds lists of individual transactions in each category.

When printing is finished, the print window remains on the screen. Press Esc to return to the Main Menu. For more information about printing reports, refer to Chapter 7, Basic Reports.

CONCLUSION

This chapter has explained how to write and print checks, record deposits, review transactions on the Register and the Write/Print Checks screen, and reconcile your Quicken records with your bank statement. In the next chapter, you will learn how to enter additional types of transactions to tailor your Quicken records to your personal situation.

5

More Transactions

In the last chapter, you learned to record basic payments and deposits in a Bank account and to reconcile your bank records with your statement. These features barely scratch the surface of Quicken's ability to record almost any type of event that affects your financial life.

In this chapter, you'll learn to use one of the program's most powerful and flexible features—split transactions. Split transactions allow you to assign a single transaction to up to 30 different purposes. Other topics include:

- Deposits with cash back.
- Transferring money between accounts.
- Cash transactions in Bank and Cash accounts.
- Managing Credit Card accounts, reconciling statements, and paying bills.
- Using Other Asset accounts and Other Liability accounts to keep track of noncash assets and liabilities.

Together, these features allow you to set up a full-fledged accounting system for a small business or to tailor Quicken to your personal needs. In special cases, such as payroll, accounts receivable, accounts payable, and other advanced topics, more detailed explanations are offered in later chapters.

Split Transactions

Sometimes a single transaction includes several items for different purposes. A mortgage payment, for example, usually includes payments for principal, interest, taxes, and insurance. Or you might write a check at a department store for a video tape, a shirt, a new valve for the toilet, and a gift for Uncle Ed. Or a single bank deposit might come from several sources.

Quicken's split transaction feature is designed for just such occasions. It allows you to divide a single transaction into as many as 30 parts, each with its own category and/or class, description, and amount. Quicken even helps with the math. The first 15 lines of a split transaction appear on the voucher portion of voucher checks, but not on regular checks or wallet checks.

You can also use the split transaction window to:

- Assign parts of the same transaction to subcategories of one main category.
- Add up the total amount of a transaction when, for example, you are writing one check to cover several items or depositing several checks at once.
- Write memos longer than the 31 characters that will fit on the memo line.
- Record transactions, such as cash purchases, that do not affect your account balance.

Split transactions can add useful detail to your Quicken records. The way they appear in your Quicken reports depends on the type of report. In Summary Reports, they are treated as if they were completely separate transactions. In Transaction Reports, a split transaction is usually treated as single entry, with the notation that the transaction is split. However, you can elect to show split transaction details. In Account Balance reports, split transactions are not a factor, unless you elect to show class detail as explained in Chapter 7.

This section explains the general uses of split transactions. More specific applications are suggested in later chapters.

Using the Split Transaction Window

You can open the Split Transaction window any time the Write/Print Checks screen or the Register is displayed. If you are splitting a previously recorded transaction, first select the transaction on the Register or display the check on the Write/Print Checks screen. The cursor can be anywhere within the selected transaction.

You can open the Split Transaction window (Figure 5.1) by pressing Ctrl-s or by selecting 3. Split Transaction from the Edit pull-down menu (F3). This window is basically an extension of the category, memo, and amount blanks of any Quicken transaction, and the same basic rules for entering information apply.

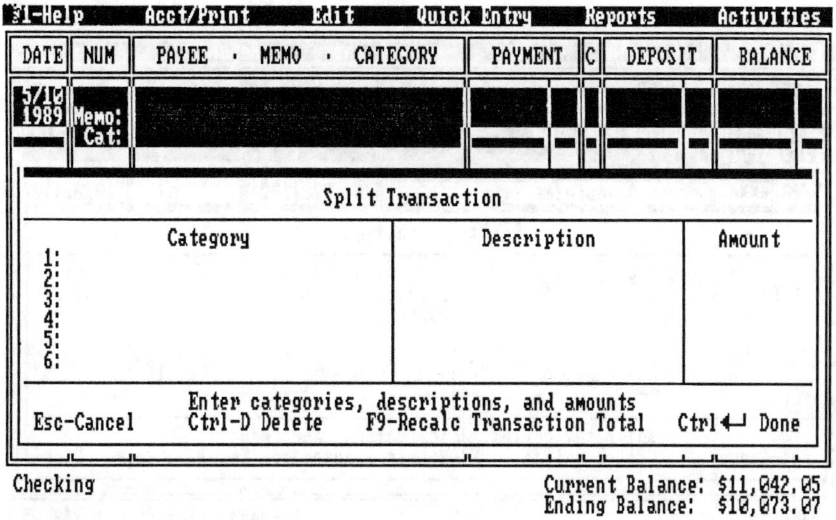

Figure 5.1. The Split Transaction window.

Splitting Transactions

The most common use for split transactions is to assign a single payment or deposit to several categories or classes. As always, you can type out the entry in the category column, or make selections from the Category and Class Lists. The description column is the equivalent of the memo line for an unsplit transaction.

Suppose, for example, you write a check on your business checking account for $96.66 at a computer store for a printer repair (say, $67.32) and a 3,000-sheet carton of computer paper ($27.95 plus 5 percent sales tax, a total of $29.34). (Sales tax for personal expenses is no longer deductible, but sales tax on business purchases is included in the cost of the item.) You want to assign these expenses to expense categories called Repairs and Office.

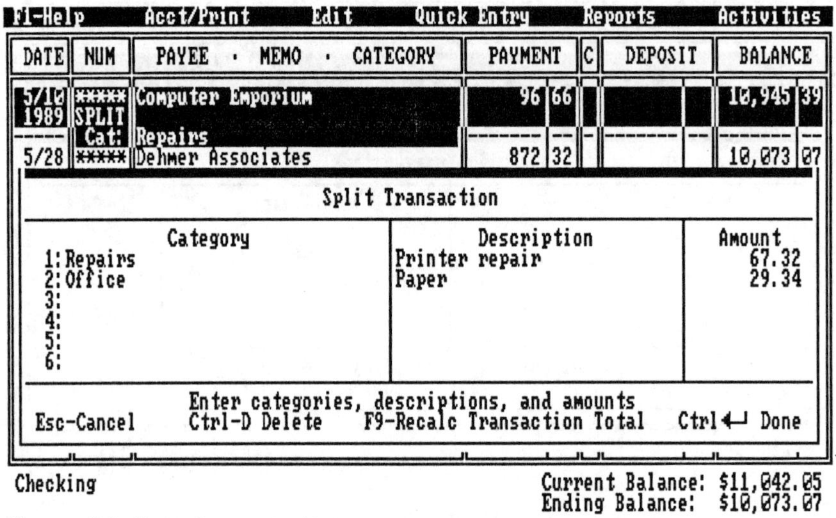

Figure 5.2. Entering a check in the Split Transaction window.

This transaction is shown in Figure 5.2. Follow these steps to record it:

1. Call up the Register for your business checking account and fill transaction for the total amount ($96.66) as usual until you get to the category line.

2. Open the Split Transaction window (press Ctrl-s or select 3. Split Transaction from the Edit menu).

3. Enter Repairs in the category column of line 1. Type a note, such as Printer repair, in the Description column, and 67.32. Notice that each time you enter an amount, Quicken automatically balances the transaction by entering an amount below.

4. Repeat the procedure for line 2, entering Office in the category column, Paper in the Description column, and 29.34 in the Amount column.

5. Press Ctrl-Enter to complete the split. Quicken closes the Split Transaction window, and returns to Write/Print Checks or the Register, and you can record the transaction as usual.

When you record a split transaction on a Register, SPLIT appears in the NUM column. On the Write/Print Checks screen, SPLIT appears below the category line. These notations will not affect your printed checks or reports.

If you later change your mind about splitting a transaction, you can easily turn it back into a simple transaction. To unsplit a transaction, highlight it on the Register or display it on Write/Print Checks, open the Split Transaction window, and press Ctrl-d until you have erased all of the information in it. When you press Ctrl-Enter to close the window, the transaction becomes a simple transaction, and you can finish recording it as usual. You may need to enter a new category and/or class on the category line.

Split transactions allow you to keep your records in as much detail as you want. You can do any other type of transaction. Additional examples are provided later in this chapter.

Balancing Split Transactions

Occasionally, you may enter a total amount for a transaction, then find that your transaction splits don't equal the amount you originally entered. As a simplified example, you might enter a total of $100, with splits of only $50 and $45. When a split transaction doesn't balance, Quicken automatically enters the balance in the next line on the Split Transaction window. Your Split Transaction window in this example might look like Figure 5.3.

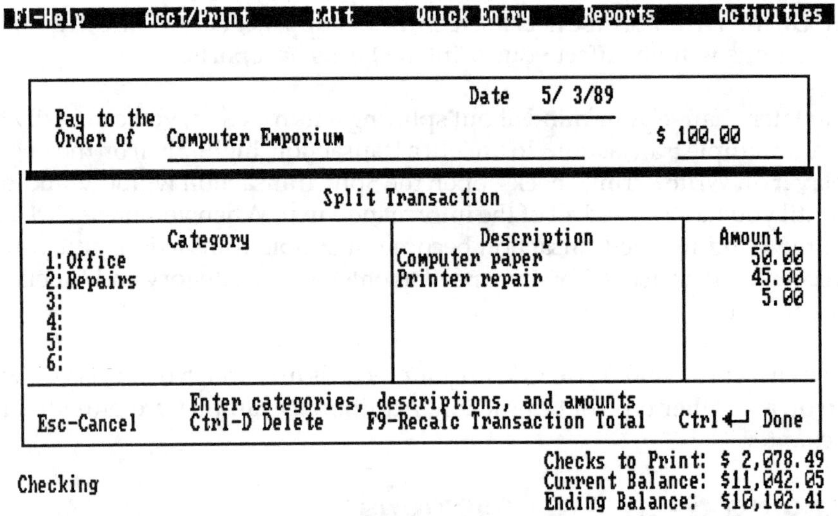

Figure 5.3. An unbalanced split transaction.

You may need to revise the information in the window. But if the problem is that you entered the incorrect amount on the Write/Print Checks screen or a Register, Quicken can automatically adjust it for you.

The procedure is simple: Press Ctrl-d to delete the last amount in the Split Transaction window, then press F9 to recalculate the amount you originally entered. Quicken automatically enters the correction on the main transaction screen. You can now complete the transaction as usual.

Adding Up Split Transactions

You can use the Split Transactions window as an adding machine when you write a single check to cover several items or make a deposit that comes from several sources. When you use this technique, you initially leave the amount line of the main transaction screen blank.

On the Write/Print Checks screen, Quicken knows that you are entering a payment, and you enter the amounts within the split as usual. On the Register, however, deposits are entered as positive numbers and payments are entered as negative, because Quicken does not know which type of transaction you are recording until you complete the split transaction window. That is, for a $100 check, you would enter -100 in the amount column of the Split Transaction window; for a $100 deposit, you would enter 100.

The same principle applies to other types of accounts, as shown in Table 5.1. This is a critical point: outflows from the current account must be preceded by a minus sign (-); inflows are entered as positive numbers.

This may seem confusing at first, but it makes perfect sense. Bank accounts, Cash accounts, and Other Asset accounts are all assets. When you record an expense, the account balance *decreases,* so you need the minus sign; when you record income, the balance *increases.* Credit Card and Other Liability accounts are liabilities, so they work in opposite fashion. Expenditures *increase* the account balance, while payments to creditors *decrease* it.

These rules apply *only* when you are entering a new transaction. Once you record the transaction, Quicken puts the total in the Payment or Deposit column of the Register, as appropriate. When you reopen the Split Transaction window, the amounts will be positive as usual.

When you use the Split Transaction window as an adding machine, amounts may be positive or negative, depending on the type of transaction and the type of account (Table 5.1.).

Table 5.1. Using the Split Transaction Window As an Adding Machine.

Bank Accounts	PAYMENTs are negative, DEPOSITs are positive.
Cash Accounts	Amounts you SPEND are negative, amounts you RECEIVE are positive.
Credit Card Accounts	Amounts you CHARGE are negative, PAYMENTs are positive.
Other Asset Accounts	DECREASEs are negative, INCREASEs are positive.
Other Liability Accounts	INCREASEs are negative, DECREASEs are positive.

To use the Split Transaction window to add up a transaction total:

1. Leave the amount line of the main transaction blank and open the Split Transaction window.

2. Type the categories and/or classes, Descriptions, and Amounts of the split transaction in the window.

3. Press Ctrl-Enter to close the Split Transaction window. Quicken automatically enters the total in the Amount blank of the main transaction.

4. Press Ctrl-Enter again to record the entire transaction.

You can also have Quicken recalculate the total of a split transaction when you edit amounts on the Split Transaction window. Remember that the record is now a normal split transaction, and you don't have to worry about the positive and negative entries discussed earlier.

To use Quicken as an adding machine while editing a split transaction:

1. Highlight the transaction on the Register and open the Split Transaction window.

2. Make any changes, additions, or deletions you want. Quicken automatically adds an amount on the line below the last split to balance the transaction.

3. Move the cursor to the line occupied by the balancing amount and press Ctrl–d to delete the amount.

4. Press F9 to have Quicken recalculate the total on the Register. You can now close the window and record your changes as usual.

These examples work when all of the amounts in a split transaction are the same type—when you are adding up invoices to write a check or receipts to make a deposit, for example. Some split transactions will include *both* positive and negative amounts—deposits with cash back and payroll checks with deductions withheld, for example. Examples are given below in this chapter and in later chapters.

Extending Memos

The memo line of a Quicken transaction provides space for 31 characters. You can use the Split Transaction window to record additional information without assigning a transaction to additional categories or classes.

To record an extended memo, fill out the transaction as usual, then open the Split Transaction window. Now you can record whatever information you want in the description blanks of the Split Transaction window, pressing Enter to bypass the category and amount blanks. When finished, close the window and record the transaction as usual.

> NOTE: The Change Settings Menu provides an alternative way to record additional memo information. Select the option 4. Extra message line on check to add an additional message to the right of the address box on the Write/Print Checks screen. This message will be printed to the right of the address on your Quicken checks, but it will not be recorded in the Register or appear on reports.

Additional Transactions

There are other types of transactions you might want to record in a Bank account. In addition, the procedure for recording transactions in each of the other types of is slightly different. Using various techniques and account types, you can record almost any event that affects your financial life. The following examples make the point.

A Deposit with Cash Back

Many people deposit part of a check and take the rest in cash. Such deposits are quite easy to record as split transactions in your Bank account.

Suppose, for example, that you receive a check for $500 from a client. When you go to the bank, you deposit $400 in your Bank account and take the other $100 in Cash. You want to assign the $500 to an Income category called Receipts. You do not want to record every expenditure you make with the $100, so you assign it to an Expense category called Miscellaneous.

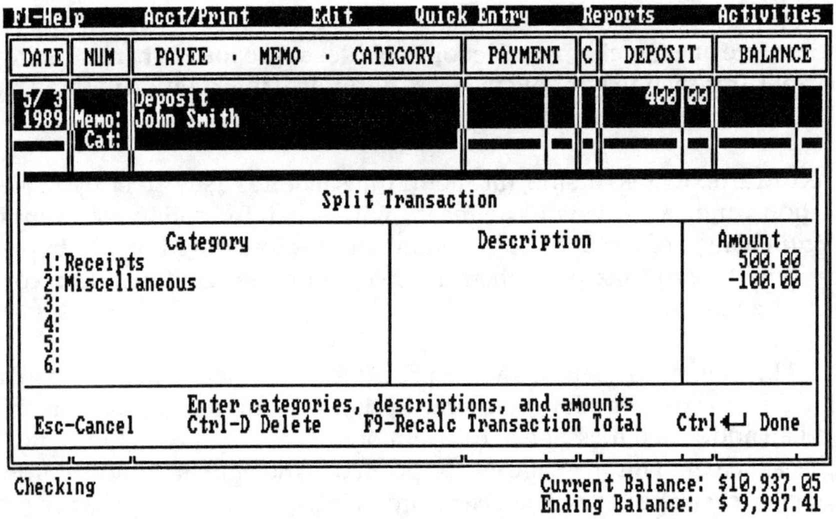

Figure 5.4. Recording a deposit with cash back.

Figure 5.4 shows the deposit entered on the Register of a Bank account. The Date, Payee, and Memo blanks are completed as usual. To record the split transaction:

1. Enter 400—the amount you actually deposit in your account—in the Deposit column and open the Split Transaction window.

2. Enter Receipts (the name of your Income category) in the category blank and enter a description if you want.

3. Enter 500—the total amount of the check—in the amount column. Quicken automatically enters -100 in the amount column of the next line to balance the transaction.

4. Enter Miscellaneous (the name of your Expense category) in the next category blank. Now you can close the Split Transaction window and complete the transaction as usual.

You have recorded three things: a deposit of $400, income of $500, and an expense of $100. Your reports of income and expenses and Cash Flow Reports will reflect the transaction accurately.

Many people routinely handle deposits in this fashion. However, your bank records will not match your records in Quicken, because the $100 assigned to Miscellaneous goes through the Quicken Bank account but is never actually deposited at the bank. You will have no paper record that accurately reflects the transaction. Quicken reports will handle the transaction correctly, but you might want to consider depositing the entire $500, then making a separate withdrawal.

Transfers

Everyone transfers money from one account to another. A typical example is transferring money from your checking account to a bank money market account. No income or expense is involved; you're simply shifting money from one place to another.

Quicken treats all transactions between two accounts the same way, even though two actual bank accounts may not be involved. If you use a Cash account to record cash purchases, for example, you can record a cash withdrawal as a transfer from your Bank account to the Cash account. No expense is incurred until you spend the money and record the transaction in the Cash account.

Quicken also treats payments of credit card bills as transfers—the check reduces the balance in your Bank account and the balance in your Credit Card account. In this case, you have decreased an asset and reduced a liability. Expenses are recorded when you enter purchases in the Credit Card account.

Suppose you want to transfer $2,000 from your checking account to your money market account at the bank. You can enter the transaction either as a payment in your checking account (Figure 5.5), or as a deposit in your money market account (Figure 5.6). Quicken automatically records the transfer in the Register of the corresponding account.

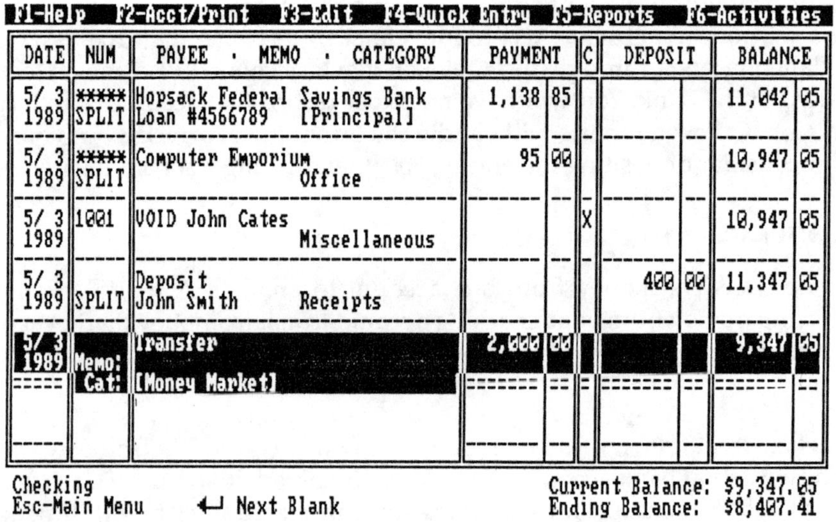

Figure 5.5. Entering a transfer in a checking Bank account.

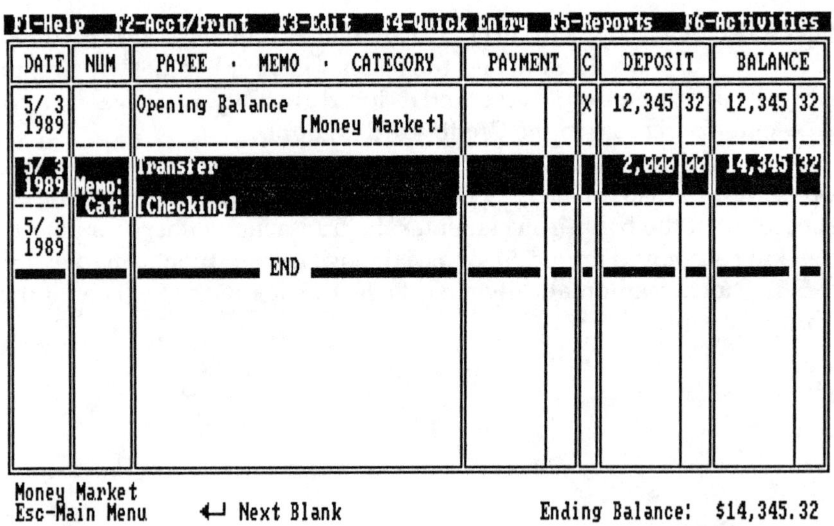

Figure 5.6. A transfer from checking as it appears in a money market Bank account.

Just fill out the transaction as usual, entering the corresponding account on the category line. You can type the name of the transfer account or select it from the

Category List. Either way, Quicken automatically encloses the entry on the category line in brackets to indicate a transfer.

When you make a transfer, the Edit pull-down menu provides a way to switch immediately to the same transaction in the corresponding account. Just highlight the transaction on the Register of your current account, then press Ctrl-x or select 8. Go to Transfer from the Edit menu (F3). The Register of the corresponding account appears, with the transaction highlighted.

The two transactions involved in a transfer are paired. You can edit the payee and memo lines independently, but changes in any other blanks will automatically be entered in the other transaction.

Transfers involving Other Asset accounts and Other Liability accounts may require more thought. Examples include paying cash from your Bank account for securities, principal payments on car loans and mortgages, the purchase of capital equipment, the sale of depreciated business equipment, and home improvements that increase your basis in your house.

Other Assets and Liabilities are advanced features. In formal business accounting, transfers are as straightforward as transfers between Bank accounts. If you are keeping records more informally, however—especially for personal record keeping—these accounts may behave in ways you don't expect. Other Asset and Liability transactions are discussed in more detail below.

Cash Transactions

Most people don't need to keep track of every minor cash expenditure. The easiest way to record personal cash expenditures is to treat withdrawals from your Bank accounts as simple expenses. Even if you classify cash transactions this way, you can still use split transactions to record significant cash purchases in your Bank account without disrupting the balance.

If you use this method, you should consider assigning your withdrawals to an expense category, such as Miscellaneous, rather than leaving them uncategorized. Otherwise, they will turn up in your reports under the heading of Other. That's fine if you never unintentionally omit a category from a transaction. But when you assign cash withdrawals to Miscellaneous, you know how you intended to classify them. If the Other classification unexpectedly shows up in reports because of a mistake, you can easily locate uncategorized transactions and correct them.

A Cash account allows you to keep more detailed records of cash transactions. If you use a Cash account for personal finances, it is unlikely that you will want to record every quarter you spend for a newspaper or lunch at McDonalds. Fortunately, you can easily update your Cash account balance and assign whatever is left over to Miscellaneous expense.

For business bookkeeping, on the other hand, you may want to monitor your cash transactions as carefully as you manage your checking account. Since Quicken Cash accounts work almost exactly like Bank accounts, entering transactions is almost the same.

Cash Transactions in a Bank Account

Even if you do not record most of your cash transactions, you can use split transactions to record important cash expenditures in a Bank account without disrupting the balance. Again, if you use this method, it is recommended that you assign withdrawals to a Miscellaneous Expense category rather than leave them uncategorized.

Suppose, for example, that you withdraw $100 and spend $45.45 on office supplies. The simplest solution is to record the withdrawal as a simple split transaction, with $45.45 assigned to Office Supplies and $54.55 to Miscellaneous. (You can go back and split the original withdrawal after you record it if necessary.) As shown in Figure 5.7, 100 is entered in the payment column of the Register, and the amounts are entered in the Split Transaction window.

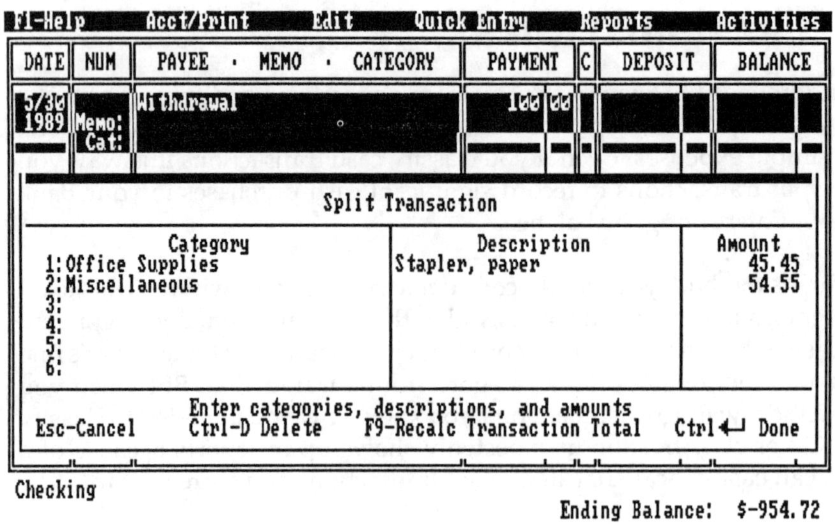

Figure 5.7. Recording a cash expense by splitting a withdrawal.

This transaction decreases the bank balance by $100, split between Office Supplies and Miscellaneous. The purchase is recorded as though it occurred on the day of the withdrawal, whether it actually did or not. For more detail, or more accuracy, a Cash account may be the solution.

CASH ACCOUNT TRANSACTIONS

The above methods of recording cash transactions work well on an occasional basis. However, if you frequently record cash transactions, it may be easier and more accurate to record them in a Cash account, particularly if you need to make a complete accounting of transactions—in a petty cash fund, for example. In addition, using a Cash account allows you to date your transactions more accurately than splitting transactions in a Bank account.

The Register for a Cash account (Figure 5.8) is similar to a Bank account Register. These columns are labeled differently, but work like their Bank account counterparts, as shown in Table 5.2.

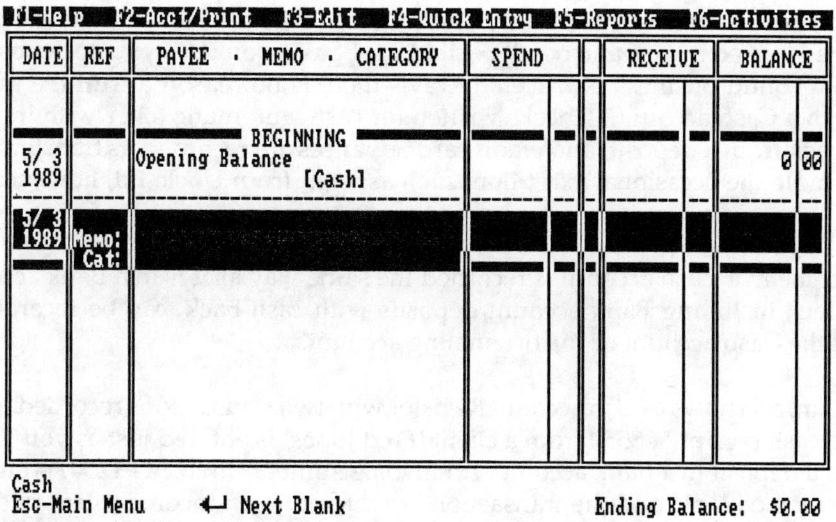

Figure 5.8. The Cash Account Register.

The REF, Spend, and Receive entries in a Cash account work like NUM, Payment, and Deposit in a Bank account (Table 5.2).

Table 5.2. Comparison of a Cash Account to a Bank Account.

REF	Allows you to enter a reference number of a cash transaction. Designed with petty cash accounts in mind.
SPEND	Is the equivalent of the Payment blank in a Bank account. Used for any cash outflows, including expenditures and transfers to other accounts.
RECEIVE	Is comparable to the Deposit blank in Bank accounts. For recording any inflows of cash, including transfers from other accounts.

There are only two kinds of transactions in Cash accounts—those that put cash in your hand and those that take it out.

Receiving Cash

There are basically only two legal sources of cash: receipts assigned to Income categories and transfers from other accounts. We have just seen one example, income received in cash and not deposited in a Bank account. (If you do deposit the cash—a sound business practice anyway—there is no reason to run the money through a Cash account.) Checks written for cash, automatic teller withdrawals, cash back from a deposit, and credit card advances are recorded as transfers. You can handle the occasional exception, such as a gift from Uncle Ed, however you want.

Income in a Cash account is recorded the same way as it is in a Bank account. Transfers, including Bank account deposits with cash back, can be recorded in either the Cash account or the originating account.

Figure 5.9 shows a Cash account Register with two transactions recorded. In the first, a cash receipt of $550 from a client (Fred Jones) is entered just as you would record a deposit in a Bank account. An invoice number (Invoice #1234) is entered in the memo blank, and the transaction is assigned to an income category called Receipts. The second transaction is an automatic teller withdrawal for $100, recorded as a transfer from Bank account called Checking. The account name is enclosed in brackets ([ ]) to designate a transfer.

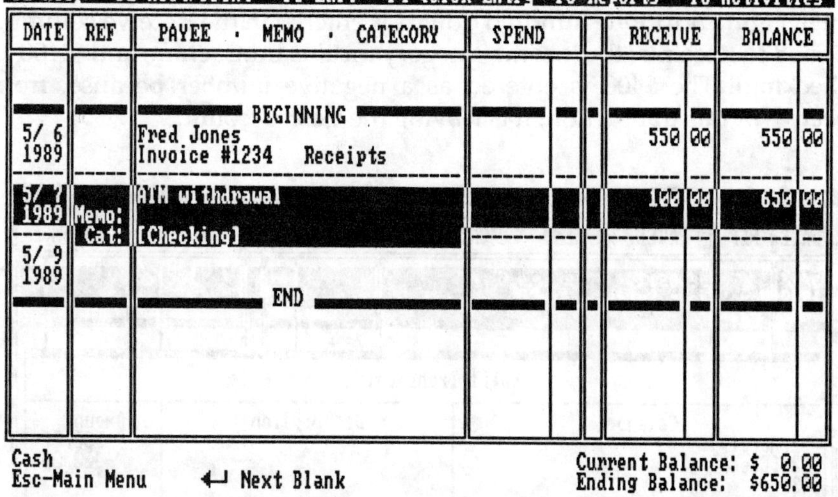

Figure 5.9. Recording a cash receipt and an automatic teller withdrawal in a Cash account.

Quicken also records the ATM transaction in the Checking Bank account, with [Cash] entered in the category blank there. The same withdrawal could just have easily been entered in the Checking account, assigned to [Cash] on the category line. The record in the Cash account would look the same.

As with any transfer, you can switch to the same transaction in the corresponding account by pressing Ctrl-x or by choosing 8. Go to Transfer from the Edit pull-down menu.

Deposits with Cash Back

You can record a deposit with cash back in a Cash account rather than a Bank account. Either way, the transaction will be recorded in the Registers of both accounts.

Earlier, we recorded a check from $500 from a client named John Smith, with $500 assigned to an Income category called Receipts; $400 was deposited in a Checking Bank account, and $100 was assigned to a Miscellaneous expense category. To assign the cash back to a Cash account rather than a Miscellaneous expense account, you could record the transaction in exactly the same way in your Bank account, entering [Cash] in the category blank, instead of Miscellaneous.

You could also enter the transaction as a split transaction in a Cash account as shown in Figure 5.10. One hundred dollars is entered in the Receive column; $500 is assigned to Receipts, the income category for this transaction; and -$400 is sent to [Checking]. The $400 is entered as a negative number because, from the perspective of this transaction, it is leaving the Cash account.

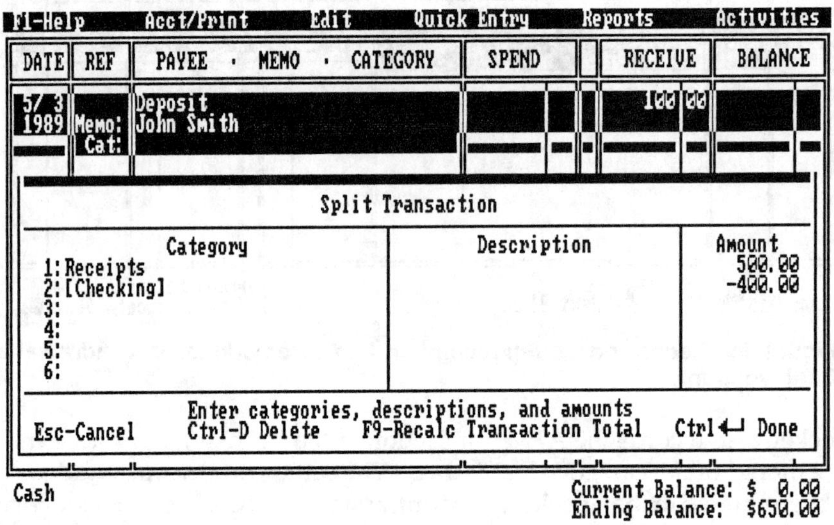

Figure 5.10. Recording a deposit with cash back in an Cash account.

SPENDING CASH

Recording cash expenditures in a Cash account is essentially the same as entering payments in the Register of a Bank account. The only difference is that the column for entering the expenditure is labeled Spend instead of Payment. You can split transactions if you want.

Figure 5.11 shows a simple expenditure—a beach cottage rental at a real estate company that requires cash payment—recorded in the Cash account Register.

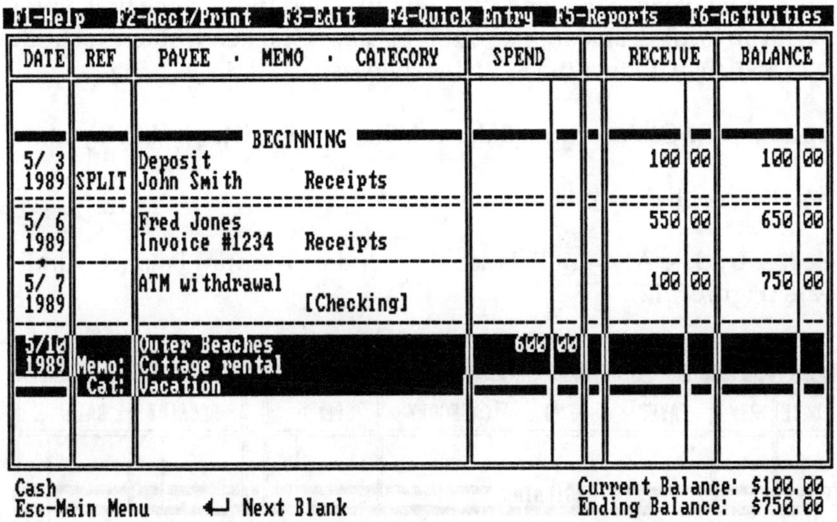

Figure 5.11. Recording an expenditure in a Cash account.

Balancing a Cash Account

If you use a Cash account for business purposes, such as tracking petty cash, your account should balance. For personal finances however, there just isn't any point in recording every single cash purchase— and even less in trying to deal with the hoard of loose change under the cushions of your sofa.

The Update Account Balance option on the Activities pull-down menu will get your Cash account back in balance. You don't have to assign the amount of an account update to a category—but again, uncategorized transactions turn up classified as Other in your reports, and it may be difficult to interpret what that means. The best solution is to assign the balance to a Miscellaneous expense category or another category.

You should update the balance only *after* you have recorded all of your other cash transactions because the transaction appears in the Register as a Balance Adjustment *on the date you make the adjustment*. Any subsequent transactions will be added or subtracted from the updated balance.

Suppose, for example, that you have $50 cash on hand and a handful of receipts for $150 in cash expenditures. You should record the expenditures first, then update the balance. The $150 in expenditures will be assigned to appropriate categories and your ending balance will be $50. If you updated the balance first, you would end up with an incorrect balance of -$100, because Quicken would first update the balance to $50, then deduct the $150 in expenses.

To update your Cash account balance when the Register is displayed:

1. Press F6 to pull down the Activities menu.
2. Select 2. Update Account Balance. The Update Account Balance window appears (Figure 5.12).

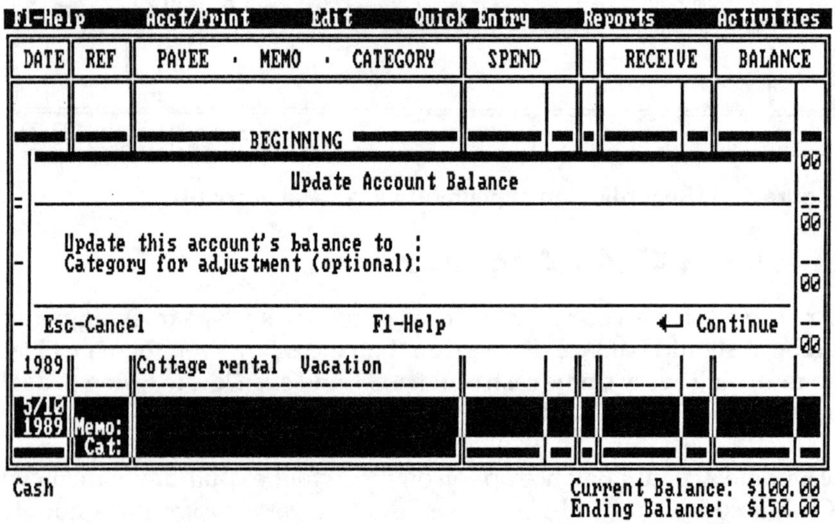

Figure 5.12. The Update Account Balance window in a Cash account.

3. Type the ending balance at the blank labeled: Update this account's balance to, then press Enter.
4. Enter a category in the blank labeled: Category for adjustment (or leave it blank), then press Enter or Ctrl-Enter to complete the transaction.

Quicken records the update as a transaction labeled Balance Adjustment and increases or decreases the balance in your Cash account.

Credit Card Transactions

Quicken treats credit card purchases and payments as if they were cash transactions. (The IRS agrees.) The expenditure occurs when you make the purchase; the payment is a transfer from your Bank account to the Credit Card account. As with cash transactions, you can record your credit card purchases and payments in any level of detail that suits your needs.

Here are some possibilities:

- Simply record credit card payments as Miscellaneous expenses in your checking account. Individual purchases won't be itemized, and the expense will be recorded when you pay the bill rather than when you make purchases.

- When you pay your bill, use a split transaction in a Bank account to itemize your purchases—or itemize significant purchases and assign the balance to Miscellaneous expense. This will provide a detailed record, but purchases will be reported on the date you pay the bill rather than when you make them.

- In a Credit Card account, itemize significant purchases and assign the balance to Miscellaneous when you pay your bill. Again, the Miscellaneous expenditure will appear to occur when you pay the bill rather than when you actually make the purchases.

- Manage your Credit Card account just as if it were a Bank account for checking, recording each purchase on the date you make it. You can enter transactions as you make them or wait until you receive your bill. When you pay the bill, record it as a transfer to the Credit Card account.

If you've already learned to use a Bank account, any of these methods should come easily.

Credit Card Transactions in a Bank Account

If you don't need to itemize credit card transactions, you may not need to set up a Credit Card account. When you pay the bill, you can simply write a check and assign it to a Miscellaneous expense category. But you can also keep more detailed records in a Bank account.

Figure 5.13 shows a simple credit card payment recorded as a split transaction in a Bank account Register. The procedure is the same as for any other split transaction. Simply enter a date, Payee, and an amount in the Payment column, then press Ctrl-s to open the Split Transaction window and record the individual items. Quicken automatically calculates the remaining balance of the transaction as you go along. If you want to record only some transactions individually, record those first, then assign the balance on the last line to Miscellaneous, as shown on line 6 of Figure 5.13.

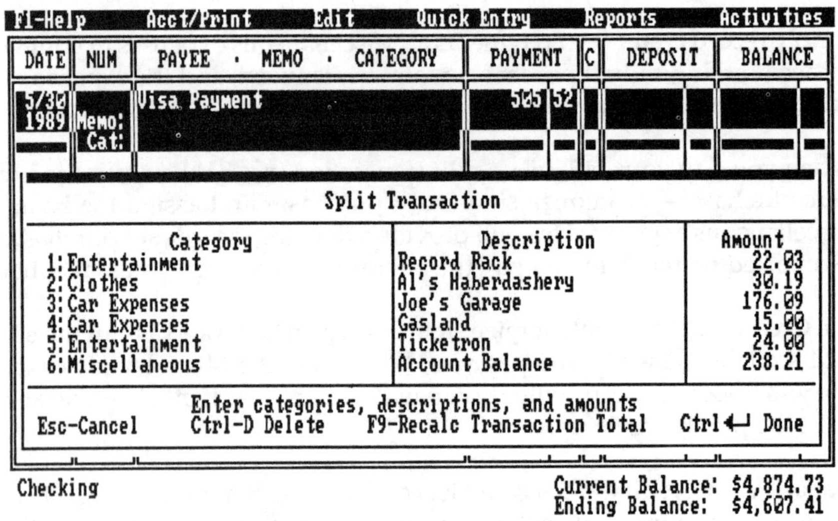

Figure 5.13. Itemizing a credit card payment as a split transaction in a Bank account.

This method allows you to record purchases in as much detail as you want, but again, the transactions are recorded on the date you write the check, not when you actually make the purchases.

Using Credit Card Accounts

The Credit Card Register works essentially the same way as a Bank account Register, only charges *increase* the account balance, while payments *decrease* it. If you entered a credit limit when you set up the account, Quicken automatically calculates Credit Remaining at the lower right corner of the screen.

Purchases are entered in the Charge column; credits, such as a credit for returned merchandise, in the Payment column. You can pay your bill either by making a transfer from checking or by using the special Pay Credit Card Bill feature on the Activities pull-down menu (F6).

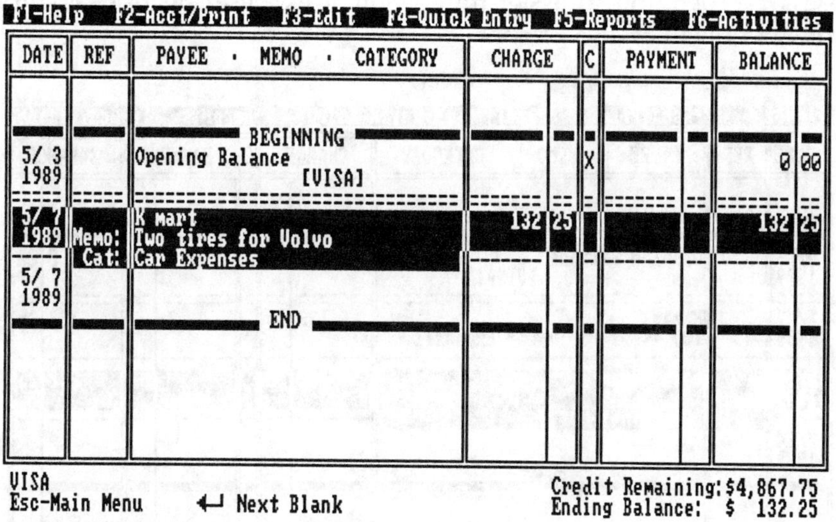

Figure 5.14. A simple credit card transaction.

Figure 5.14 shows a simple credit card purchase recorded in the Credit Card Register. The columns should be familiar. The C(leared) column on the Credit Card Register is similar to the one in a Bank account. You can use it to mark cleared items when you reconcile your records with your statement using the Pay Credit Card Bill feature. (If you enter transactions directly from your statement rather than from charge slips during the month, type an asterisk or c in the C(leared) column of each transaction as you record it.) You can use the REF column to record an identifying number, such as a purchase order or invoice. The rest of the columns function just as they do in any other account.

CREDIT CARD TRANSFERS

Some credit card transactions are transfers to or from other accounts. For example, you might record a $100 cash advance on your card as a transfer to a Bank account or to a Cash account. Similarly, when you pay your credit card bill, you are transferring money from your Bank account to your Credit Card account.

Figure 5.15 shows a $100 cash advance recorded as a transfer to a Checking Bank account. This transaction is entered exactly like a purchase, except that you type the name of the corresponding account in the category line or select the account from the Category List. Either way, Quicken supplies the brackets around the account name automatically. Note that the Credit Card account Balance increases, but no expense is recorded. You can assign transactions to expense categories as you spend the money from your Bank account.

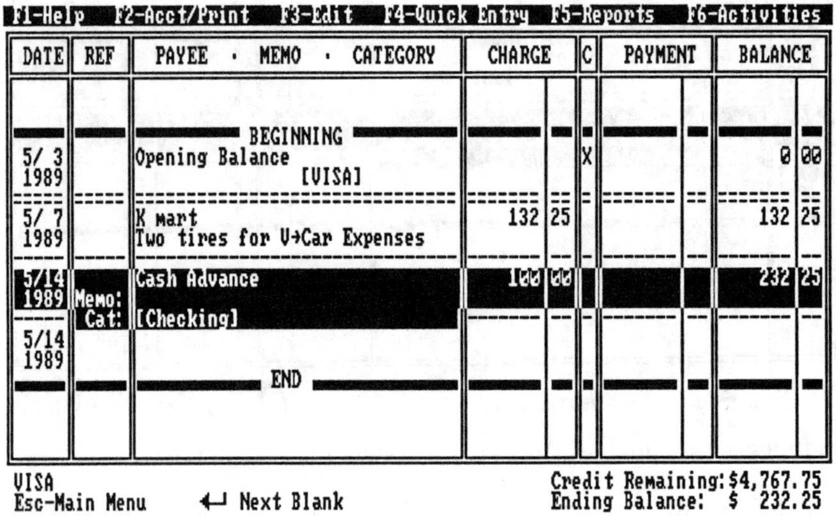

Figure 5.15. Transferring a cash advance from a Credit Card account to a Bank account.

The most common type of transfer that will appear in your Credit Card account is payment of your monthly bill. The Pay Credit Card Bill option, discussed in the next section, automatically writes a check and allows you to reconcile your Quicken account with your statement.

If you prefer, however, you can simply pay your bill by check and record the transaction as a transfer from a Bank account to a Credit Card account. Figure 5.16 shows how a payment appears in your Credit Card account. You can switch immediately to the corresponding check in your Bank account by pressing Ctrl-x or by selecting 8. Go to Transfer from the Edit pull-down menu.

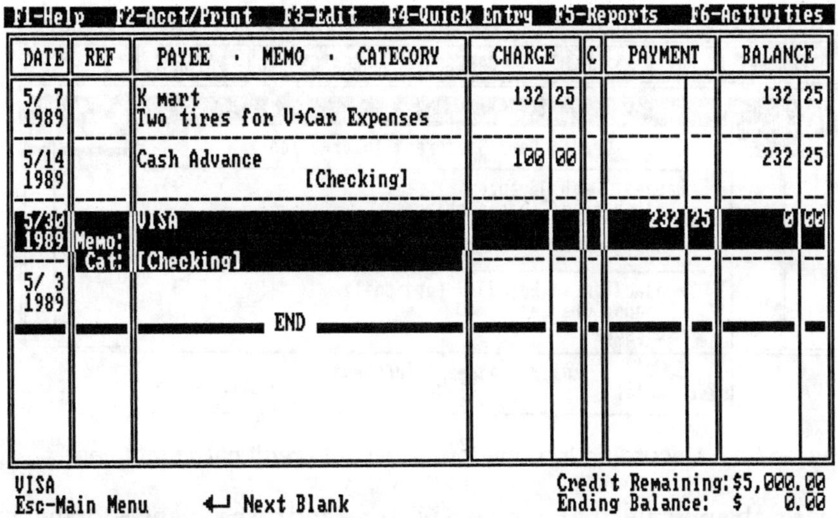

Figure 5.16. Credit card payments are recorded as transfers between a Bank account and the Credit Card account.

PAYING YOUR CREDIT CARD BILL

The Pay Credit Card Bill option on the Activities pull-down menu does much more than record your monthly credit card payment. The procedure is very similar to bank reconciliation. It allows you to:

- Reconcile your Quicken records with your statement.
- Create a lump-sum transaction to balance the account and record any transactions you don't want to enter individually.
- Automatically enter a transaction to record a finance charge.
- Automatically write a check to pay your bill.

Before you begin, the Register of your Credit Card account should be displayed. To process your monthly statement, select 2. Pay Credit Card Bill from the Activities pull-down menu. The window shown in Figure 5.17 appears. Your statement provides the information you need to complete this screen. Just type the numbers, and press Enter after each entry.

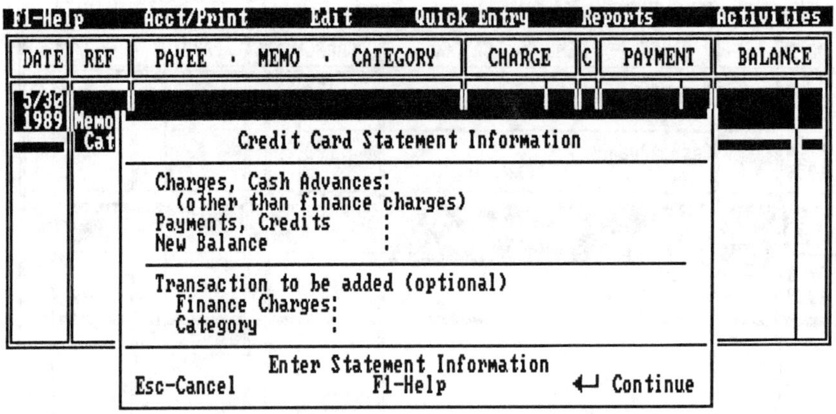

Figure 5.17. Recording information from your credit card statement.

In the first blank, enter the total of new charges and cash advances for the current statement. If these are listed separately on your statement, you can use the pop-up calculator to compute the total. Just press Ctrl-o to pop-up the calculator, add the numbers, then press F9 to paste the result into the blank. You can also use the calculator to add payments and credits if necessary. The New Balance is the balance shown on your bill.

In the bottom half of the window, you can have Quicken automatically record a transaction for any monthly finance charge. If you want, you can assign the expense to a category—and you definitely should if you are using Quicken for tax record keeping. You should have expense categories to separate personal interest from business and mortgage interest. The latter two are still fully deductible. You can deduct 20 percent of your personal interest in 1989, 10 percent in 1990, and none thereafter.

When you press Enter or Ctrl-Enter to record the window, a Reconciliation Summary screen appears, listing uncleared items (Figure 5.18). Note that the finance charge is entered automatically and marked as cleared.

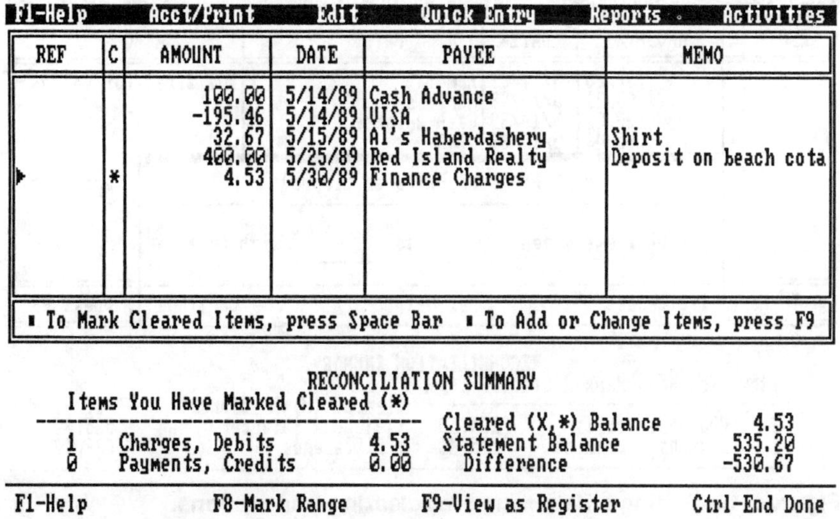

Figure 5.18. The Reconciliation Summary screen.

The Reconciliation Summary at the bottom of the screen doesn't balance at first. It includes only items you have cleared since the last reconciliation. As you check off each transaction on the list against your statement, highlight it on the list and press the space bar or Enter to mark it cleared. (Repeat the procedure to unclear an item.)

If you find that all of the transactions on the screen match your statement, you can simultaneously clear all of the transactions between two dates. To do this, press F8. You will see a window labeled: Mark Range of Dates as Cleared (Figure 5.19). Type the beginning and ending dates in the usual format (11/30/89, for example). To scroll forward or backward from the current date, press + or - before typing anything else in the blank. The date automatically appears—no typing required! When you have finished, press Enter to record the date range. Asterisks will be entered in the C(leared) column of all transactions in the range.

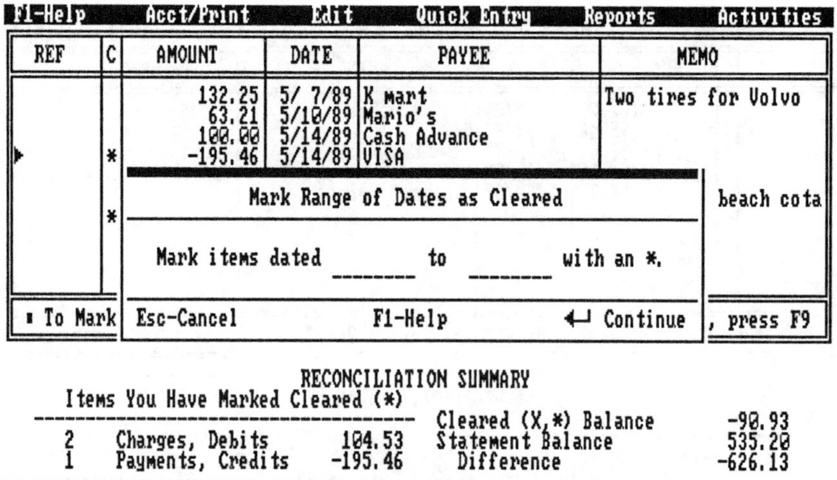

Figure 5.19. Setting a date range for clearing transactions.

When you have finished clearing transactions, the Reconciliation Summary should balance—the Cleared Balance should equal the Statement Balance, and the Difference should be 0.00. If it is, press Ctrl-End (not Ctrl-Enter) to complete reconciliation. You are ready to print your check (or record a handwritten check).

If there is a disparity, you need to make corrections or additions to your records to balance your account. Go to the next section.

Balancing Your Account

If your account does not balance at this point, you can either recheck your work and make corrections or enter a lump-sum transaction to balance your account.

Check the total of Charges, Debits, Payments, and Credits against the comparable items on your statement. When you locate the discrepancy, press F9 to call up the Register. This is a special version of the Register with the Reconciliation Summary displayed at the bottom of the screen to help you measure your progress toward balancing your account. Otherwise, it works like the normal Register, and you can add, delete, or revise transactions as usual. If you record new transactions, enter an asterisk (*) in the C(leared) column to indicate that the transaction is shown on your statement. (If you need to go back to the Reconciliation Summary screen, press F9 again.)

If your account balances after your corrections, press Ctrl-End (not Ctrl-Enter) to complete reconciliation and go on to the procedure for writing a check to pay the bill.

If your account does not balance, you can make additional changes or have Quicken make an automatic lump-sum adjustment to balance your account. If you choose the latter, make certain that any discrepancy represents unrecorded transactions and not errors. Otherwise, your reports may be inaccurate and other accounts may be thrown out of balance.

When you are ready to record lump-sum adjustments, press Ctrl-End to complete the Reconciliation Summary. When your account does not balance, a screen for making lump-sum adjustments (Figure 5.20) appears. This window may have one to three entries, depending on what disparities Quicken has found between your statement information and your records. The problem may be in your opening balance, or you may have missed one or more charges or payments.

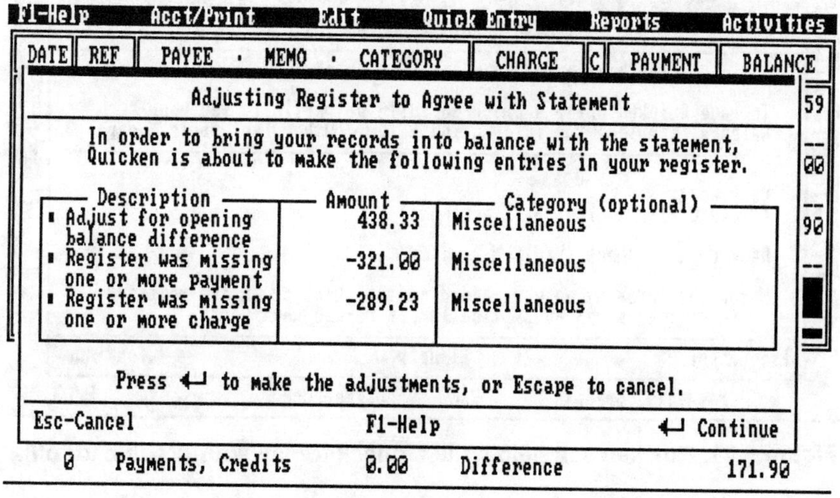

Figure 5.20. Adjusting the Credit Card Register to agree with your statement.

You can assign any of these adjustments to categories or classes. Just complete the category blanks as usual. You can type the entries or make selections from the Category List (press Ctrl-c to open the window) or Class List (Ctrl-l). Press Enter to accept the adjustments or Esc to go back to the Register for further revisions.

Adjusting the Register is an all or nothing opportunity—you can't record transactions for some adjustments but not others, and you can't change the amounts. You can, of course, later go back and revise or delete the lump sum transactions on the Register, but changing amounts will probably throw your records out of balance with future statements.

Writing a Check to Pay a Credit Card Bill

You can automatically write a Quicken check or record a check written by hand to pay your credit card bill. When you complete the reconciliation procedure, you will see the window shown in Figure 5.21. To have Quicken write or record the check, simply fill in the blanks. This is another one-time opportunity. If you press Esc to cancel, you won't be able to get back to the Make Credit Card Payment window until the next time you reconcile your account.

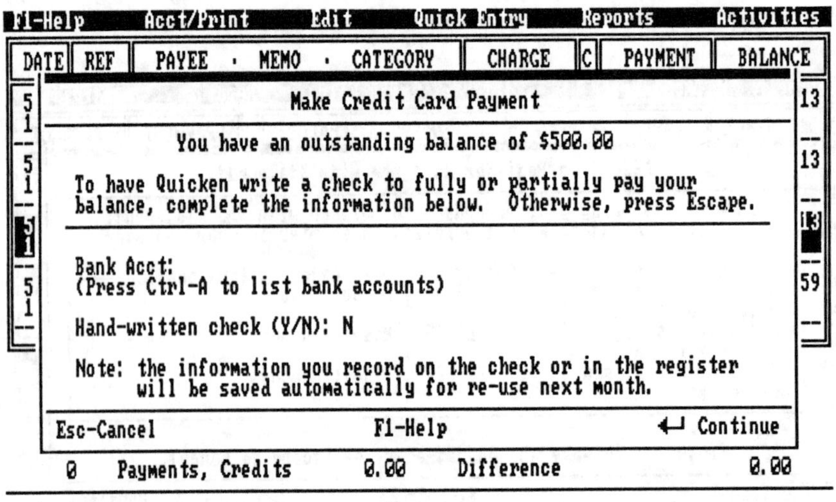

Figure 5.21. Quicken can help write a check to pay your credit card bill.

To write or record a check, enter the name of a Bank account on the first blank. You can type the name or press Ctrl-a to make a selection from the Account List. On the next line, Hand-written check, leave the entry N(o) to write a Quicken check or change it to Y(es) to record a handwritten check.

When you press Enter to complete the screen, you will see the Write/Print Checks screen or the Register of the Bank account you have selected. Your Credit Card balance is entered as the amount of the check. The current date and the name of your Credit Card account are entered in the appropriate blanks.

Once you have completed a credit card payment, Quicken will recall the payee, address, and memo, Quicken will recall this information when you make future credit card payments with the Pay Credit Card Bill option.

Other Asset and Other Liability Accounts

Other Asset and Other Liability accounts are among Quicken's advanced features. Basically, they are intended for recording noncash assets and liabilities. Examples are shown in Tables 5.3 and 5.4. This is essential for a full accounting of your personal or business financial picture—but then not everyone needs to account for every transaction.

The basic accounting equation, remember, is:

$$\text{Net Worth} = \text{Assets} - \text{Liabilities}$$

and that includes noncash assets and liabilities.

Quicken handles the equation perfectly. Other Asset and Other Liability accounts are very well suited for such tasks as keeping track of depreciable capital equipment, stock and real estate investments, loans, accounts payable and receivable, and many other financial and business accounts.

The complication is that the basic accounting equation does not distinguish between cash transactions and noncash transactions. This is no problem if you're running a full-blown accrual accounting system, where income and expenses are recorded when they are incurred, rather than when they are paid. Such items as invoices, bills, cash receipts and outflows, depreciation, and unrealized capital gains flow through the system without a hitch. Most individuals and a high percentage of small businesses operate on a cash basis—and that also poses no problem as long as you stay away from Other Assets and Liabilities.

However, many Quicken users find a need to set up a sort of hybrid system, mixing what is basically a cash system with noncash Other Assets and Liabilities. A small business might, for example, want to track payables and receivables, but still report income and expenses on a cash basis. You might want to record the appreciation on your house to keep up with your net worth, or changes in value of your investments, without recording income or expenses in the process. You might want to record the purchase of a sofa in an expense category and also add it to an Other Asset Account called Home Inventory. When you do any of these things, you may need to adapt Quicken to your situation.

Quicken's Cash Flow Reports resolve these situations for many users. They detail inflows and outflows of cash into and from Bank accounts, Cash accounts, and Credit Card accounts, without regard to activity in Other Asset and Other Liability accounts. Still, you may need to use special tactics if you want to treat some outflows as expenditures and some inflows as income, but not others. Examples are given in the chapters on specific applications, such as accounts receivable.

Table 5.3. Applications for Other Asset Accounts.

Home Equity	The purchase price of your home, plus improvements (not repairs) for determining capital gains when you sell the house.
Home Appreciation	Increase in the value of your home (an unrealized gain), for determining net worth.
Home Inventory	A record of personal property, useful for insurance purposes and determining net worth. Should usually be recorded at market value.
Investments	Purchases, sales, and market changes for investments in stocks and other securities.
Real Estate	Tax basis and depreciation of investment properties.
Capital Equipment	Purchases and current depreciation of business equipment.
Accounts Receivable	Invoices and payments by client. This is easiest to do on an accrual basis, but you can adapt Quicken to record receivables on a cash basis.

Table 5.4. Applications for Other Liability Accounts.

Loans	Outstanding balances and payments on principals for mortgages, car loans, or any other type of loan.
Accrued Taxes	Amounts deducted for state and local taxes and social security (FICA), for which you make periodic payments.
Accounts Payable	Quicken provides a simple method of cash-basis reporting of payables; all you have to do is post-date checks when bills arrive and have Quicken print the checks when the bills are due. If you want to keep payables on an accrual basis you can do so in an Other Liability account.

The Other Asset Register

Transactions are recorded in the Other Asset Register almost exactly as they are on a Bank account Register. Other than the way Quicken reports handle certain transfers, the main difference is that the amount columns are labeled Decrease and Increase rather than Payment and Deposit. Also, you will not have occasion to make entries in the C(leared) column, because there is no reconciliation procedure for Other Asset accounts.

Suppose, for example, you have just bought a house for $100,000 and you spend $5,000 remodeling a bathroom. This increases your tax basis in the house, because it is an improvement that enhances its value rather than a repair. The result might look like Figure 5.22. (You could get considerably more complicated about recording the purchase, but we're going for simplicity here.)

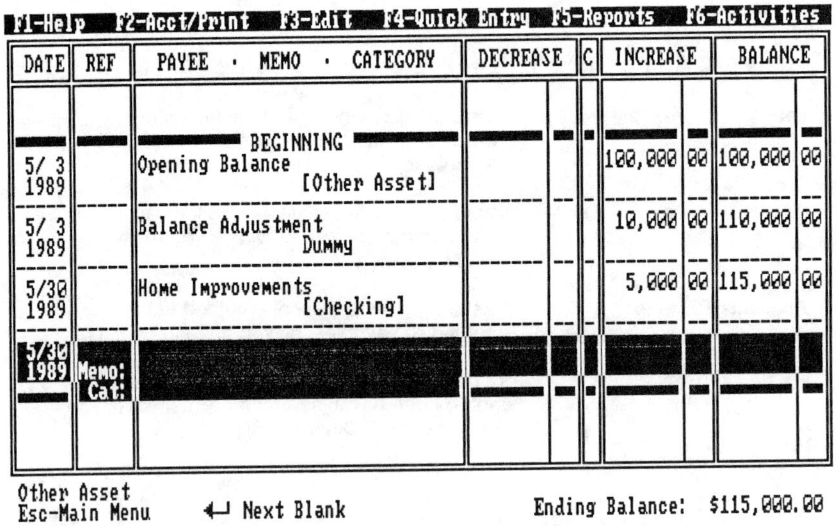

Figure 5.22. The Other Asset Register.

The opening balance is $100,000, and the remodeling increases it to $105,000, the second transaction on the Register. No expense is recorded, because the remodeling is treated as a transfer from a Bank account called Checking. However, a Cash Flow Report will show an outflow of $5,000 from your Bank account to the Other Asset account.

Suppose further that your home office occupies one-sixth of the house, and at the end of the year, you want to record a depreciation expense for tax purposes. Seven months' depreciation might come to about $340. The depreciation is recorded as a Decrease on the Register and assigned to an expense category called Depreciation. This transaction will be reflected in income and expense reports, but not in Cash Flow Reports. Meanwhile, the balance of the account is decreased to $104,660, because depreciation decreases your basis in the property for tax purposes.

> **NOTE:** The IRS has become very sticky about allowing home office deductions, but you probably will not have a problem if your home is legitimately your principal place of business and in certain other situations. Check with a tax professional if you have any doubts.

THE OTHER LIABILITY REGISTER

In most cases, other transactions that affect the balance in an Other Liability account will be recorded in other types of accounts. Other Liability accounts most often represent loans, and the only thing you can do is repay them; the check will be written on a Bank account.

When you buy a house, you will probably also take out a substantial mortgage. Figure 5.23 shows the opening balance and first payment for a $85,000 loan as it appears in the Other Liability Register. The first payment decreases the balance in the account by only $37.60. Most of the rest of the $1,100 payment goes to interest, with the remainder paid into an escrow account for insurance and taxes.

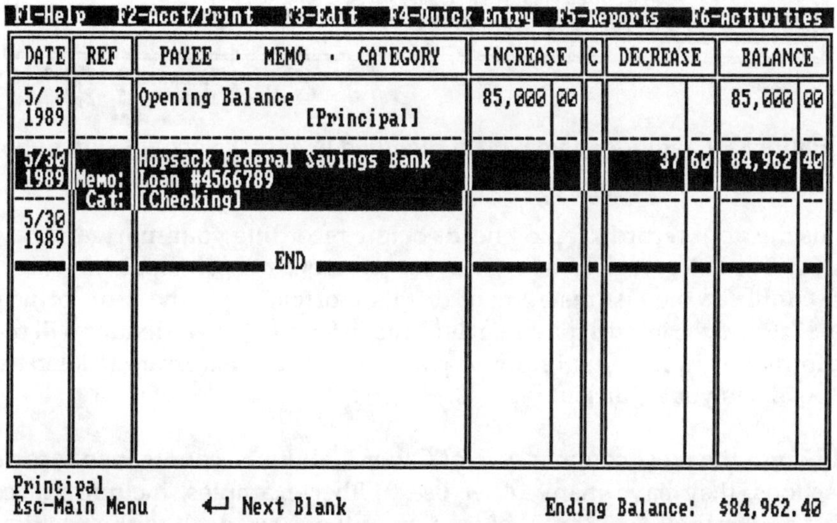

Figure 5.23. The opening balance and first payment for a mortgage on the Other Liability Register.

Figure 5.24 shows how the loan payment is entered in the Bank account Register. The payment on principal is a transfer to the Principal Liability account. The amounts are assigned to a Mortgage expense category, with subcategories for Interest, Insurance, and Taxes. All of these splits will be treated as Outflows in Cash Flow Reports. On an income and expense report, however, only the last three splits are recorded as expenses. The payment on principal is treated as a transfer.

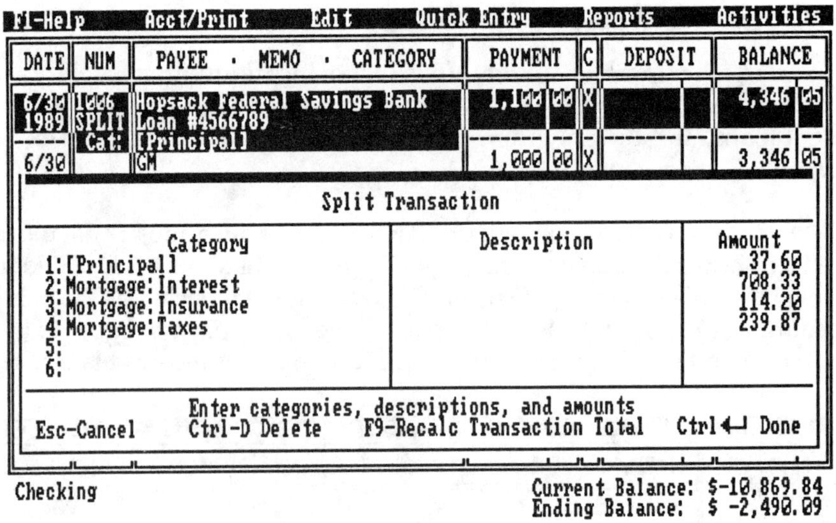

Figure 5.24. A mortgage payment recorded in a Bank account with principal assigned to an Other Liability account.

Consider your record keeping needs before recording your mortgage payment this way. The interest decreases and the payment on principal increases each month, until for the last installment of this mortgage, payment on principal is nearly $740 and the interest payment is only a little over $6. The lender will provide this information in an annual summary, so it may not be necessary to keep track of these details in your Quicken records.

Although the most common use of Other Liability accounts is to record loan transactions, they have many other uses. Other examples, including accounts payable and payroll taxes withheld, among others, are dealt with specifically in later chapters.

Updating Account Balances

From time to time, you may want to update the balances of Other Asset or Other Liability accounts. For example, you might update the balance of an Other Asset account to reflect appreciation of your house. In an Other Liability account, you might want to update the balance of a loan if you elect not to keep track of the balance on a regular basis by splitting transactions into payments on principal and interest.

You can enter these updates as regular transactions that increase or decrease the balance of the account assigned to catagories and classes. Just calculate the difference between the balance shown in your records and the actual balance. If your house has increased in value from $200,000 to $225,000, for example, you could enter an increase of $25,000 in your House Other Asset account, perhaps assigned to an Income category called Appreciation. If your car has depreciated from $20,000 to $18,000, you would enter a decrease of $2,000.

If there is only one asset or liability in an account—such as a house, a mutual fund, a single stock, or a loan—Quicken will make the calculation for you. The Update Account Balance option on the Activities pull-down menu (F6) is the same for both Other Assets and Other Liabilities—and in fact the same as for a Cash account.

To update your account balance when the Register is displayed, press F6 to pull down the Activities menu, then select 2. Update Account Balance. The Update Account Balance window appears. Type the ending balance at the blank labeled Update this account's balance to: and record a category for the adjustment transaction if you want. Finally, press Ctrl-Enter to complete the window. Quicken records the update as a transaction labeled Balance Adjustment and increases or decreases the balance in your account.

Eliminating Unwanted Transactions from Reports

The basic accounting equation says that any amount that turns up in an account, positive or negative, has to come from somewhere. It might be income, an expense, or a transfer, but an offsetting amount has to be recorded somewhere to keep the equation in balance. If you avoid the issue by leaving the category line blank in a transaction, Quicken simply classifies it as Other.

Quicken allows you to produce reports that include exactly the information you want, with no extraneous information. You can specify exactly which categories, classes, and accounts you want included. You also have control over how transfers are reported.

For informal reports, you may want to do some things "off budget" in ways that technically violate the basic equation. For example, if you record loan payments as expenses, then update the loan balance, you're basically recording the same payments twice—and the money to decrease the loan balance has to come from somewhere. The same is true if you record receivables in an Other Asset account when you send a statement but no income until the check arrives, or when you treat a furniture purchase as an expense, then add the item to your Household Inventory Other Asset account. In each case, the "second half" of the transaction, which would indicate the source of funds, is missing.

In a strict accounting system, none of these arrangements would be permissable, but such maneuvers can be very useful for managing personal finances and certain types of business bookkeeping. With judicious use of Quicken's ability to "filter" and customize reports, you should be able to produce exactly the results you need by eliminating the "second half" of certain off-budget transactions.

Conclusion

At this point, you should be able to record almost any type of transaction in any type of Quicken account. In the last chapter, you learned to record transactions in a Bank account, print checks, and reconcile your Quicken records with your bank statement. This chapter adds split transactions to assign transactions to two or more purposes and enter transactions in other Quicken accounts.

In the next chapter, you will learn to streamline your record keeping by using memorized transactions for individual records and transaction groups for recording an entire set of transactions in regular sessions with Quicken.

6

Streamlining Transactions

When you frequently record similar transactions, you don't have to type out all of the information every time. Two of Quicken's most powerful features—memorized transactions and transaction groups—can help you streamline repetitive record keeping.

Memorized transactions allow you to record information from any frequent transaction—paycheck deposits, regular bills, payments to your doctor and dentist, or checks to the local grocery store. Memorized transactions are added to the Memorized Transactions List. It is similar to other Quicken screens that allow you to make selections, such as the Select Account window or the Category List. Once you have recorded a memorized transaction, it takes only a few keystrokes to recall it to the Write/Print Checks screen or the Register.

Transaction groups are groups of memorized transactions that you can recall all at once for such purposes as paying monthly bills, writing payroll checks, or writing checks for quarterly taxes. If you want, you can even have Quicken's Billminder feature remind you when transaction groups are due. When you recall a transaction group, Quicken enters all of the transactions on the Register at once, allowing you to make revisions and deletions as necessary.

Once recorded, any memorized transaction or transaction group can be recalled in any account. This means, for example, that if you sometimes pay a particular bill by check, sometimes in cash, and sometimes by credit card, you can always recall a memorized transaction in the appropriate account.

The commands governing memorized transactions and transaction groups, summarized in Table 6.1, appear on the Quick Entry pull-down menu. (Options 4 and 5 on the menu deal with categories and classes.) To execute a command, press F4 to pull down the menu, then type the number corresponding to the command you want to use. You can also execute the memorized transaction commands with Control key commands (Ctrl-t for Recall Transaction, Ctrl-m for Memorize Transaction). Once you are familiar with memorized transactions, you will probably find it more convenient to use the Control key commands.

Table 6.1. Control Key Commands That Execute Transactions.

1. Recall Transaction (Ctrl-t)	Allows you to recall a memorized transaction from the Memorized Transactions List.
2. Memorize Transaction (Ctrl-m)	Memorizes the information in the current transaction .
5. Execute Transaction Group	Records transactions from the group you select in the current account.
6. Set Up Transaction Group	Allows you to create a transaction group from memorized transactions previously recorded on the Memorized Transactions List.

In addition to saving time and effort, these features help ensure that you record transactions consistently. Typographical errors are eliminated; a transaction's Memo is always the same; and categories, classes, and split transactions will be recorded the same way time after time.

MEMORIZED TRANSACTIONS

You can memorize a transaction in advance, while you're entering it, or after you've recorded it. You can record and recall any transaction on either the Write/Print Checks screen of a Bank account or the Register of any account. The procedure is the same on either. Generally, you should record Quicken checks on the Write/Print Checks screen. Deposits, checks you write by hand, and other transactions should be recorded on the Register.

Quicken can memorize all of a transaction, or only part of it. Rent payments, for example, are the same every month; you might want to memorize the payee, amount, address, memo, and category and/or class. Other transactions, such as utility bills, vary; you will probably want to leave the amount blank.

Once you have recorded a memorized transaction, it takes only a few keystrokes to recall it from the Memorized Transactions List. Quicken automatically enters the memorized information. You need only fill in the blanks the remaining blanks and record the transaction.

Table 6.2. The Columns of the Memorized Transactions List.

Description	Information from the payee blank.
Split	If the transaction is split, an S appears here.
Memo	Information from the memo blank.
Category	Category and/or class memorized with the transaction. In split transactions, the category and/or class of the first split is displayed.
Clr	If you memorize a cleared transaction on the Register, an asterisk will appear here. You will seldom do this.
Amount	For transactions that are always the same amount, such as a paycheck deposit or rent, you can record the amount along with the rest of the transaction.
Type	Indicates whether the transaction is a check (Chk), Payment (Pmt), or a Deposit (Dep). Checks are written only on Write/Print Checks. (See note.)
Grp	Indicates a group number if the transaction is part of a transaction group.

When you memorize a transaction, Quicken adds it to the Memorized Transactions List. Figure 6.1 shows the list with some typical transactions recorded. Most of the headings on the list should be familiar. Each transaction may include information in any or all of the columns on the list. The contents of each column are summarized in Table 6.2.

NOTE: Register transactions are classified as Payments or Deposits regardless of the type of account in which they are recorded. This may be confusing in accounts where the Amount columns are labeled differently. In a Credit Card account, for example, a Charge will be labeled Pmt, while a Payment (when you pay your bill) will be labeled Dep.

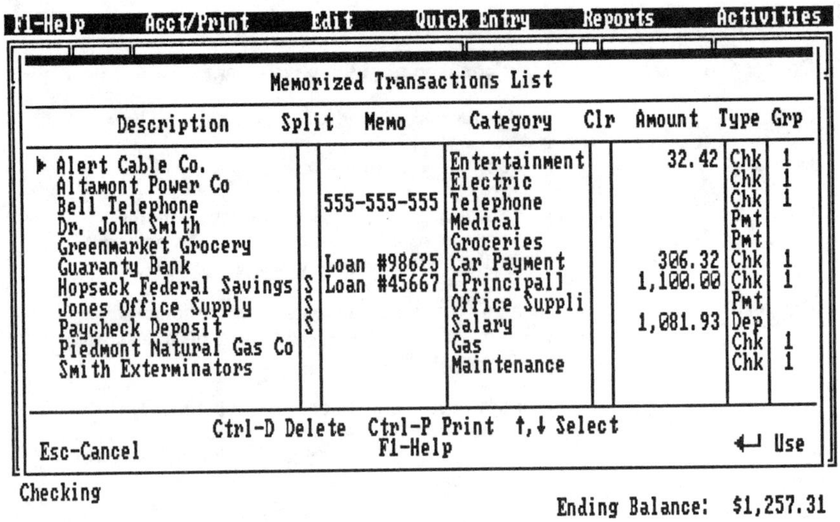

Figure 6.1. The Memorized Transactions List.

CREATING MEMORIZED TRANSACTIONS

To add a transaction to the Memorized Transactions List, first type the information you want to record as usual on the Write/Print Checks screen or any Register. When an entry—like the amount of a utility payment or an hourly employee's paycheck—varies leave that line blank. (Quicken never memorizes the date of a transaction.)

Once the information is entered, press Ctrl-m or select 2. Memorize transaction from the Quick Entry menu. Quicken highlights the information, and this message appears: The marked information is about to be memorized. When you press Enter to complete the procedure, Quicken adds the transaction to the list. After memorizing a transaction, you can finish filling it out on the Write/Print Checks screen or the Register and record it as usual. If you don't want to record the transaction now, just press Ctrl-d to delete the memorized information you have just typed. Quicken will delete the information just memorized from the screen.

The procedure for memorizing a previously recorded transaction is basically the same. Just display the transaction on the Write/Print Checks screen or highlight the transaction on the register, then press Ctrl-m to memorize it. (All of the information in the transaction, including the amount will be memorized, but you can revise the memorized transaction later, as explained below.)

Recalling Memorized Transactions

You can recall memorized transactions on either the Write/Print Checks screen or the Register. Before you recall a transaction, make sure a blank check is displayed on the Write/Print Checks screen or a blank transaction is highlighted on the Register. (Otherwise, Quicken will replace the current transaction with the memorized transaction, and you may lose an important record.)

To recall a memorized transaction, you simply select it from the Memorized Transactions List. To call up the list, press Ctrl-t or select 1. Recall Transaction from the Quick Entry pull-down menu. When the list appears, highlight the transaction you want to recall and Enter. (If the list is extensive you can save time by typing the initial of the description of the transaction you want to select. The first transaction with that initial will be highlighted. You can still use the arrow keys to select another.)

Quicken automatically enters the information from the memorized transaction on the screen. You can now add or change information and record the transaction as usual.

Revising Memorized Transactions

When you need to change a memorized transaction, you don't have to start over; memorized transactions are easily revised. To change a memorized transaction, recall the transaction to the Write/Print Checks screen or the Register as usual, make the changes, then memorize the transaction again.

Unless you have changed the transaction description, a window appears when you record the new version warning you: Transaction Already Memorized. Select 1. Replace to replace the old version or 2. Add to add the new version to the list as a separate memorized transaction.

You can also delete a memorized transaction you no longer need. Just call up the memorized transactions window, highlight the transaction to be deleted, then press Ctrl-d. A window warning that your are about to delete a memorized item appears. Press Enter to execute the deletion or Esc to cancel.

Printing the Memorized Transactions List

When the Memorized Transactions List is displayed, you can make a printed copy by pressing Ctrl-p. A printer selection window appears. Make a selection, then press Enter. Quicken prints your list, complete with transaction splits and addresses.

Transaction Groups

Once you have recorded memorized transactions, you can set up transaction groups to further streamline your Quicken check writing and record keeping. You can recall the entire group with a few keystrokes, then review, revise, and record each individually.

A transaction group can include any combination of checks, payments, deposits, or other transactions. When you recall the group, Quicken automatically enters the memorized transactions on the Register. Those memorized as checks to print on the Write/Print Checks screen are also appear there. You can add or revise any information—or delete entire transactions—as you record each transaction.

In addition to streamlining your record keeping, transaction groups allow you to schedule regular payments, whether or not you receive bills. (You may even want to set up a group with a single regular transaction to take advantage of this feature.) Quicken's Billminder feature reminds you when transaction groups are due. You can use the Change Setting Menu to set how far in advance Quicken reminds you of due bills. (See Chapter 13 for details.)

Setting Up a Transaction Group

You can set up as many as 12 transaction groups, starting on either the Write/Print Checks screen or on any Register. Each memorized transaction can be a member of only one group. If you select a transaction that is already in a group, it is removed from the first group. (To include a transaction in two transaction groups, you must memorize it twice.)

To set up a transaction group, first record the memorized transactions you want to include in the group, then press F4 to pull down the Quick Entry menu and select 6. Set Up transaction group. The Select Transaction Group window (Figure 6.2) appears. Size is the number of transactions in the group; Frequency indicates the interval at which Billminder will remind you to execute the group; and the last column shows the next scheduled time to execute the group (along with the day of the week that date falls on).

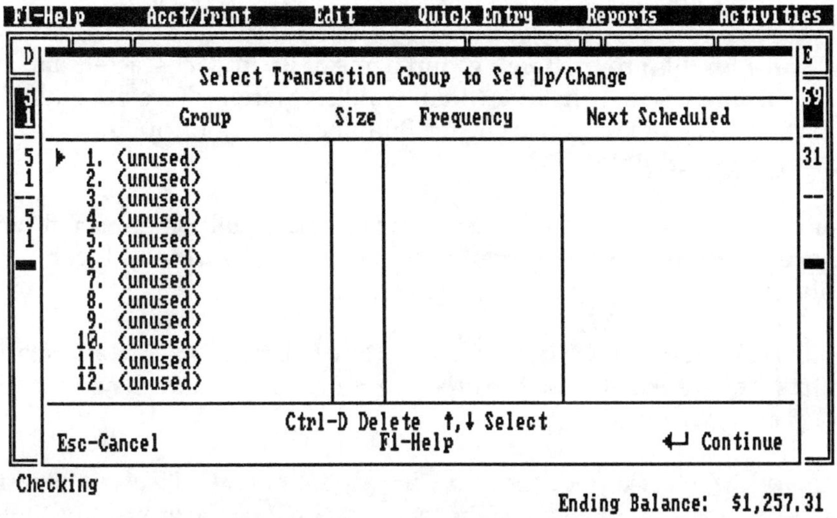

Figure 6.2. The Select transaction group window.

Next, highlight the first <unused> group (or select a previously defined group to modify), then press Enter. The Describe Group window (Figure 6.3) appears.

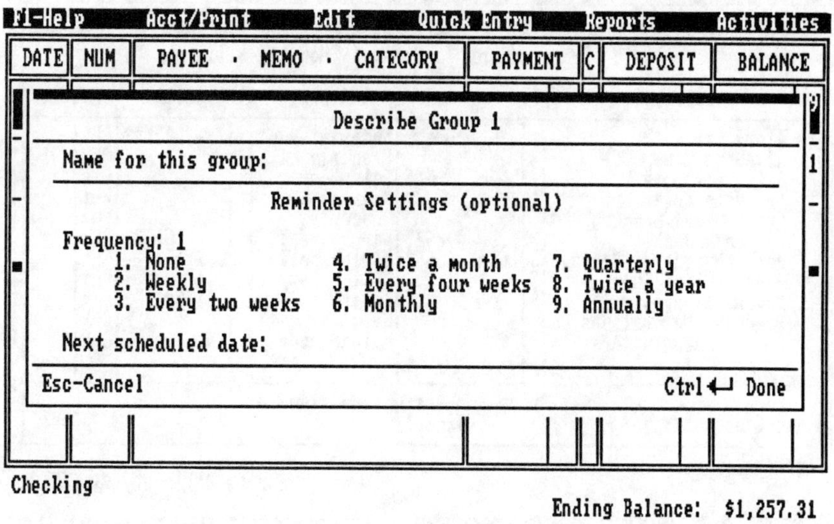

Figure 6.3. The Describe Group window.

To complete this window:

1. In Name for this group, type a group name of up to 20 characters and press Enter. Examples might include Monthly Bills, Quarterly Taxes, or Payroll. The next two blanks allow you to engage Billminder. They are optional. To bypass them, press Ctrl-Enter.

2. For Frequency, select the interval at which you want Billminder to remind you to execute the group. For example, you might choose 6. Monthly for monthly bills or 3. Every two weeks for a biweekly payroll.

3. Enter the Next scheduled date that this group falls due. Quicken automatically enters the current date. You can type over it or use the + and - keys to scroll forward or backward.

Once you have set a frequency and scheduled date, Quicken automatically calculates the next scheduled date whenever you execute the group. For example, if the frequency is monthly and the next scheduled date is 5/1/89, Quicken schedules the next payment for 6/1/89. The program even tells you the day of the week the transactions are due, so you will know whether it's a business day.

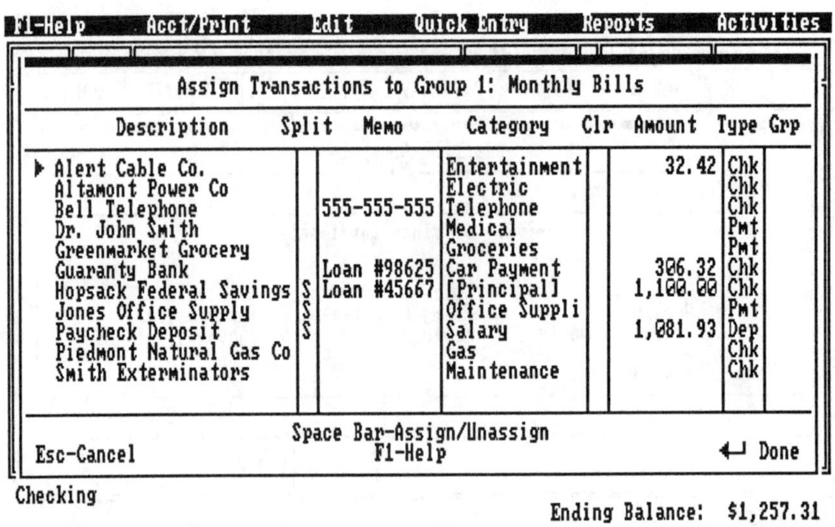

Figure 6.4. Selecting memorized transactions for a transaction group on the Assign Transactions window.

When you press Enter to complete the description window, the Assign Transactions window appears (Figure 6.4). To add a transaction to the group, use the arrow keys to highlight it, then press the space bar. The group number appears in the right column. Add as many transactions to the group as you want. (If you change your mind about one, highlight the transaction and press the space bar again to remove it.)

Finally, press Enter to confirm your selections. The Write/Print Checks screen or the Register reappears, and the transaction group is ready to use.

Executing a Transaction Group

Executing a transaction group is similar to recalling a memorized transaction, except that Quicken retrieves the entire group at once. Memorized transactions originally recorded on the Write/Print Checks screen will be entered both there and in the Register. All others are entered only in the Register.

Once the group is executed, you record each transaction separately, revising or deleting as you go along. You can execute a transaction group from either the Write/Print Checks screen or the Register.

To execute a transaction group:

1. Press F4 to pull down the Quick Entry menu, then select 5. Execute transaction group.

2. When the familiar Select Transaction Group window appears, highlight the group you want to use and press Enter.

3. Next, a transaction group Date window appears. If you have set a frequency for the group, the next scheduled date appears. Otherwise, the current date is displayed. As usual, you can change the group date either by typing over it or by using the + and - keys to advance or roll back the day. Quicken automati cally enters this date for each transaction in the group. (You can, of course, change the dates of individual transactions later.)

When you press Enter to confirm the date, Quicken records the transactions in the group on the Register, and you will see a message that the transaction group has been entered.

When you press Enter to continue, Quicken highlights the first transaction in the group. (Note that checks are marked by asterisks in the NUM column. These transactions are automatically added to the Write/Print Checks list for printing.) As you review each transaction, make whatever changes you want, then press Ctrl-Enter to record it.

Revising or Deleting Transaction Groups

You can always add to, revise, or delete a transaction group. The procedure is basically a repeat of setting up a group. To begin, select Set Up Transaction Group from the Quick Entry pull-down menu (F4) and highlight the group you want to change or delete.

To revise the group, press Enter to continue. The Describe Group window appears, and you can complete the definition the same way you would set up a new group, making whatever changes you want as you go along.

To delete a group, highlight it on the Select Transaction Group window, then press Ctrl-d. A warning appears that you are about delete the group permanently. Press Enter to confirm the deletion. The transaction group will be deleted, but the memorized transactions the group comprised will remain intact.

Conclusion

The previous two chapters covered Quicken transactions, from the basics to the program's most sophisticated features. In this chapter, you learned to streamline your record keeping by using memorized transactions for individual records and transaction groups for recording an entire set of transactions in regular sections with Quicken.

If you're using Quicken to manage your personal or business finances, rather than simply to print checks, the purpose of all of this work is to organize your records so you can take control of your finances. In the next chapter, you'll learn to do this with basic Quicken reports. After that, we'll move on to some more sophisticated special applications.

7

Basic Reports

You have already learned to use Quicken to write checks and balance your accounts. By classifying transactions by category and/or class, you have also laid the groundwork for producing Quicken reports to retrieve information from your financial records in almost any form you need to manage your personal or business finances.

You don't have to be an accounting whiz to begin using Quicken reports. The Personal Reports and Business Reports options on the Reports Menu (Figure 7.1) allow you to select predefined reports that meet the needs of most home and business users. To create these reports, you need only to make a selection from the Personal or Business submenu, enter a title (optional), and set the date range you want the report to cover.

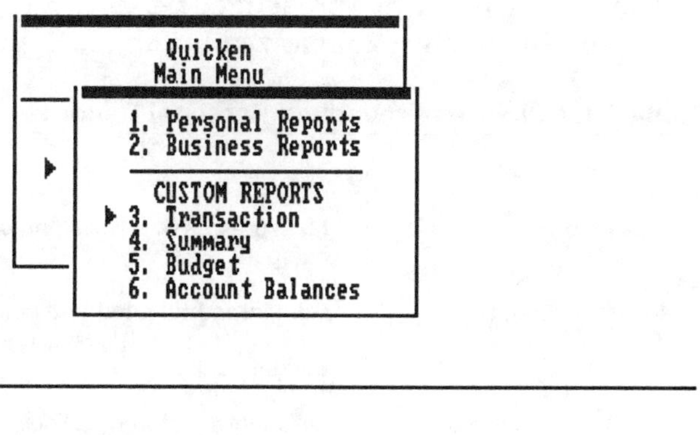

Figure 7.1. The Reports Menu.

The predefined reports are all variations of the four basic types of custom reports listed at the bottom of the Reports Menu. The Personal Cash Flow Report, for example, is a Summary Report that lists cash inflows and outflows by category. The Business P&L Statement is another variation of a Summary Report. It reports income and expenses (as opposed to cash flow), also with subtotals for each category.

While the predefined reports are likely to meet most of your reporting needs, you can easily customize them to suit yourself. If you prefer, you can begin from scratch by selecting one of the four custom report options. The techniques for customizing a predefined report and creating a custom report from scratch are basically the same.

This chapter introduces the basics of Quicken reports. First, you will learn to create and print a predefined report. Following is a general introduction to creating custom reports. This information is used throughout the remainder of the book for specific applications, including balance sheets, budgeting and taxes, accounts payable and receivable, and more business uses. Once you understand Quicken reports, you will be able to focus on the financial tasks at hand, rather than on your computer, as you create reports for those purposes.

USING PREDEFINED REPORTS

Quicken's predefined reports are a good place to start in summarizing information in your Quicken records, even if you later decide to create custom reports. Intuit knows how its customers use the program, and there may be no need to strike out on your own. The five predefined personal reports and seven predefined business reports are briefly summarized in Tables 7.1 and 7.2.

Table 7.1. Quicken's Predefined Personal Reports.

Personal Reports	
Cash Flow	Measures cash inflows and outflows by category.
Monthly Budget	Compares budgeted and actual inflows and outflows by month, just like a typical household budget (Chapter 9).
Itemized categories	Lists individual transactions, subtotaled by category.
Tax Summary	Lists tax-related transactions, subtotaled by category (Chapter 9).
Account Balances	Your net worth as of the current date, based on the balances in your Quicken accounts (Chapter 8).

Most individuals manage their finances on a cash flow basis. Your monthly mortgage payment and car payment, for example, seem like expenses, since they deplete your bank account. This is despite the fact that part of the payments

Table 7.2. Quicken's Predefined Business Reports.

Business Reports	
P&L Statement	Income and expenses by category.
Cash Flow	Cash inflows and outflows by category to measure actual cash activity.
A/P by Vendor	Lists totals for unprinted checks by payee and by month (Chapter 11).
A/R by Customer	Accounts receivable by customer and by mont(Chapter 11).
Job/Project Report	Income and expenses to specific job or project, subtotaled by class (Chapter 12).
Payroll Report	Summary of payroll income and expenses, by category and subcategory (Chapter 12).
Balance Sheet	A business balance sheet as of today (Chapter 8).

decrease your loan balances—and so are technically transfers, rather than expenses. Thus, Quicken's Cash Flow Report and Monthly Budget Report work on a cash flow basis, measuring the money that comes into and leaves your Bank accounts, Cash accounts, and Credit Card accounts.

On the other hand, not everything that affects your financial life involves cash. For example, you may want to include the appreciation in your house or changes in the value of your investments in calculating your net worth. Depreciation or casualty losses may affect your tax picture. Accordingly, in addition to cash transactions, Quicken's personal predefined Itemized Categories, Tax Summary, and Account Balances reports include transactions recorded in your Other Asset and Other Liability accounts.

Businesses tend to be more heavily oriented toward income and expenses (or profit and loss), but they still need to keep track of their cash transactions. The Business Cash Flow Report serves the latter purpose. The other reports on the Business submenu are appropriate for reporting profits and losses and taxes. The P&L Statement, Cash Flow Report, and Balance Sheet should be quite familiar. The other predefined business reports are dealt with in more detail in later chapters.

Creating a Predefined Report

The steps for creating a predefined report are basically the same for all types of reports. All Quicken reports are created from the Reports Menu. You can call up this menu either by selecting 3. Reports from the Main Menu or by pressing F5 to pull down the Reports Menu any time the Write/Print Checks screen or any Register is displayed.

To create a predefined report, select 1. Personal Reports, or 2. Business Reports from the Reports Menu, then make a selection from the submenu that appears next. A report definition screen appears. Figure 7.2 shows the definition screen for a Cash Flow Report. Definition screens for other types of reports are the same except for the heading. You can enter a report title if you want. (Otherwise the title will be the name that appears at the top of the window). When you have finished the window, press Ctrl-Enter to display the report on the screen. Figure 7.3 shows a Personal Cash Flow Report for June.

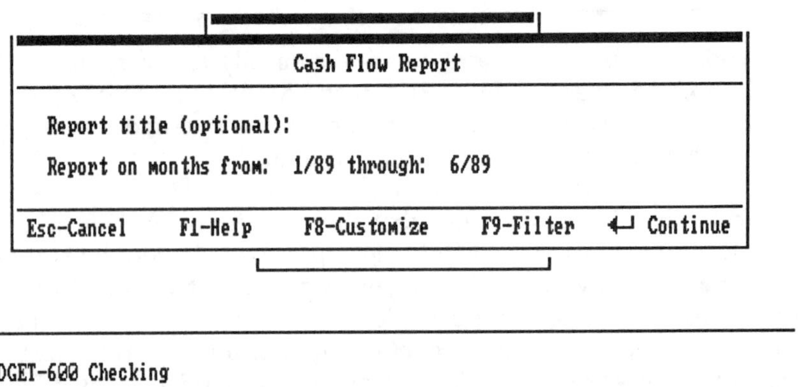

Figure 7.2. Defining a Cash Flow Report.

CASH FLOW REPORT
6/ 1/89 Through 6/30/89

Bank,Cash,CC Accounts　　　　Page 1
6/30/89

Category Description		6/ 1/89-6/30/89
INFLOWS		
Receipts		1,000.00
Salary		1,538.47
Inflows - Other		0.50
TOTAL INFLOWS		2,538.97
OUTFLOWS		
Car Expenses		191.09
Clothes		63.44
Depreciation		340.00
Entertainment		46.03
Federal Tax		246.21
FICA		115.54
Miscellaneous		341.55
Mortgage:		
Insurance	114.20	
Interest	708.33	
Taxes	239.87	
Total Mortgage		1,062.40
Office		129.34
Repairs		1,095.87
State Tax		94.79
Utilities		131.22
Outflows - Other		259.96
TO Principal		37.60
TOTAL OUTFLOWS		4,155.04
OVERALL TOTAL		-1,616.07

Figure 7.3. A predefined Cash Flow Report.

The procedure is the same for all predefined reports, except the Personal Monthly Budget Report. For that report, you must press F7 to set budget amounts before you can create the report from the report definition window, as explained later and in more detail in Chapter 9. In addition, while the report definition window for any predefined report is on the screen, you can press F8 to customize the report or F9 to filter it. The latter option allows you to exclude transactions assigned to a particular category or that contain other information you specify.

If you do not want to print a report after it is displayed, press Esc to cancel. You may have to press Esc several times before you return to the part of Quicken where you want to continue working.

Viewing Large Reports

Some Quicken reports are too large to display on the screen at once. A Personal Monthly Budget Report, for example, is too wide to display on a standard 80-column monitor if it covers more than one month. In fact, any report that subtotals by columns (horizontally) is likely to be too wide to display. Any report can also be too long to display vertically at once if it includes enough information.

Fortunately, Quicken provides special cursor commands to help you view large reports, as shown in Table 7.3. These commands are logical extensions of the cursor commands you use on the Register or the Write/Print Checks screen, but some of them work slightly differently.

Table 7.3. Cursor Controls for Viewing Large Reports.

Tab, Ctrl—>	Right one screen.
Shift-Tab, Ctrl-<-	Left one screen.
Page Up, Page Down	Up or down one screen.
Home	Top left corner of the report.
End	Bottom left corner of the report.
F9	In Transaction Reports, switches between full column width and half column width to expand or condense the report horizontally.

The last option in the table, switching from full and half-column width (F9), applies to only the Personal Itemized categories and the Tax Summary among the predefined reports. (These are both variants of the Custom Transaction Report, and the option applies to all such reports.) These reports summarize transaction information and include payee, memo, and category entries. At the half-column setting, these are displayed in truncated form, and the report will fit on an 80-column screen. With the full-column setting, you will see all of the information in these fields, but the report will be too large to display at once on the screen.

If you have a high-resolution monitor (EGA or VGA), you can expand the display through the Change Settings Menu. Select 6. Other Settings from the Change Settings Menu. Then on the Other Settings submenu, change the setting for 43 line register/reports (option 10) to Y(es). This option will not work for other types of monitors.

When you print large reports, Quicken automatically divides them into sections that are easy to assemble, as explained in the next section.

PRINTING A REPORT

Once you have created any type of Quicken report on your screen, you can print it for your records. Just press F8 to select the Print option, which is always displayed at the bottom right of a report on your screen.

When the Print Report window appears (Figure 7.4), you can select a printer. If in doubt, select 1. Report Printer. (If you have not set up your printer and need to, you can press F9 to go to the Printer Setup submenu. See Chapter 13 for details.) When you press Enter to confirm your printer selection, Quicken prints your report, and the on-screen report reappears. At this point, you can press Esc to back through the reports menus until you reach the point from which you want to continue your work.

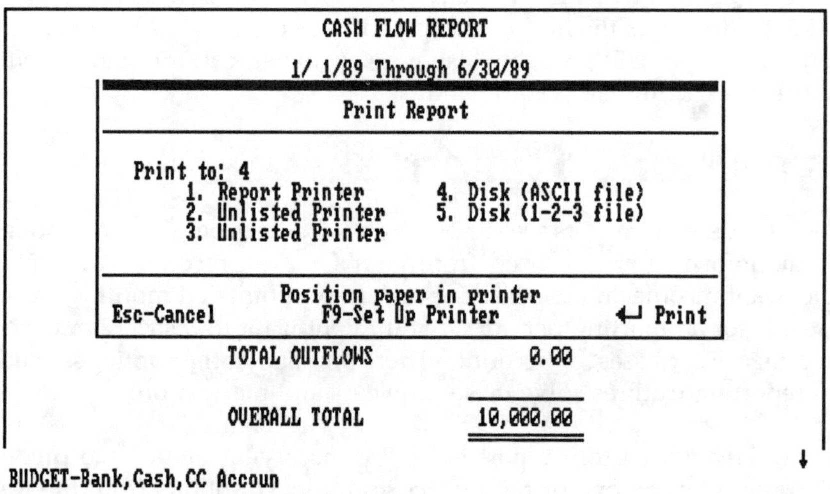

Figure 7.4. The Print Report window.

When you print a large report, vertical space should not be a problem. Quicken divides the report into pages (66 lines per page, unless you set up your printer differently). If a report is too wide to fit on a single page horizontally, Quicken automatically prints the report in strips. If you have an 80-column printer, for example, the first 80 columns will be printed on the first page, the next 80 columns on the next, and so on.

If your printer can print compressed type (usually 17 pitch) or can handle wide paper (usually 11 inches or 132 columns), you can print wider reports without having to tape pages together. (Again, see Chapter 13.)

You can also "print" a file to disk for use with other programs. In the Print Report window, option 4. Disk (ASCII file) creates a file on your data disk that you can call up into your word processor or other program. Option 5. Disk (1-2-3 file) sets up a file on your data disk that can be read by Lotus 1-2-3, Lotus Symphony, or compatible spreadsheet programs.

When you select either of the last two options, you will see a window asking for a file name. Type the *full* path and file name. If you do not include a drive letter or subdirectory, Quicken will copy the file to the same location as your Quicken program files. For example, on a dual floppy system, you should enter b:filename to copy the file onto your Quicken data disk.

> **NOTE:** Quicken will automatically add a .prn extension when you set up a 1-2-3 file. To call up the file in your spreadsheet, use the /File Import Numbers command. You will probably also need to adjust column widths with the /Worksheet Column Set command.

Customizing Reports

Quicken's predefined reports are simple and easy to use, but they may not gather exactly the information you need from your Quicken records. You might, for example, want income and expenses or cash flow subtotaled monthly, instead of in aggregate for a reporting period. Or you might want to restrict your report to certain categories, classes, or accounts. There are many other options. Quicken's custom reporting features solve these problems and many more.

You can create a custom report either by modifying one of the predefined reports or by selecting one of the four custom report options from the Reports Menu. Either way, the procedure is almost the same, because all predefined reports are variations of the four basic types of custom reports—Transaction, Summary, Budget, and Account Balances—designed for particular purposes. You could create any of the predefined reports yourself by changing the settings for one of the custom reports.

The options for customizing reports vary slightly—but not much—among the four basic report types. In each case, Quicken provides three different screens for setting custom options:

- The Create Report screen is the focal point of all customized reports. It allows you to enter a report title, set a date range, select report headings, and choose which accounts to include in the report.

- The Filter Report Transactions window, which you can reach from the Create Report screen, allows you to restrict the report to information from transactions that meet certain criteria, such as those assigned to selected categories or classes.

- The Report Options window, also accessible from the Create Report screen, allows you to create a report on the basis of income and expenses or of cash flow. You also have options for how the report will treat transfers among your Quicken accounts.

In short, Quicken allows you to create exactly the report you want, whether you start with a predefined report or one of the custom reports. The next sections explain the Create Report screen for each of the four basic report types. The following sections cover the Filter Reports Transactions window and the Report Options window.

The procedures for viewing and printing custom reports are identical to those for predefined reports, explained in the last two sections of this chapter.

THE CREATE REPORT SCREEN

The Create Report screen is home base for specifying information about a custom report. It determines the basic structure of the report you are about to create. This screen is somewhat different for each of the four basic report types, but the procedures for calling it up are always the same. The Create Report screen appears immediately when you select one of the four custom reports from the Reports Menu. If you start by selecting one of the predefined reports, the report definition screen appears first. From there, press F8 to call up the Create Report screen. Whichever you choose, you will simply fill out the blanks on the screen, then press Ctrl-Enter to create the report. The first of the custom options is the Transaction Report.

> **NOTE:** All of the Create Report screens allow you to set a date range. Quicken defines a week as Sunday through Saturday, two weeks as Sunday through the second Saturday, a half month as the 1st through the 15th and the 16th through the end of the month, and a half year as January 1 through June 30 or the rest of the year. These settings can be quite important. There is a

significant difference, for example, between writing payroll checks every two weeks and writing checks twice a month.

CUSTOMIZING A TRANSACTION REPORT

Transaction Reports list individual transactions, subtotaled by time period, category, class, payee, or account. (On the Report Options window, explained below, you can choose to have the report show totals only, omitting individual transactions.) On the Personal Reports submenu, the Itemized Categories Report and the Tax Summary Report are variations of the custom Transaction Report. None of the predefined business reports are based on the Transaction Report.

```
                              ITEMIZED CATEGORY REPORT
                               6/ 1/89 Through 6/30/89
All Accounts                                                                Page 1
7/30/89

  Date   Acct      Num         Payee          Memo        Category     Clr  Amount
 ----- -------- ------ --------------- ---------- --------------- - ---------

                 INCOME/EXPENSE
                   INCOME
                     Receipts
                     --------
  6/ 3 Checking       S Deposit                       Receipts          X     500.00
  6/ 3 Cash           S Deposit                       Receipts                500.00
                                                                           ---------
                     Total Receipts                                         1,000.00

                     Salary
                     ------
  6/30 Checking       S Paycheck Deposit Gross Pay    Salary            X   1,538.47
                                                                           ---------
                     Total Salary                                           1,538.47

                     Income - Other
                     --------------
  6/ 3 Checking       S Deposit                                         X       0.50
  6/30 Stocks           Revalue                                               200.00
                                                                           ---------
                     Total Income - Other                                     200.50
                                                                           ---------
                   TOTAL INCOME                                             2,738.97


                   EXPENSES
                     Car Expenses
                     ------------
  6/30 Checking       S Visa Payment     Joe's Garag  Car Expenses      X    -176.09
                                         Gasland      Car Expenses      X     -15.00
                                                                           ---------
                     Total Car Expenses                                      -191.09
```

Figure 7.5. The top of an Itemized Categories Report, one type of Transaction Report.

Figure 7.5 shows the beginning of a predefined Itemized Categories Report on the same transactions shown in the Cash Flow Report in Figure 7.3. This is a Transaction Report that lists individual transactions subtotaled by category. You can customize this type of report to do many other things.

The first step is to go to the Create Transaction Report screen (Figure 7.6). There are two ways to reach this screen. The first is to select 3. Transaction from the Reports Menu. The second is to select 3. Itemized Categories or 4. Tax Summary from the Personal Reports submenu, and then press F8 (Customize) when the report definition screen appears. The Create Report screen offers three selections.

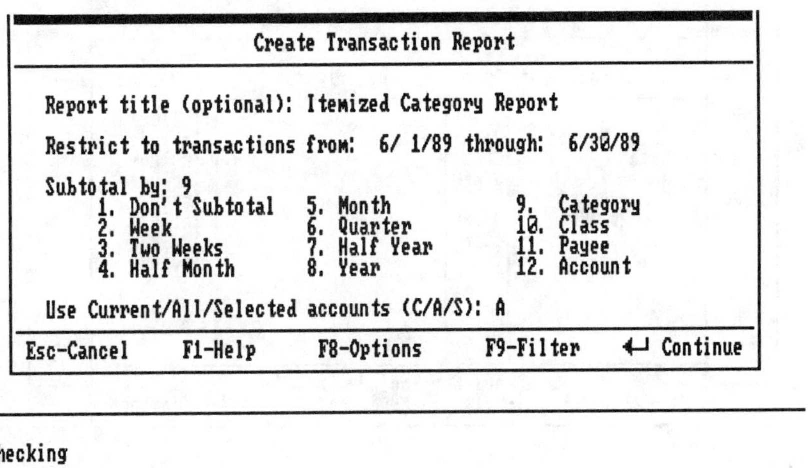

Figure 7.6. The Create Transaction Report screen.

On the first line, Report title (optional) you can enter a title if you want. (If you arrived at the Create Report window by selecting a predefined report, a title will be entered automatically). If you leave this line blank, Quicken will provide a descriptive title, such as Transaction Report by Category.

The second line, Restrict transactions from...through, simply defines the time period covered by the report. To create a report for the first half of 1989, for example, enter 1/1/89 and 6/30/89. You can subtotal transactions by period—a week, a month, a quarter, for example—in reports covering an extended period, such as a year, by making a selection in the Subtotal by blank. (If you do not subtotal, transactions will be listed in chronological order.) You can also subtotal by category, class, payee, or account. The option you choose will replace the category column in the Itemized Categories Report shown in Figure 7.5, and Quicken will sort and subtotal transactions accordingly.

The last line on the Create Transaction Report screen allows you to select accounts to include in the report. If you enter C(urrent) or A(ll), the report will immediately appear when you press Ctrl-Enter to complete the Create Transaction Report screen. If you choose S(elected), the Select Accounts to Include screen appears (Figure 7.7). Initially all accounts are included. To exclude an account, highlight it and press the space bar. (You can reinstate an account by highlighting and pressing the space bar again.) You can also switch all accounts from include and exclude (or vice versa) by pressing F9. When you complete the Select Accounts window, press Enter to return to the Create Report screen.

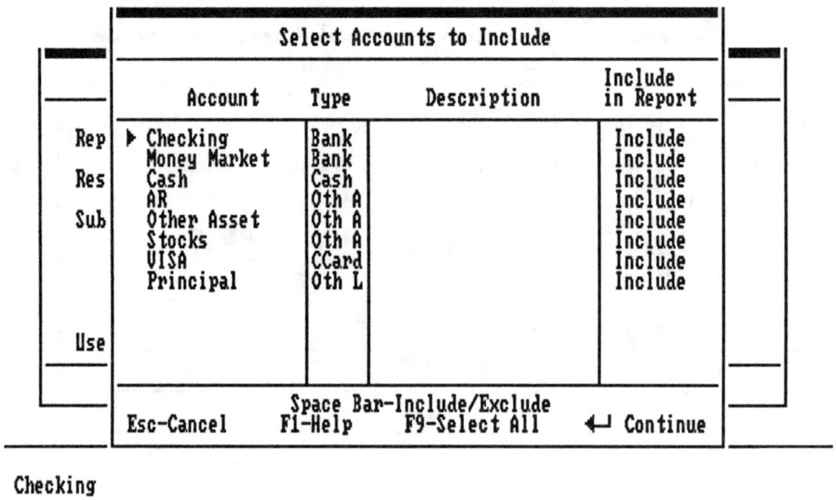

Figure 7.7. The Select Accounts to Include screen.

When you complete the Create Report screen, you can display the report by pressing Ctrl-Enter. But first you may want to filter the transactions included in the report or select options, as explained later in the Filter Report Transactions screen and the Report Options screen sections. First, let's look at the Create Report screen for other types of reports.

Customizing a Summary Report

A Summary Report does not list individual transactions, only the totals you choose. You have already seen an example in the predefined Cash Flow Report in Figure 7.3. That report provides subtotals only by category, with row headings down the left side of the report. You can select a different classification for row headings, as well as column headings (across the top). Perhaps the most natural example is a report that uses Income and Expense categories down the left side of the report and monthly totals across the top (Figure 7.8). The other predefined reports based on the Summary Report are the Business P&L Statement, Cash Flow, A/P, A/R, the Job/Project, and Payroll reports.

SUMMARY REPORT BY MONTH
1/ 1/89 Through 3/31/89

SUMMARY-All Accounts Page 1
7/30/89

Category Description	1/89	2/89	3/89	OVERALL TOTAL
INFLOWS				
Salary	5,500.00	5,500.00	5,500.00	16,500.00
TOTAL INFLOWS	5,500.00	5,500.00	5,500.00	16,500.00
OUTFLOWS				
Car Expenses	370.60	213.36	38.00	621.96
Car Loan	246.00	246.00	246.00	738.00
Clothes	295.95	124.99	46.00	466.94
Entertainment	132.87	69.88	165.00	367.75
Food	228.14	214.64	265.00	707.78
Home Repairs	71.55	0.00	127.00	198.55
Medical	250.00	132.00	0.00	382.00
Miscellaneous	447.34	379.55	480.00	1,306.89
Mortgage	700.00	700.00	700.00	2,100.00
Telephone	145.32	102.11	165.23	412.66
Utilities	392.60	347.48	212.12	952.20
Bal Fwd-Visa	0.00	0.00	0.00	0.00
TOTAL OUTFLOWS	3,280.37	2,530.01	2,444.35	8,254.73
OVERALL TOTAL	2,219.63	2,969.99	3,055.65	8,245.27

Figure 7.8. A Summary Report of cash flow with monthly subtotals.

The Create Summary Report screen (Figure 7.9) is similar to the Create Transaction Report screen, except that you can select row headings and column headings instead of a single classification for subtotals. As usual, you can call up this screen two ways. The first is to select 4. Summary from the custom reports section of the Reports Menu. The second is to press F8 (Customize) when the report definition screen is displayed for any of the predefined reports based on the Summary Report.

```
                     Create Summary Report

  Report title (optional):

  Restrict to transactions from:  1/ 1/89 through:  3/31/89

  Row headings (down the left side): 1
       1. Category          3. Payee
       2. Class             4. Account

  Column headings (across the top): 5
       1. Don't Subtotal    5. Month             9. Category
       2. Week              6. Quarter          10. Class
       3. Two Weeks         7. Half Year        11. Payee
       4. Half Month        8. Year             12. Account

  Use Current/All/Selected accounts (C/A/S): A

Esc-Cancel     F1-Help     F8-Options     F9-Filter     ↵ Continue

SUMMARY-Checking
```

Figure 7.9. The Create Summary Report screen.

As with Transaction Reports, you can enter a report title in the first blank of the screen. If you leave the entry blank, Quicken will supply a title based on your column headings selection, such as Summary Report by Month. You can also set a date range to be included in the report on the line labeled: Restrict to transactions from...through.

The next two choices are Row headings (down the left side) and Column headings (across the top). These options provide dozens of possibilities. Think of row headings as your primary classification and column headings as a secondary classification. If you manage rental properties, for example, you might want a report that shows income and expenses by property. (This is explained in detail in Chapter 10.) If you identify the properties by class, you could choose 1 (category) to yield income and expenses under row headings and 10 (class) to provide subtotals for each property.

On the last line of the Create Summary screen you can select (C)urrent, (A)ll, or S(elected) accounts. If you choose one of the first two options, Quicken will automatically restrict your report to the current account or include all of your accounts.

If you opt to select accounts, the Select Accounts window, shown in Figure 7.7, appears when you press Ctrl-Enter to complete the report screen. Select Accounts works the same way as described above. You can include or exclude an account by highlighting it on the screen and pressing the space bar. The setting in the right column will switch. You can also switch all accounts from include and exclude (or vice versa) by pressing F9. When you complete the Select Accounts window, press Enter to return to the Create Report screen, then press Ctrl-Enter to display your report on screen.

As with any report screen, the Create Summary Report screen allows you to select F9 to filter the report or F8 to select Report Options. These are described later.

Customizing Budget Reports

Budget Reports differ from other types of Quicken reports in that they require you to set budget amounts before you can create the report. You can establish a budget for a month, or for almost any other period you choose. The report will list categories down the left side and the time period across the top. You will see your budgeted amount for each category, the actual total, and the difference. The Personal Monthly Budget, which provides monthly subtotals by category, is the only predefined report based on the custom Budget Report.

You can establish a monthly budget by category simply by selecting 2. Monthly Budget from the Personal Reports submenu. If you want to customize the report, there are, as always, two ways to get to the Create Budget Report screen (Figure 7.10). You can select 5. Budget from the Reports Menu, or you can select the Monthly Budget Report from the Personal Reports submenu, then press F8 (Customize) when the report definition screen appears.

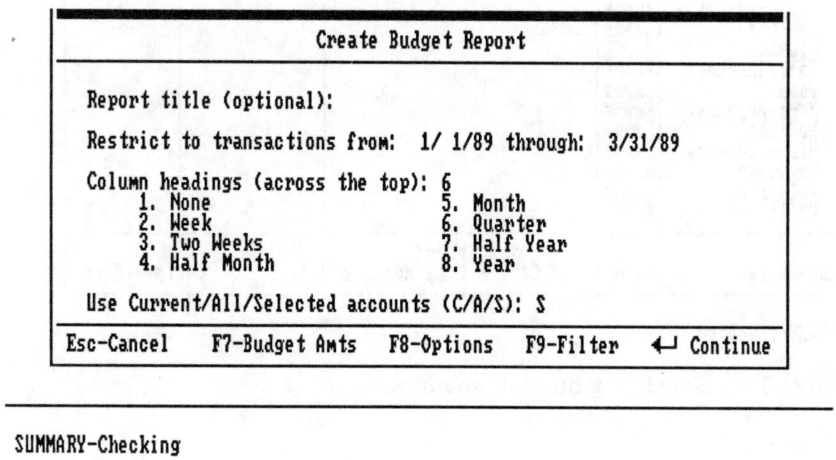

Figure 7.10. The Create Budget Report screen.

On the Create Budget Report screen, you can enter a title if you want. (If you do not enter a title, Quicken will provide one, such as Budget Report by Quarter). You can also set a date range for the report.

The Column headings option allows you to select the periods for which you want to budget. If you select 1 (none), your budgeted amounts will be for the period of the report. Otherwise, they will be for the period you select as a column heading. Budget reports always provide subtotals by category, listed down the left side of the report. Subcategories and classes are not shown.

To set budget amounts, press F7 to call up the Specify Budget Amounts screen (Figure 7.11). You can enter a monthly amount for each category or press Ctrl-e to set variable monthly budgets (Figure 7.12). Notice the option, F9-Fill w/Amt, at the bottom of the screen. When you press F9, Quicken automatically fills in the amount you have entered for the month indicated by the cursor for the rest of the year. You always set budget amounts on a monthly basis, even if you choose another budget period for column headings. Quicken uses the monthly amount to calculate your budget for the period you choose. Both the monthly budget window and the Specify Budget Amounts screen are closed by pressing Ctrl-Enter. When you have finished setting budget amounts, the Create Report screen reappears.

Specify Budget Amounts

Category	Type	Description	Budget Amount	Monthly Detail
▶ Salary	Inc			
Car Expenses	Expns			
Car Loan	Expns			
Clothes	Expns			
Entertainment	Expns			
Food	Expns			
Home Repairs	Expns			
Medical	Expns			
Miscellaneous	Expns			
Mortgage	Expns			
Telephone	Expns			
Utilities	Expns			

↑,↓ Select

Esc-Cancel F1-Help Ctrl-E Edit Monthly Detail Ctrl↵ Done

SUMMARY-Checking

Figure 7.11. Specifying budget amounts.

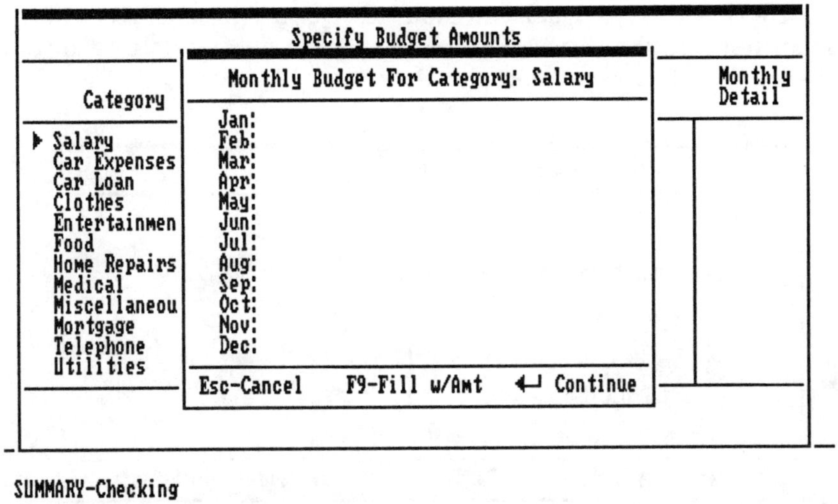

Figure 7.12. Setting variable monthly budgets.

On the last line of the Create Report screen, you can choose to include C(urrent), A(ll), or S(elected) accounts. As with all custom reports, if you take the last option, the Select Accounts screen shown in Figure 7.7 appears after you finish defining the report. You can include or exclude accounts by highlighting them and pressing the space bar. Again, pressing F9 shifts the settings for all accounts.

As with other types of reports, you can press F9 to filter a budget report or F8 to set report options, as explained below.

Customizing Account Balances Reports

The final custom report is the Account Balances Report. This report yields a balance sheet or net worth report (which is the same thing) by adding the totals of your assets and liabilities (including postdated checks), then calculating the difference. The predefined Personal Account Balances Report and the Business Balance Sheet Report both provide a balance sheet as of the current date.

Many businesses and individuals use balance sheets to measure their progress toward meeting financial goals. The Create Account Balances Report screen (Figure 7.13) allows you to create a report that shows your net worth at intervals ranging from a week to a year. You can reach this screen by selecting one of the predefined balance sheets, then pressing F8, or by selecting 6. Account Balances from the Reports Menu. As usual, you can enter a report title and a date range and include C(urrent), A(ll) or S(elected) accounts. For a current date balance sheet, choose 1 (none) as the report interval.

```
                 Create Account Balances Report

  Report title (optional):

  Report balances on dates from:  1/ 1/89 through:  8/ 4/89

  Report at intervals of: 1
       1. None                          5. Month
       2. Week                          6. Quarter
       3. Two Weeks                     7. Half Year
       4. Half Month                    8. Year

  Use Current/All/Selected accounts (C/A/S): A

Esc-Cancel    F1-Help    F8-Options    F9-Filter   ↵ Continue

SUMMARY-Checking
```

Figure 7.13. The Create Account Balances Report screen.

As with other reports, you can filter Account Balances Reports by pressing F9 or choose Report Options by pressing F8 while the Create Report screen is displayed.

The Account Balances Report normally shows only the balances for each of your Quicken accounts. However, when you choose S(elected) accounts, the Select Accounts window provides a special feature that allows you to select the option Detail, in addition to including and excluding accounts. When you select that option, the report provides subtotals by classes and subclasses. For example, if you use classes to identify customers in accounts receivable, the report will show the outstanding balance for each. (See Chapter 11.) Detailed Account Balances Reports are also useful for managing investments and real estate (Chapter 10), for reporting on inventory (Chapter 12), or other purposes for which you want balances by class. As always, you can change the setting for an account by highlighting it on the Select Accounts screen and pressing the space bar—once to switch from Include to Detail, and again to exclude the account, and once again to go back to Include. You can also switch settings for all accounts simultaneously by pressing F9.

FILTERING REPORTS

On any of the Create Report screens, you can press F9 to filter reports. The Filter Report Transactions window is shown in Figure 7.14. This screen allows you to generate reports on very specific groups of transactions. For example, the predefined Personal Tax Summary "filters" transactions to include only those assigned to categories designated as tax-related. Among the Business predefined reports, A/P by Vendor includes only unprinted checks; A/R by Customer includes only uncleared transactions; and the Payroll Report includes only transactions assigned to a category called Payroll. These are only a few of the possibilities. Filtering transactions allows you to produce reports that include *precisely* the information you need—no more, no less.

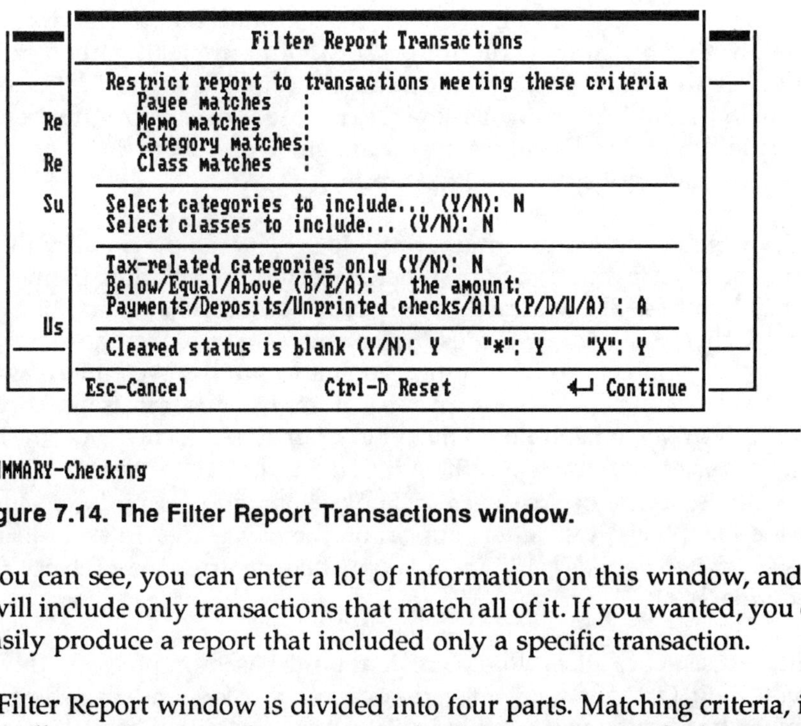

Figure 7.14. The Filter Report Transactions window.

As you can see, you can enter a lot of information on this window, and your report will include only transactions that match all of it. If you wanted, you could quite easily produce a report that included only a specific transaction.

The Filter Report window is divided into four parts. Matching criteria, in the first box, allows you to use the same search criteria you use to find a transaction with Find on the Edit pull-down menu, plus a few more. You can also select categories and classes to include only those you need. This is useful not only for producing specific reports, but also for excluding irrelevant categories, such as unrealized capital gains or home appreciation. In the window's third box, you can elect to confine your report to tax-related categories; to transactions below, equal to, or above a certain amount; or to payments, deposits, or unprinted checks. Finally, you can include or exclude transactions that are not cleared (the cleared column will be blank), that are provisionally cleared (marked with an asterisk) or reconciled with your bank statement (marked with an X).

Any time the Filter Report window is displayed, you can press Ctrl-d to return all of the settings to their normal position.

MATCHING CRITERIA

The first four options on the Filter Report Transactions window help you locate transactions recorded with a particular payee, memo, category, and/or class. If you simply make an entry in one of these blanks, your report will include only transactions that match that criterion *exactly*. For example, if you enter Dr. Fred Smith under payee and Medical under category, Quicken will find transactions made out to Dr. Fred Smith and assigned to the Medical category, but not transactions made out to Dr. Fred Smith and assigned to a Dental category, or any transactions made out simply to Fred Smith.

Quicken's flexible search criteria provide considerable flexibility in locating transactions, even if you have been somewhat erratic in recording them. There are three search entries: .. is a wildcard for any combination of characters; ? is a wildcard for a single character; and ~ excludes any key entry that matches the search criteria. For example, ..smith.. finds Dr. Smith, Fred Smith, Smith & Wesson, Alias Smith & Jones, or Arrowsmith Booksellers. An entry of smith.. will locate transactions made out to Smith & Wesson, but not to the other examples. An entry of ..smith locates transactions made out to Dr. Smith and Fred Smith, but not to Smith & Wesson, Alias Smith & Jones, or Arrowsmith Booksellers, and ~..smith.. excludes any transaction in which those letters appear on the payee line. To exclude all blank entries, enter two periods (..); to include only blank entries enter the not sign plus two periods (~..).

Wildcard searches allow you to create reports based on precisely the transactions you want. Obviously, however, they carry the risk of unexpected results. For example, a transaction you want to include may be omitted because of a simple typographical error. Similarly, you may inadvertently include unwanted transactions because your search criteria were not specific enough. For example, you might enter ..smith.., intending to include Dr. Smith, Alias Smith and Jones, and Arrowsmith Booksellers—but have forgotten all about the check last January to Capital Locksmiths, which would be included too.

Wildcard searches are a powerful tool for creating reports that meet precise criteria. But use them with caution.

SELECTING CATEGORIES AND CLASSES

The next box of the Filter Report Transactions window allows you include or exclude any of the entries on your Category List or Class List. To select categories, change the entry beside Select categories to include from N(o) to Y(es). To select classes, do the same on the next line. You can select both.

The procedure is the same for selecting categories and classes. If you take the first option, the Select Categories window (Figure 7.15) or will appear when you press Ctrl-Enter to confirm the information in the Filter window. This window works exactly like the Select Accounts window. You can exclude any category by highlighting it and pressing the space bar. To reinclude a category, just repeat the procedure. You can also press F9 to shift the setting for all categories. When you have finished your selections, press Ctrl-Enter to continue. You can use the same methods on the Select Classes window.

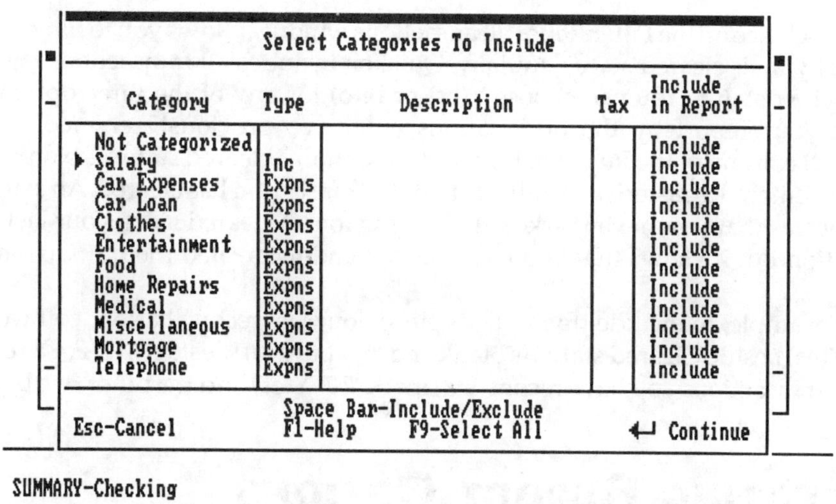

Figure 7.15. Selecting categories for a custom report.

When you have finished, the Create Report window reappears. If you want to make more changes on the Filter Report Transactions window, you can press F9 to call it up again. Your previous work will remain intact.

Tax-Related Categories, Amount, and Transaction Type

The three choices in the next box of the Filter Report Transactions window are not related, but their purpose is straightforward. Under Tax-related categories only, you can choose to include only transactions assigned to categories you have designated as tax-related. For Below/Equal/Above you can restrict your report to reflect transactions below, equal to, or above a certain amount. Under Payments/Deposits/Unprinted checks/All, you can include or exclude transactions based on their type. To produce an expense report, for example, you could enter P(ayments); an income report might include only D(eposits); for accounts payable, you could include only U(nprinted checks). Or you can leave the entry A(ll) to include all types of transactions.

> **NOTE:** Payments are decreases to Cash and Other Asset accounts, increases for Credit Card and Other Liability accounts.

Cleared Status

The final choice on the Filter Report Transactions window allows you to filter transactions by their cleared status. Initially, Quicken includes all transactions regardless of their status. You can choose Y(es) or N(o) for any of the three options to restrict your report by the designations you have previously entered in the C(leared) column of the Register. When a transaction's cleared status is blank, you have not entered an asterisk to indicate that the transaction has cleared. An asterisk (*) indicates that you have marked the transaction as cleared since your last reconciliation. An X shows that you have cleared and reconciled the transaction

For example, to include transactions since your last reconciliation, you would enter Y(es) beside Cleared status is blank and "*," but N(o) beside "X." For a report of only transactions you have reconciled, mark "X" Y(es) and the other two blanks N(o).

Selecting Report Options

The Report Options window (Figure 7.16) serves two purposes. You can choose whether to report transactions on the basis of income and expenses or on cash flow, and you can exclude transfers between accounts that basically cancel each other out. For Transaction Reports, the Report Options window also allows you to specify the amount of detail to include in your report.

```
                         Report Options
Re   Report organization: 1
         1. Income and expense   2. Cash flow basis
Re
     Transfers: 1
Su       1. Include all    3. Include only transfers to
         2. Exclude all       accounts outside this report

     Show totals only (Y/N): N
     Show split transaction detail (Y/N): N
     Show memo/category/both (M/C/B): B
Us
   Esc-Cancel             Ctrl-D Reset           ↵ Continue

SUMMARY-Checking
```

Figure 7.16. The Report Options window.

The difference between cash flow and income and expense reports is discussed in detail in Chapter 3. Briefly, income and expenses consist of all transactions that change the balance in any account *except* transfers from one account to another. Cash flow, on the other hand, consists of all inflows and outflows from your cash accounts, namely Bank accounts, Cash accounts, and Credit Card accounts.

Suppose, for example, you buy $1,000 worth of stock and record the transaction as a transfer from your Bank account to an Other Asset account, then update the Other Asset account to reflect your good fortune that the value of the stock has increased to $1,200. In an income and expense report, the purchase will be shown as a transfer, not an expense, but the update will appear as income. In a cash flow report, the purchase will be shown as an outflow, and the update will not be shown at all.

For Transaction Reports, the Report Options window offers three more options (See Figure 7.17.). Usually a Transaction Report lists individual transactions, subtotaled by time period or purpose. If you elect to show totals only, the report will show only totals. The result is similar to a Summary Report, except that income or cash inflows are shown as positive numbers, while expenses and outflows are negative (See Figure 7.18.).

```
                         Report Options
Re   Report organization: 1
          1. Income and expense    2. Cash flow basis
Re
     Transfers: 2
Su        1. Include all    3. Include only transfers to
          2. Exclude all       accounts outside this report

     Show totals only (Y/N): Y
     Show split transaction detail (Y/N): N
     Show memo/category/both (M/C/B): C
Us
     Esc-Cancel              Ctrl-D Reset          ↵ Continue

Checking
```

Figure 7.17. The Reports Options Window for Transaction Reports.

```
                        TRANSACTION REPORT BY CATEGORY
                          10/ 1/89 Through 10/31/89
All Accounts                                                        Page 1

12/31/89

                            Description                      Amount
           ---------------------------------------------  ---------
           INCOME/EXPENSE
             INCOME
               Receipts                                     8,147.52
                                                           ---------
             TOTAL INCOME                                   8,147.52

             EXPENSES
               Office                                        -336.25
               Rent                                        -1,500.00
               Utilities:
                 Electric                                    -131.22
                 Telephone                                   -436.22
                                                           ---------
               Total Utilities                               -567.44
                                                           ---------
             TOTAL EXPENSES                                -2,403.69

                                                           ---------
           TOTAL INCOME/EXPENSE                             5,743.83
                                                           =========
```

Figure 7.18. A Transaction Report Showing totals only.

The default for Show split transaction detail is N(o), meaning that your report will not include the details of split transactions, unless you subtotal by category, class, payee, or amount. Change the setting to Y(es) if you want to include the information in transaction splits. Finally, you can elect to show the memo, the category, or both in your report. If you don't change the setting, your report will show both the memo and category line of each transaction. You can condense reports horizontally by selecting one or the other.

Conclusion

This chapter provided a basic introduction to Quicken reports. You should now be able to create any of the five predefined Personal Reports and seven predefined Business Reports. The latter part of the chapter explained how to customize these reports and to create reports from scratch with the four Custom Reports selections on the Reports Menu.

Feel free to experiment. It's the best way to get a feel for how Quicken reports organize information.

The following chapters provide more specific examples of how to use Quicken to record transactions and create reports for particular purposes, starting with balance sheets and budgets in the next chapter.

8

The Balance Sheet

A balance sheet sums up your assets and liabilities, then calculates the difference. If you keep track of all of your assets and liabilities with Quicken, the overall total will be your personal net worth or your equity in your business.

The basic accounting equation, remember, is:

Net Worth = Assets - Liabilities

Thus, in theory at least, your balance sheet presents a snapshot of your financial situation; it summarizes all of the transactions you or your business has ever made. Income increases assets or decreases liabilities; expenditures do the opposite; and your net worth rises or falls accordingly. That is why any lender will ask for a personal financial statement or a balance sheet before making a loan.

Keeping constant track of everything you own and owe is not worth the effort for many people. Nevertheless, the options for using Quicken balance sheet reports are many. You don't have to keep track of all of your assets and liabilities. You might simply want to monitor your cash position by watching the balances in your Bank, Cash, and Credit Card accounts. You can also use balance sheets to keep track of individual assets and accounts, such as your investment portfolio, real estate investments, depreciable capital equipment, and loans.

SETTING UP A BALANCE SHEET

Quicken provides three balance sheet reports: Account Balances on the Personal Reports submenu, the Balance Sheet on the Business Reports submenu, and Account Balances under custom reports on the main Reports Menu. All of these do the same thing. They add up the balances in your Bank accounts, Cash accounts, and Other Asset accounts, then the balances in your Credit Card accounts and Other Liability accounts, and finally, calculate the difference.

The personal and business versions are identical. They provide a current balance sheet—as of today—summarizing the balances in all of the accounts in the current account group. The simplest way to create a balance report is to select one of these options. A report window appears with blanks for entering a title and a different date. To display the report on screen, simply press Ctrl-Enter when the information in the window is correct.

The Custom Account Balance option also creates the same report if you do not change any of the settings. The only difference is that this option takes you directly to the Create Account Balances Report screen (Figure 8.1), which allows you to set up periodic balance sheets.

```
                    Create Account Balances Report

  Report title (optional):

  Report balances on dates from:  1/ 1/89 through: 11/ 8/89

  Report at intervals of: 1
       1. None                        5. Month
       2. Week                        6. Quarter
       3. Two Weeks                   7. Half Year
       4. Half Month                  8. Year

  Use Current/All/Selected accounts (C/A/S): S
Esc-Cancel     F1-Help     F8-Options     F9-Filter   ↵ Continue

NETWORTH-Checking
```

Figure 8.1. The Create Account Balances Report window.

NOTE: You can also customize a predefined balance sheet report. First, select the report type from the Personal or Business submenu. When the report window appears, select F8-Customize to call up the Create account Balances Report screen, or F9-Filter to reach the Filter Report Transactions screen.

After the blanks for a report title and a date range, the Create Report screen prompts you to: Report at intervals of... Most balance sheets show your account balances on a certain date. If you select 1. None, for example, your report will show account balances as of the current date—the same as the personal and business predefined reports.

However, you can create a report that shows your balances at intervals of one week to a year. For example, you could create a quarterly balance sheet to gauge your progress in increasing your net worth or else a monthly balance sheet of your Bank, Cash, and Credit Card accounts to help keep tabs on your cash position. A current date balance sheet provides a snapshot of your financial situation, but it doesn't tell you where you've been or where you're going. A periodic balance sheet can help you spot trends, so you can tell whether your are meeting your financial goals or headed for trouble.

The final option on the Create Account Balance Report screen is Use Current/All/Selected accounts. By definition, a balance sheet usually includes all assets and liabilities—and thus all accounts. However, you may want to choose only the current account or selected accounts for special purposes. Monitoring your cash position has already been offered as one example. You can also select accounts to create separate business and personal balance sheets from the same account group. Or you might want to create a balance sheet for just your investment portfolio.

When you choose S(elected) accounts, the Select Accounts window (Figure 8.2) appears when you complete the screen. There are three possibilities for each account: Include (Include appears in the right column), Detail (also indicated in the right column), and Exclude (the right column is blank).

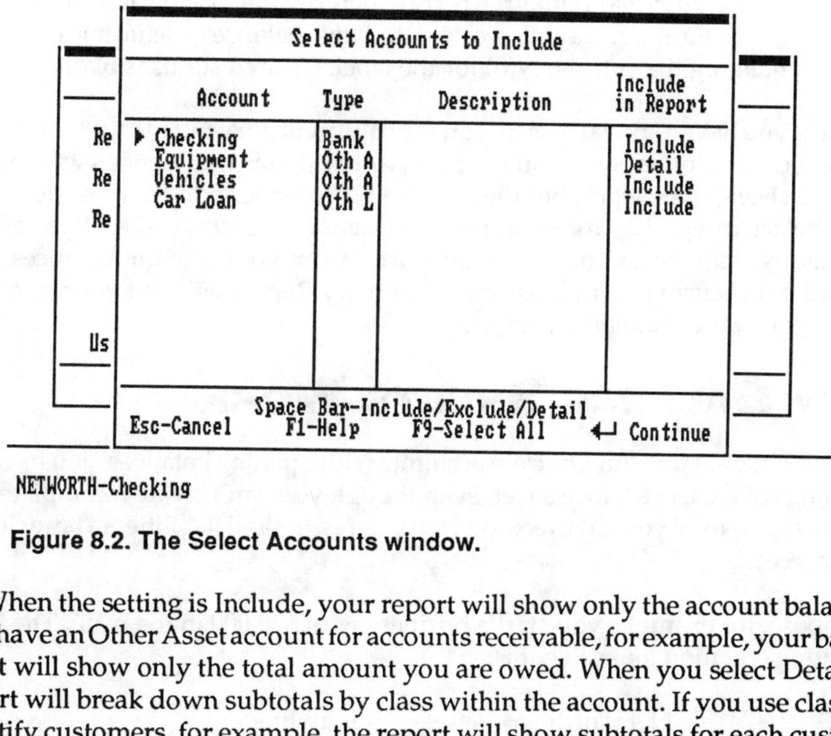

Figure 8.2. The Select Accounts window.

When the setting is Include, your report will show only the account balance. If you have an Other Asset account for accounts receivable, for example, your balance sheet will show only the total amount you are owed. When you select Detail, the report will break down subtotals by class within the account. If you use classes to identify customers, for example, the report will show subtotals for each customer.

Initially, all accounts are included on the Select account window. To change an individual setting, highlight the account and press the space bar. The setting will switch to Detail; press again to exclude the account, and again switch back to

Include. You can also toggle through the three settings for all accounts simultaneously by pressing F9. To show Class detail for all accounts, for example, press F9 once.

You can further customize your balance sheet with the Filter Report Transactions window. (Press F9 when the report window or the Create Report window is displayed.) The Filter window works just as it does for any other report. You can restrict the report to transactions that match certain criteria, to select classes or categories to include, and specify other information about transactions to be included in the report. (See Chapter 6 for details.)

If you use classes to identify items in an Other Asset account, for example, you can create a balance sheet for an individual stock identified by a class in your portfolio or an individual rental property when several are recorded in a single Other Asset account. You can also calculate bank balances excluding uncleared items by changing the entry to N(o) for the label: Cleared status is blank.

Unless you have a special reason, you probably will not want to select categories, matching criteria, or any of the other options on the Filter Transactions window for a balance sheet—they work, but the results will be rather odd for most purposes. If you select categories, for example, Quicken will exclude the effect of any transactions assigned to unselected categories from your account balances, as if they had not occurred. In most cases, a Summary Report will suit your purposes better if you want subtotals by category.

How Balance Sheets Work

As soon as you set up your Quicken accounts with opening balances, you have the beginnings of a basic balance sheet, even though you can't create a complete and accurate report until you have recorded all of the assets and liabilities to be included in your records.

Suppose, for example, you start a business with $20,000 in the bank. The basic accounting equation looks like this:

Net Worth	=	Assets	- Liabilities
$20,000	=	$20,000	- $0

And your first Quicken balance sheet is shown in Figure 8.3.

```
                  ACCOUNT BALANCES REPORT

                       As of 5/30/89
NETWORTH-Checking
11/ 8/89
                                                5/30/89
               Account                          Balance
------------------------------------------    ----------
ASSETS
  Cash and Bank Accounts
    Checking                                   20,000.00
                                              ----------
  Total Cash and Bank Accounts                 20,000.00

                                              ----------
TOTAL ASSETS                                   20,000.00

LIABILITIES                                         0.00
                                              ----------
OVERALL TOTAL                                  20,000.00
                                              ==========

NETWORTH-Checking
Esc-Create report          F1-Help                F8-Print
```

Figure 8.3. A beginning balance sheet for a new business.

Purchasing capital assets—such as equipment, vehicles, or a house—does not affect the overall total unless you record a depreciation expense or the asset appreciates. Suppose, for example, you buy a computer system for $5,000 cash. You set up an Other Asset account called Equipment and record the transaction as a transfer from Checking to Equipment. Now the balance sheet looks like Figure 8.4. Net worth—the Overall Total—is still $20,000, because there are no income, expenses, or liabilities. You have merely traded one asset ($5,000 cash) for another of equal value (the computer system).

Finally, let's look at the balance sheet after several more transactions:

- You pay $1,000 rent, recorded as a check in your checking account.
- The first month's depreciation on the computer is, say, $100, recorded as an expense in your Equipment Other Asset account.
- You receive $1,500 for services to a client, a deposit in your checking account.
- You borrow $8,000 and purchase a $10,000 car.

```
                         BALANCE SHEET
                         As of 5/30/89
NETWORTH-All Accounts                                          Page 1
5/30/89
                                                  5/30/89
                    Account                       Balance
        ---------------------------------- ----------
        ASSETS
          Cash and Bank Accounts
            Checking                              15,000.00
                                                 ----------
          Total Cash and Bank Accounts            15,000.00

          Other Assets
            Equipment                              5,000.00
                                                 ----------
          Total Other Assets                       5,000.00

                                                 ----------
        TOTAL ASSETS                              20,000.00

        LIABILITIES                                    0.00
                                                 ----------
        OVERALL TOTAL                             20,000.00
                                                 ==========
```

Figure 8.4. A balance sheet showing a capital expenditure, but no depreciation.

The loan and the car purchase are actually two transactions. Here is one way to record them:

1. Set up an Other Liability account called Car Loan and an Other Asset account called Vehicles. Both have opening balances of $0.00. (Otherwise there would be no way to record accurately the activity that is about to occur in your checking account.)

2. Enter the loan as a deposit in your checking account, assigned to the Car Loan account.

3. Write the check for $10,000, assigned to the Vehicles Other Asset account.

Now your checking account Register looks like Figure 8.5. (The depreciation transaction does not appear because it is recorded in the Equipment Other Asset account and does not affect the checking account.) And your balance sheet is shown in Figure 8.6.

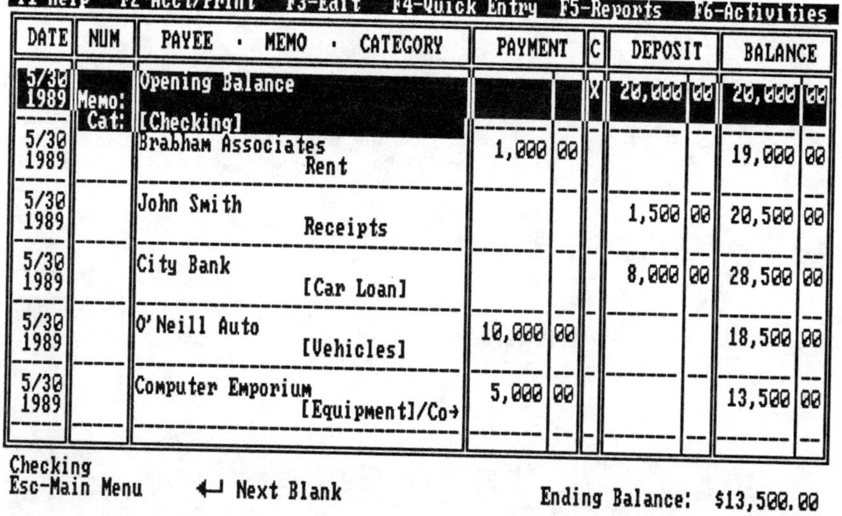

Figure 8.5. The opening transactions of a new business, shown on a Quicken Register.

NOTE: Many businesses prefer to keep track of accumulated depreciation on their balance sheets. This is easily accomplished in Quicken by using classes and subclasses. In this example, you could record the computer purchase in the business checking account, with this entry on the category line:

[Equipment]/Computer:Cost.

This increases the balance of the Equipment Other Asset account. To record the depreciation, enter a $100 decrease in the Equipment account, with this entry on the category line: Depreciation/Computer:Acc Dep. Now you have a record of the depreciation expense for the current year, and a detailed balance sheet will show the original cost of the computer, accumulated depreciation, and the current depreciated value of the equipment.

```
                         BALANCE SHEET
                         As of 6/30/89
NETWORTH-All Accounts                                           Page 1
6/30/89
                                                    6/30/89
                        Account                     Balance
            ---------------------------------- ----------
            ASSETS
              Cash and Bank Accounts
                Checking                            13,500.00
                                                   ----------
              Total Cash and Bank Accounts          13,500.00

              Other Assets
                Equipment                            4,900.00
                Vehicles                            10,000.00
                                                   ----------
              Total Other Assets                    14,900.00

                                                   ----------
            TOTAL ASSETS                            28,400.00

            LIABILITIES
              Other Liabilities
                Car Loan                             8,000.00
                                                   ----------
              Total Other Liabilities                8,000.00

                                                   ----------
            TOTAL LIABILITIES                        8,000.00

                                                   ----------
            OVERALL TOTAL                           20,400.00
                                                   ==========
```

Figure 8.6. A balance sheet for a new business after several transactions.

When you compare the latest balance sheet with the first, you can see that:

- Various transactions have reduced the checking account balance from $20,000 to $13,500, even though the only expense recorded in the account is the $1,000 in rent.
- The business has two other assets—the car, valued at $10,000, and the computer system, now valued at $4,900 ($5,000 cost less $100 depreciation expense).
- The business also now has an $8,000 Other Liability, the car loan.
- Income has exceeded expenses by $400 (the $1,500 fee, less $1,000 rent and $100 in depreciation on the computer system), leaving a net worth or Overall Total of $20,400.

Now the basic equation looks like this:

Net Worth	= Assets	- Liabilities
\$20,400	= \$28,400	- \$8,000

Thus, the balance sheet reflects, in simple form, all of the transactions that have occurred to date. If you had set up your Quicken system the day after all of these transactions occurred, you could have gotten the same result by adding up assets and liabilities, then subtracting the difference—without recording a single transaction other than the opening balances of the accounts. The balance sheet, in short, is a snapshot summary of all of the transactions you or your business has ever made.

You may already have noticed, however, that the purchases of the computer and the car are handled differently than the way many individuals think of their personal finances. When you buy a home computer, you may think of that as an outright expense. And when you buy a car, the relevant consideration is probably down payment and the monthly payments, rather than a complex transaction involving assets, liabilities, and depreciation.

Formal business accounting is precisely accurate and perfectly suited to its purpose. But it's not necessarily the best way to manage personal finances. Fortunately, you can get Quicken to keep exactly the records you want.

Personal Balance Sheets versus Business Balance Sheets

Formal business balance sheets are based on what is known as cost basis or historical accounting. No expense is recorded when the company acquires a capital asset, such as equipment, an office building, or a plant. Instead, the asset is "capitalized"—in Quicken terms, treated as a transfer from a Bank or Cash account to an Other Asset account. The expense is recorded as the asset is depreciated.

Depreciation, in fact, is something of a misnomer. When you think of the depreciation of your personal car, you usually think about the decline in its *market value*. You paid \$10,000 for it, and now it's worth only \$7,000, so it has depreciated by \$3,000. But that's not what an accountant means by depreciation at all. What the accountant does is to *amortize* the cost of the car over a certain period of time, using one of several methods. Even after the car is *fully depreciated*, it may still be worth \$5,000, but on the accountant's balance sheet, it no longer has any value.

An asset *never* appreciates on the accountant's books, unless it is sold, when it may turn up as a capital gain. In this case, the gain is not the difference between original cost and selling price, but between the asset's depreciated value and the selling price. If you sell your $5,000 computer system for $2,000 after it is fully depreciated, you have a $2,000 capital gain—not a loss of $3,000—because the entire cost has been amortized, or treated as an expense.

At the same time, the company owners' (or stockholders') equity, their ownership interest, is basically defined as their investment plus retained earnings. These are listed as *liabilities* on the balance sheet. This is because equity is theoretically the amount the owners would get, after everyone else had been paid, if the company were liquidated. It is the amount the company "owes" its investors.

Thus, the formal accounting equation comes down to this:

Assets = Equity (or Net Worth) + Liabilities

Or, more simply:

Assets = Liabilities

Always. By definition, the balance sheet balances.

For all of its precision, formal accounting defies the common sense of personal finances in two important ways. First, the accountant's *book value* of noncash assets has no direct relationship to their actual *market value*. Suppose you buy a rental property for $100,000. If you use the straight-line method to depreciate the property over 30 years, its book value, or basis, after 15 years will be $50,000. If you then sell the property for $200,000, your capital gain will be $150,000—and that's the amount the IRS will expect you to pay taxes on. On the other hand, if you buy the same home for $100,000 and apply for a second mortgage 15 years later, you can list its value as $200,000 on your financial statement—and that's the number the bank wants to see.

Even for businesses, historical or book value has little to do with market value. If it did, you could theoretically calculate the value of a share of stock in, say, IBM by dividing shareholders' equity by the number of shares outstanding, and there would be no such thing as stock speculation. Consequently, some businesses keep *both* historical balance sheets, required for tax and accounting purposes, and market value balance sheets, which may give a more accurate picture of the company's borrowing capacity, among other things. Even assigning market value to assets may yield only the company's liquidation value—how much would be left if everything were sold and all debts were paid. That may have little to do with the business's market value as a going concern.

The second point is that the common sense idea of net worth is not the same as the accountant's concept of equity. Personal net worth is not really either an asset or a liability, but a measure of your financial progress, of whether you're getting ahead or falling behind. Nevertheless, its position in Quicken's basic accounting equation makes it close enough to serve as an equity account for a proprietorship or one-person service business. Where there are partners or stockholders, however, you will need to devise a more sophisticated method for calculating equity, as explained below.

The upshot of all of this is that many Quicken users need to keep records in ways that do not exactly fit the basic accounting equation that governs the operation of the program. You may want to adjust the value of your home and cars on your balance sheet to reflect the market without generating income, expenses, or cash flow on other Quicken reports. For some assets, such as securities and your home, you may want to record both your cost basis for tax purposes and the market value. Or, when you buy a piece of furniture, you may want both to record it as an expense and add it to your household inventory for insurance purposes.

All of these situations require special record keeping tactics to produce exactly the results you want.

Personal Balance Sheets

Many financial advisers consider a net worth statement the best starting point for managing personal finances. As noted earlier, it summarizes the results of all of the transactions you have ever made. By keeping track of your net worth on a periodic basis you can measure your financial progress, or identify warning signs if you're spending yourself into a hole in ways that might not show up on an Income and Expense report or a Cash Flow Report.

It's no coincidence that a personal financial statement is one of the key items a bank or other lender will want to see when you apply for a loan. A balance sheet shows, for example, whether you have borrowed too much against your assets (a second mortgage, for example) or have enough equity or net worth to support additional loans. And, coupled with an income statement, the net worth report can show whether you can afford additional debt payments.

Cash Balance Sheets

Quicken, remember, has three types of cash accounts: Bank accounts, Cash accounts, and Credit Card accounts. A Credit Card account is technically a liability, but credit card purchases are generally treated as if you paid by cash or check. As long as you are working with only these types of accounts—and you may not have any compelling reason to get more complicated—keeping track of account balances is simply a matter of recording your routine transactions. No special techniques are necessary; the simple process of entering income and expenses and reconciling your accounts will provide the information required to produce an accurate Account Balances Report.

To create a personal net worth statement under these circumstances, select 1. Personal Reports from the Reports Menu, then 5. Account Balances from the Personal Reports submenu. When the report window appears, fill in the title (optional) and the date (if different from the one shown), then press Ctrl-Enter to create the report. You can print the report by pressing F8 and following the usual printing procedure.

What you get is a snapshot of your cash position:

Overall Total = Bank Balances + Cash - Credit Card Balances

In fact, this information is quite useful, and you may want to create cash Account Balances Reports even if you record all of your assets and liabilities in Quicken.

To create a cash Account Balances Report when you have Other Asset accounts and/or Other Liability accounts, select Personal Reports from the Reports Menu, then Account Balances from the Personal Reports submenu. When the Account Balances Report window (Figure 8.7) appears, press F8 to select Customize. The Create Account Balances Report window appears. You can now do what you want with the first three options: Report title, Report balances on dates and Report at intervals of.

Figure 8.7 shows the Account Balances Report Window; the Create Account Window is what you see when you press F8.

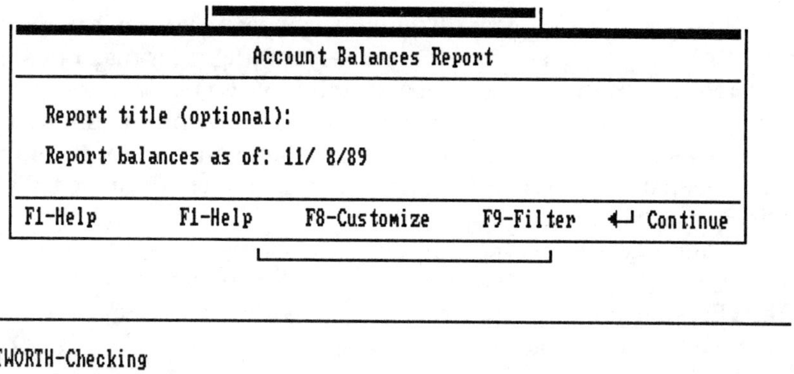

Figure 8.7. The Account Balances Report Window.

For most Quicken users, a cash Account Balances Report is a distant cousin of a full-fledged net worth statement, but it still provides very useful information. If the overall total of your cash accounts is eroding, you may be spending yourself into trouble even if your net worth is showing healthy gains. On the other hand, if your cash balance is increasing, you may have an opportunity to make long-term investments with higher yields—or to spend the increase on a scuba diving trip to the Great Barrier Reef. That's a personal choice, but you'll know where you stand.

Financial advisers unanimously recommend that you keep a cash emergency fund sufficient to cover at least six months' expenses. A year may be better. The reasoning is simple. No one's job is 100 percent secure, and you don't want to be forced to sell securities or other noncash assets at the bottom of the market just because the roof leaks.

Adding Other Liabilities and Other Assets

A full accounting of your personal net worth will probably include noncash assets and loans. These can be recorded in Other Asset accounts and Other Liability accounts. Assets include your home if you own it, other real estate, vehicles, securities investments, household inventory, debts owed to you, life insurance, collectibles, or other items of value. For life insurance, you should include only the cash value—not the face value—of whole life insurance and its variants. Term policies have no cash value, and should not be included. Liabilities, other than your Credit Card accounts, will probably be limited to mortgages or other loans.

All of these affect your net worth, but the way you record such items in Quicken is a matter of personal preference. Formal accounting rules may not apply. If you buy a stereo, for example, you probably think of it as an expense rather than a transfer to capital equipment, as a business would. But you still might want to add it to your household inventory at a value less than you paid for it. You may think of your car loan payment as an expense—and you may not want to split payments into principal and interest (the amounts change with each installment) or to figure the depreciation every month.

> **NOTE:** Recording securities investments requires special Quicken techniques, as explained in Chapter 10.

With Quicken, you can adopt a common sense approach, but you have to cheat the basic accounting equation a little to do it. The problem in the stereo and car loan examples is essentially the same: You need to change the balance in an Other Asset or Other Liability account without generating income or an expense. You will probably encounter this sort of situation often if you use Quicken to track personal net worth or to set up a market value business balance sheet.

Adjusting Balances

For personal accounting, you may want to record a transaction as both an expense and a change in an Other Asset account balance. This is technically cheating, because the same transaction can't be both an expense and a transfer to an Other Asset account.

Household purchases are an example. Suppose you buy a stereo for $1,000, paid by check. You want to record that as an expense and add the stereo to your home inventory at a value of $800, with a notation of its original cost. This requires two transactions:

1. In your checking account, record the purchase as an expense assigned to an appropriate Expense category.
2. In an Other Asset account named, say, Inventory, enter the stereo as an increase of $800. You can use the payee and memo lines to record the brand, components, serial number, and original cost for insurance purposes. Split the transaction if you need additional memo space. On the category line, assign the item to a class—/Stereo, for example.

You still have a problem. Quicken will assume that the second transaction represents income—which of course it doesn't—because you have already treated the original purchase as an expense and the $800 value of the stereo system has to come from somewhere. That won't matter on a Cash Flow Report, because inflows into Other Asset accounts are not included. But in a report of income and expenses, the addition of the stereo to Inventory will turn up as income.

Here are two ways to solve the problem:

1. On the Create Report screen, choose S(elected) accounts on the last line of the screen, then exclude the Other Asset or Other Liability account from the report.

2. Assign Other Asset and Other Liability Transactions to a special category, such as Dummy, then filter the report to exclude the category.

These tactics also work for excluding opening balances of any type of account from reports of income and expenses. (Left uncategorized, opening balances show up under the heading of Income—Other or Expenses—Other because they shift the balance of the accounting equation.)

Houses and Mortgages

There remains the question of what information to record in Other Asset and Other Liability accounts. Suppose, for example, that you buy a house for $125,000 with a $100,000 mortgage. For tax purposes, you need to keep track of your basis in the house, in order to figure your capital gain when you sell it.

Your basis is Cost + Improvements - Depreciation. Improvements are expenditures that increase the value of the property; routine maintenance is excluded. Remodeling the kitchen or adding a room increases your basis; painting, replacing the roof, or putting in a new furnace usually does not, unless the job is part of an overall renovation. Depreciation is not ordinarily a factor for a primary residence unless you rent out part of your house or claim depreciation as a home office expense. As usual, the IRS rules are complicated, so get professional advice if you have any doubts.

Also for tax purposes, you need records of payments for interest and local taxes, since both are deductible. And you need to keep track of the current market value of the house and the outstanding principal on the mortgage to calculate your net worth when you apply for a loan. You do not necessarily have to keep all of this information up to date on a daily basis, however.

Let's start with the basis. The original transaction is easy enough to record:

1. Create a House Loan Other Liability account and a House Other Asset account, both with balances of 0.00, and a class called Basis.

2. Transfer $100,000 from the Mortgage account to your Bank account. The Mortgage balance is now $100,000.

3. Write a check for $125,000, assigned to House/Basis on the category line. You now have an account balance of $125,000, which is your basis in the house.

If you have a mortgage when you begin using Quicken, set up the Mortgage Other Liability account with an opening balance of the amount you now owe and the House Other Asset account with an opening balance of the *amount you paid for the house,* not its current market value.

Now suppose you spend $15,000 remodeling the kitchen. This increases your basis to $140,000. Here are two ways to record the expenditure:

1. Just write the check, assigning the transaction to House/Basis. This does not create an expense, since it is a transfer from a Bank account to an Other Asset account, but it will show up on a Cash Flow Report, because it is a transfer from a cash account to a noncash account.

2. If you want to record the transaction as an expense, assign the check to an appropriate Expense category, then enter the increase in the House account, assigned to /Basis. In this case, you will need to exclude the House account from reports of income and expenses.

If you claim depreciation on your house, you can treat the transaction similarly, as a decrease in the House account assigned to, say, Depreciation/Basis. This will record a depreciation expense and reduce the basis. However, the transaction will not show up on a Cash Flow Report, because it is not a cash transaction.

Appreciation is another noncash transaction, but it is recommended that you assign it to an Income category (Appreciation, perhaps), so you can distinguish it from other noncash transactions. You also need a class, such as Market, so you can distinguish the market value of the house from your basis.

You can update the value of the house by recording an increase in the House account, assigned to Appreciation/Market. This transaction will not affect Cash Flow Reports, but, again, you will probably want to exclude it from reports of income and expenses by selecting accounts or by filtering categories.

Finally, we come to the mortgage. As suggested in Chapter 5, the mortgage payment can be treated as a fairly complicated split transaction, assigned to Expense categories for interest, taxes, and insurance, and an Other Liability account for the mortgage principal. To be completely accurate, in fact, you would need to assign the escrow payment to an Other Asset account, then record the payments for taxes and insurance there when the lender made the payment; escrow payments and disbursements are not necessarily equal for the tax year. Moreover, the payments on principal and interest change every month, and principal declines at a glacial pace in the early years of a mortgage. Further, payments on principal will not show up on a report of income and expenses, although they will be included in a Cash Flow Report.

Is all of this worth the trouble, when the lender sends you a statement summarizing all of this information anyway? Maybe not. Here's a shortcut. Treat your mortgage payments as a simple expense, assigned to a Mortgage Expense category. Then, when your statement comes from the mortgage lender, update your outstanding principal as a decrease in your Other Liability account. Again, you will probably want to remove this transaction from reports of income and expenses by excluding the account or by filtering categories.

The lender's statement provides the property tax and interest information you need to fill out your tax return. If you want to include this information in your Quicken records, you can record it as a split, zero-sum transaction. This can be done in any account, but the Other Liability account is recommended, so you will not have extraneous information in your Bank accounts.

Suppose the year-end statement for the $100,000 mortgage shows $10,000 in interest and $1,000 paid in property taxes. and you have been assigning your mortgage payments to an Expense category called Mortgage. Now you want to assign part of that expense to subcategories Mortgage:Interest and Mortgage:Local Tax. To record this transaction in the Register:

1. Type 0 for the amount of the transaction, but *do not* press Enter, then press Ctrl–s to split the transaction.

2. Enter the $10,000 and $1,000 expenses as usual, assigned to Mortgage:Interest and Mortgage:Local Tax. Quicken automatically enters -11,000.00 on the last line to balance the transaction at 0.00.

3. Assign the -11,000 on the last line to Mortgage and complete the transaction as usual.

The result is shown in Figure 8.8. You have now reassigned part of the expense originally allocated to Mortgage to Mortgage:Interest and Mortgage:Local Tax, but the overall total for Mortgage is unchanged. Thus, you now have a record of your total payments, plus the interest and local tax information you need to file your tax return.

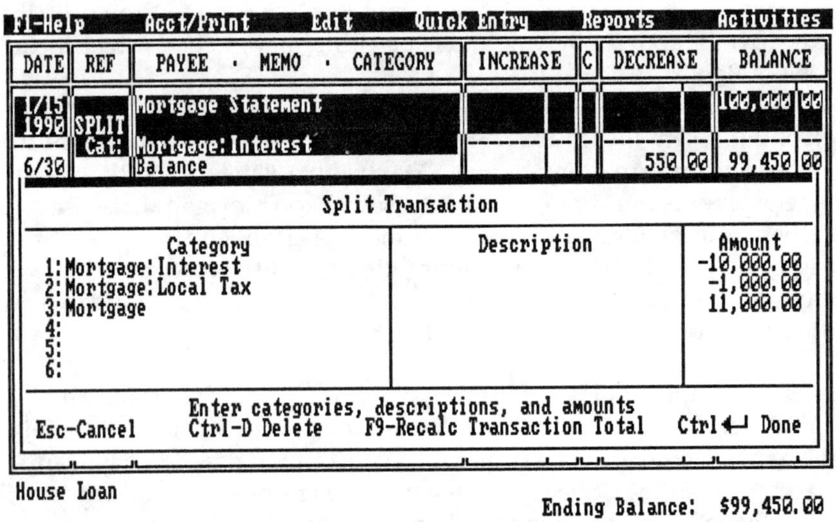

Figure 8.8. Summarizing a year's mortgage transactions.

The House Balance Sheet

After all of this, suppose that the house has appreciated by $10,000 in the course of a year; the balance on the mortgage principal has declined by $550; and the $15,000 kitchen remodeling is finished. The balance sheet for the house now looks like Figure 8.9.

To create this report, choose selected accounts on the Create Report screen and set the entry for the House Other Asset account to Detail. The house is now worth $150,000, and the basis has increased to $140,000. The owner's equity is now

$50,550. Of course, if the remodeling had been financed by a second mortgage, the balance of that loan would appear under Other Liabilities, and the Overall Total would be reduced by the corresponding amount.

```
                         ACCOUNT BALANCES REPORT
                             As of 6/30/89
BALANCE-Selected Accounts                                      Page 1
6/30/89
                                                  6/30/89
                       Account                    Balance
              -------------------------- ----------------------
              ASSETS
                Other Assets
                  House
                    Basis                 140,000.00
                    Market                 10,000.00
                                         ------------
                  Total House                          150,000.00
                                                     ------------
                Total Other Assets                     150,000.00

                                                     ------------
              TOTAL ASSETS                             150,000.00

              LIABILITIES
                Other Liabilities
                  House Loan                            99,450.00
                                                     ------------
                Total Other Liabilities                 99,450.00

                                                     ------------
              TOTAL LIABILITIES                         99,450.00

                                                     ------------
              OVERALL TOTAL                             50,550.00
                                                     ============
```

Figure 8.9. A house balance sheet.

Setting Up a Partnership

Quicken is not designed specifically to keep records for a partnership, but it can be adapted quite easily for that purpose. Suppose, for example, that Susan Smith and James Jones set up a public relations firm as a partnership. Each invests $10,000, which is deposited in the business's checking account. The partners' investments are charged to their capital accounts. A capital account represents each partner's equity, or ownership interest, in the business. The capital accounts are considered *liabilities* to the business. Quite simply, if Smith and Jones decided to back out right at the beginning, each would get $10,000 back, and the partnership would be disbanded.

At this point, the business has $20,000 in assets (the checking account) and $20,000 in liabilities (the capital accounts). The balance sheet looks like the one in Table 8.1.

Table 8.1. An Initial Balance Sheet for New Partnership

ASSETS	
Checking	20,000.00
TOTAL ASSETS	20,000.00
LIABILITIES	
Smith Capital	10,000.00
Jones Capital	10,000.00
TOTAL LIABILITIES	20,000.00
OVERALL TOTAL	0.00

As has been noted, Quicken's basic accounting equation is:

Net Worth = Assets - Liabilities

To adapt Quicken to keep books for a partnership, you will need to think of that equation this way:

0 = Assets - Liabilities - Partners' Capital

In effect, you are algebraically transforming the equation to:

Partners' Capital = Assets - (other) Liabilities.

Net worth basically disappears, because the partnership, as an entity, has none. Any value of assets over liabilities accrues to the partners' capital accounts.

This has important implications:

- Anything a partner takes from the business—a cash draw, salary, or goods—reduces his capital account and is treated as a transfer rather than an expense.

- At the end of each accounting period, the partnership's net income is distributed to the partners' capital accounts—*whether or not they actually receive it.* This may take the form, for example, of each partner's ownership interest in the office computer system (calculated as cost – depreciation) or earnings left in the business bank account.

- Everything else is treated as ordinary income and expenses, just as you would to manage your personal finances.

This doesn't mean that the partnership has to do all of this formal accounting itself in order to use Quicken. It is a perfectly valid option to use the program for routine bookkeeping and to let an accountant keep the formal books. Most partnerships need the services of an accountant anyway, and Quicken will provide all of the information the accountant needs. Consult with your accountant to make sure you set up your accounting system to provide the necessary information.

On the other hand, it is not difficult to set up capital accounts in Quicken. This requires three steps:

1. Record the partners' original investments in an Other Liability account. Net worth—the Overall Total on a Quicken balance sheet—will now be 0.00.

2. Record money the partners withdraw from the business in an Other Liability account. This is called a drawing account. Partners' salaries must also accounted for in an Other Liability account.

3. At the end of an accounting period, transfer the business's net income and the balances in the partners' drawing accounts to the partners' capital accounts.

There are a number of ways you can do this, using a combination of Other Liability accounts and classes. Your choice depends on how you want your balance sheet to look. You could, for example, set up separate Other Liability accounts for each partner's capital account, drawing account, and salary account, then make the necessary transfers at the end of each period.

The method chosen here is to set up a single Equity Other Liability account, using classes for each partner, capital account, drawing account, and salary. The advantage is that you can create either a general balance sheet, listing only Assets, Liabilities, and Equity, or a detailed balance sheet, breaking down each class by partner.

The actual transactions involved in creating a partnership vary considerably. Thus, the following examples are schematic. If you are setting up a partnership, you will probably want to enlist an accountant to help with the details.

Setting Up the Accounts

Let's go back to the opening example of the Smith and Jones public relations partnership. Each partner has invested $10,000, deposited in a Checking account, which now has a balance of $20,000.

You could record this startup as follows:

1. Set up a Bank account called Checking, with an opening balance of 0.00. (If you are beginning to use Quicken for an existing partnership, of course, the opening balances of all accounts will be determined by your current books.)

2. Set up an Other Liability account called Equity, also with an opening balance of 0.00.

3. Set up classes—Smith and Jones—so you can assign transactions to each partner. You will also need the following subclasses: Capital, for recording each partner's partnership interest in the business; Drawing, for recording assets the partners withdraw from the business; and Salary, if the partners will draw salaries.

4. To record the initial investments in the Equity Other Liability account (you could also record it in the Checking account), go to the Register and enter an increase of $10,000 for each partner, with these entries on the category line:

   [Checking]/Smith:Capital and [Checking]/Jones:Capital.

5. Press Home to go to the Opening Balance transaction and delete it. This has no effect on any balances, but it prevents a 0.00 total from showing up on your balance sheet under the heading of Equity—Other.

The Register now looks something like Figure 8.10. The balance in the Equity account is $20,000, and each partner's Capital account is credited with $10,000. You are now ready to create your first balance sheet, as described in the next section.

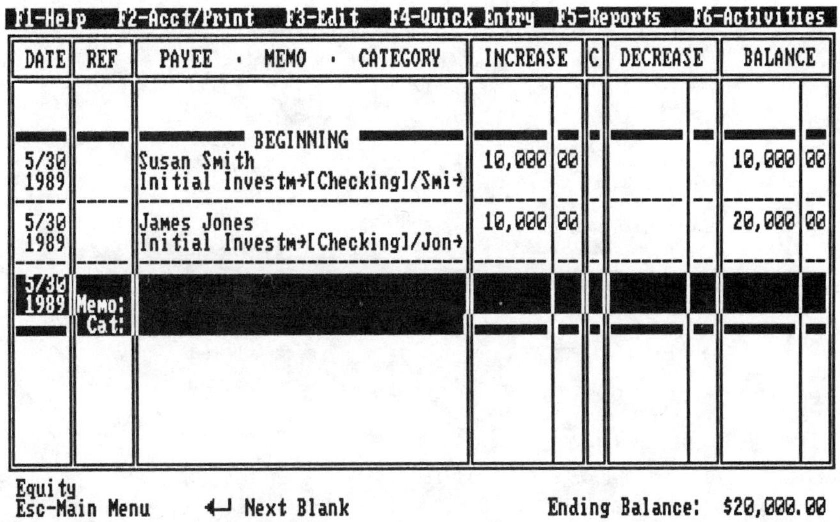

Figure 8.10. Setting up a partnership on an Other Asset account Register.

A First Balance Sheet

The firm of Smith and Jones now has $20,000 in the bank, and each partner has a Capital account (identified as a class) of $10,000. You can now create a summary balance sheet, listing only the total of the Equity Other Liability account (without breaking out each partner's Capital class), or a detailed balance sheet, listing the classes within the Equity account.

To create a summary balance sheet, select 6. Account Balances from the Reports Menu. When the Create Account Balances Report window appears, enter a title, if you want. You should not have to change the date range on the second blank. Leave the bottom line set to the default, A(ll) accounts. Finally, press Ctrl-Enter to create the report. The result is shown in Figure 8.11.

```
                              Balance Sheet
                              As of 6/30/89
PARTNERS-All Accounts                                                 Page 1
6/30/89
                                                   6/30/89
                       Account                     Balance
        ----------------------------------- ----------
        ASSETS
          Cash and Bank Accounts
            Checking                          20,000.00
                                              ----------
          Total Cash and Bank Accounts        20,000.00

                                              ----------
        TOTAL ASSETS                          20,000.00

        LIABILITIES
          Other Liabilities
            Equity                            20,000.00
                                              ----------
          Total Other Liabilities             20,000.00

                                              ----------
        TOTAL LIABILITIES                     20,000.00

                                              ----------
        OVERALL TOTAL                              0.00
                                              ==========
```

Figure 8.11. A summary balance sheet for a new partnership.

To create a detailed balance sheet, change the last line of the Create account Balances Report window to S(elected) accounts, then press Enter. The Select Accounts window appears. Highlight the Equity Other Liability account, then press the space bar to change the setting in the right column from Include to Detail, then press Enter. Now the balance sheet looks like Figure 8.12.

The only difference between the two examples is that the second splits out the balance in the Equity Other Liability account into a class for each partner and a subclass for Capital. In either case, the Overall Total, or net worth, is 0.00. Simple enough. But Smith and Jones haven't even started doing business yet. There are more techniques to learn.

```
                              Balance Sheet
                              As of 6/30/89
PARTNERS-Selected Accounts                                              Page 1
6/30/89
                                                  6/30/89
                  Account                         Balance
  ---------------------------------- ------------------------------
     ASSETS
       Cash and Bank Accounts
         Checking                                            20,000.00
                                                           -----------
       Total Cash and Bank Accounts                          20,000.00

                                                           -----------
     TOTAL ASSETS                                            20,000.00

     LIABILITIES
       Other Liabilities
         Equity
           Jones:
             Capital                10,000.00
                                   -----------
           Total Jones                           10,000.00
           Smith:
             Capital                10,000.00
                                   -----------
           Total Smith                           10,000.00
                                                -----------
         Total Equity                                        20,000.00
                                                           -----------
       Total Other Liabilities                               20,000.00

                                                           -----------
     TOTAL LIABILITIES                                       20,000.00

                                                           -----------
     OVERALL TOTAL                                                0.00
                                                           ===========
```

Figure 8.12. A detailed balance sheet for a new partnership.

Drawing Accounts

When a partner withdraws money or goods from a partnership, the effect is to reduce the balance in his capital account. However, just recording the transaction there is not sufficient. The business needs a record of how much each partner takes during each accounting period. Again, you could do this several ways in Quicken. The method chosen here is to set up a subclass called Drawing for recording each partner's withdrawals.

Suppose Smith withdraws $1,000 and Jones withdraws $2,000 from the partnership's Checking account for personal use. The withdrawals are recorded as decreases on the Checking account Register, with these entries in the category line:

[Equity]/Smith:Drawing and [Equity]/Jones:Drawing.

(You could also record the transactions in the Equity account, assigned to [Checking], with the same class designations.) You can save keystrokes by setting up Memorized Transactions for these activities, as explained in Chapter 5.

Now the Register looks like Figure 8.13. Assuming, for the sake of illustration, that nothing else has happened, the Bank account Balance has declined to $17,000 and the partners' Equity has declined to the same amount. The detailed balance sheet now looks like Figure 8.14.

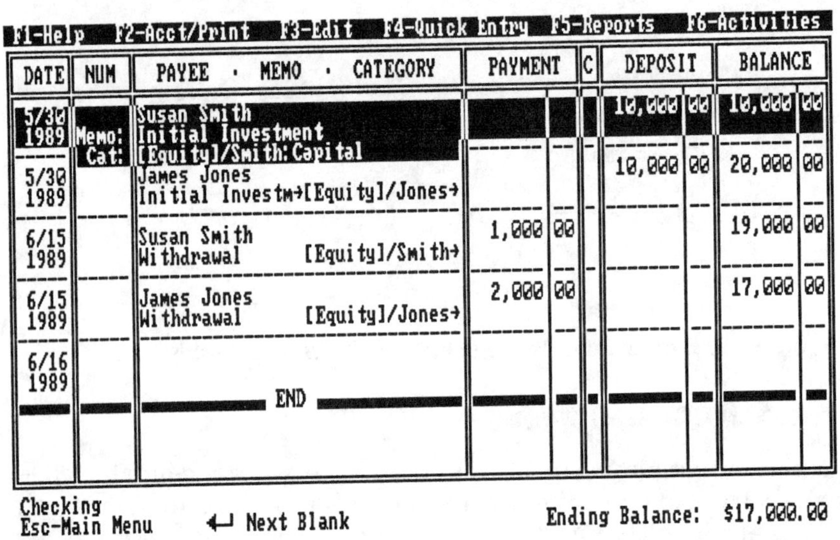

Figure 8.13. Two partners withdraw cash from the partnership's business Checking account.

```
                                   Balance Sheet
                                   As of 6/30/89
PARTNERS-Selected Accounts                                                  Page 1
6/30/89
                                                        6/30/89
                 Account                                Balance
   ---------------------------------- ------------------------------
   ASSETS
     Cash and Bank Accounts
       Checking                                                 17,000.00
                                                              -----------
     Total Cash and Bank Accounts                               17,000.00

                                                              -----------
   TOTAL ASSETS                                                 17,000.00

   LIABILITIES
     Other Liabilities
       Equity
         Jones:
           Capital                    10,000.00
           Drawing                    -2,000.00
                                     -----------
         Total Jones                              8,000.00
         Smith:
           Capital                    10,000.00
           Drawing                    -1,000.00
                                     -----------
         Total Smith                              9,000.00
                                                -----------
       Total Equity                                             17,000.00
                                                              -----------
     Total Other Liabilities                                    17,000.00

                                                              -----------
   TOTAL LIABILITIES                                            17,000.00

                                                              -----------
   OVERALL TOTAL                                                     0.00
                                                              ===========
```

Figure 8.14. Assigning partners' withdrawals from Checking to Equity reduces both the business's assets and its liabilities.

PARTNERS' SALARIES

The partners in a business often draw salaries. Unlike the salaries of employees, partners' salaries are distributed to their capital accounts. Partners' salaries are treated much like partners' withdrawals. They are, in effect, part of the partners' agreement on how to distribute the partnership's income.

One way of handling partners' salaries in Quicken is to set up a Salary subclass to be used within the Equity account. If Smith and Jones each draw $1,500 a month in salary, for example, they could enter the transactions in the Checking Bank account, assigned to [Equity]/Smith:Salary and [Equity]/Jones:Salary. Again,

Memorized Transactions, explained in Chapter 5, will simplify the task of recording these entries. Barring other transactions, the partnership's detailed balance sheet after the first month might look like Figure 8.15.

```
                         ACCOUNT BALANCES REPORT
                              As of 6/30/89
PARTNERS-Selected Accounts                                        Page 1
11/ 8/89
                                                      6/30/89
                  Account                             Balance
     ----------------------------------  --------------------------------
     ASSETS
       Cash and Bank Accounts
         Checking                                               14,000.00
                                                              -----------
       Total Cash and Bank Accounts                             14,000.00

                                                              -----------
     TOTAL ASSETS                                               14,000.00

     LIABILITIES
       Other Liabilities
         Equity
           Jones:
             Capital                      10,000.00
             Drawing                      -2,000.00
             Salary                       -1,500.00
                                        -----------
           Total Jones                                6,500.00
           Smith:
             Capital                      10,000.00
             Drawing                      -1,000.00
             Salary                       -1,500.00
                                        -----------
           Total Smith                                7,500.00
                                                   -----------
         Total Equity                                           14,000.00
                                                              -----------
       Total Other Liabilities                                  14,000.00

                                                              -----------
     TOTAL LIABILITIES                                          14,000.00

                                                              -----------
     OVERALL TOTAL                                                   0.00
                                                              ===========
```

Figure 8.15. Including partners' salaries on a balance sheet.

This, of course, is very schematic. The business also will be incurring expenses and generating income. The next section shows how a partnership squares up the balance sheet at the end of an accounting period.

End-of-Period Procedures

A partnership, remember, has no net worth. This means that all income must be distributed to the partners' capital accounts at the end of each accounting period—or at least at the end of the tax period. You may want to have your accountant take care of this task, but you can do it with Quicken.

Squaring up the balance sheet at the end of the period involves two steps:

1. Calculating the partnership's net income and distributing that amount to the partners' capital accounts. This is not necessarily the amount of cash the partners actually receive. Some of the net income, for example, may take the form of undepreciated capital assets, such as office equipment. Some of it may still be in the business Checking account. It doesn't matter; all of the partnership's net income must be distributed to the partners, and they must pay personal income taxes on it.
2. The partners' salary and drawing accounts are adjusted to zero by transferring the balances to their capital accounts. These accounts record amounts each partner takes from the business in each accounting period, and you need to start anew when a new accounting period begins.

Thus, the balance in each partner's capital account at the end of an accounting period is calculated this way:

```
Beginning Balance
+ Partner's Share of Net Income
- Salary and Draws
==================================
Ending Balance
```

This must always be the last series of transactions during the accounting period. If you later add income or expense transactions for the period, you will have to repeat the procedure to reflect them on the balance sheet.

Suppose, schematically, that as of December 31, Smith & Jones has earned $75,000 in net income. Each partner has received $18,000 in salary. In addition, Smith has drawn $10,000, and Jones has drawn $15,000. This means that the partnership's assets have increased by $14,000 ($75,000 less the $61,000 the partners have received in draws and salary). Their unadjusted balance sheet looks like Figure 8.16.

```
                          Balance Sheet
                          As of 12/31/89
PARTNERS-Selected Accounts                                   Page 1
6/30/89
                                                   12/31/89
              Account                               Balance
     ----------------------------------  ---------------------------------
     ASSETS
       Cash and Bank Accounts
         Checking                                              34,000.00
                                                              -----------
       Total Cash and Bank Accounts                            34,000.00

                                                              -----------
     TOTAL ASSETS                                              34,000.00

     LIABILITIES
       Other Liabilities
         Equity
           Jones:
             Capital                 10,000.00
             Drawing                -15,000.00
             Salary                 -18,000.00
                                   -----------
           Total Jones                          -23,000.00
           Smith:
             Capital                 10,000.00
             Drawing                -10,000.00
             Salary                 -18,000.00
                                   -----------
           Total Smith                          -18,000.00
                                               -----------
         Total Equity                                         -41,000.00
                                                              -----------
       Total Other Liabilities                                -41,000.00

                                                              -----------
     TOTAL LIABILITIES                                        -41,000.00

                                                              -----------
     OVERALL TOTAL                                             75,000.00
                                                              ===========
```

Figure 8.16. An unadjusted detailed balance sheet for a partnership at year end.

What this shows is that the partners have invested $10,000 each and withdrawn $33,000 and $28,000, respectively. Thus, they now appear to "owe" the partnership $23,000 and $18,000. The Overall Total at the bottom of the balance sheet is $75,000. Not coincidentally, this happens to be the partnership's net income. But it belongs to the partners, not the business, and it must be distributed to the partners' capital accounts.

Net income can end up anywhere in your Quicken accounts—in the form of a Bank account balance, a capital asset, or a reduction in a liability. None of these are affected by distributing net income to the partners' capital accounts. Instead, you will adjust the partnership's Overall Total—or net worth—to zero by assigning net income to the partners' Other Liability account by updating the balances.

NOTE: In the process, you will effectively wipe out the partnership's net income, since it is being transferred from the business to the partners. However, you can still create an accurate P&L Statement for the partnership. When you create the report, press F8 to select Customize. Change the last line of the screen to Use Selected accounts, then exclude the Equity Other Liability account on the Select accounts screen.

Distributing Partners' Salaries

Partners' salaries are treated differently than employees' salaries or wages. Partners' salaries are not an expense to the business, but part of the partners' agreement concerning how to divide the profits. Thus, the partners' salaries are credited to their capital accounts before the remainder of the profits is divided.

In this case, Smith and Jones each have received $18,000 in salary, recorded in the Salary subclass in the Equity Other Liability account. The purpose of this subclass is to monitor the amount each partner takes in salary. Distributing their salary shares of net income effectively cancels this item.

To record the distribution, go to the Equity Other Liability account Register and enter these two transactions as *increases* in the account. On the category line, assign one to Income/Jones:Salary and the other to Income/Smith:Salary.

These transactions accomplish two things: The balances and Smith's and Jones's Salary subclass are returned to zero, and the partnership's net income is reduced by $36,000. The rest of net income still has to be distributed, and the balances of the partners' drawing accounts have to be returned to zero for the beginning of the new accounting period.

Distributing the Rest of Net Income

After accounting for the partners' salaries, $39,000 of net income remains. Partnerships have various methods for splitting up profits, but let's say Smith and Jones divide it evenly. That means that $19,500 goes to each partner's capital account. Only the amounts would be different if they had another arrangement; you would still record the distribution the same way.

The balances in the drawing accounts also need to be "zeroed out" to give each partner a clean slate for the new period. One way to do this is to deduct the drawing account balance from each partner's share of net income.

Smith's transaction is easy to record as a split transaction in the Equity account Register. The amount of the transaction is $19,500, with $10,000 assigned in the category blank to Income/Smith:Drawing and $9,500 to Income/Smith:Capital, as shown in Figure 8.17. As a result of this transaction, the balance in her drawing account is increased from -$10,000 to $0.00, and her capital account is increased by $9,500, to $19,500.

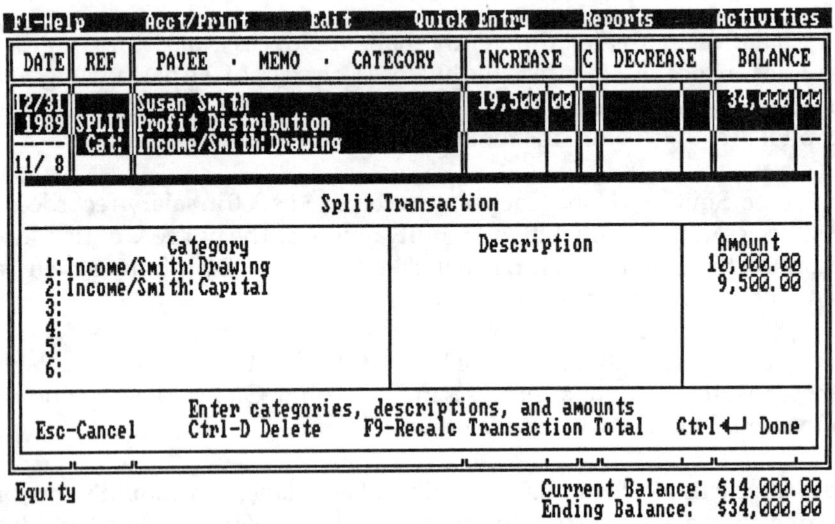

Figure 8.17. Distributing net income and balancing a partner's drawing account.

Jones's transaction is recorded the same way, with $15,000 assigned to Income/Jones:Drawing and $4,500 assigned to Income/Jones:Capital. The balance in his drawing account is now 0.00 and his capital balance is $14,500. The partners' investment in the business stands at $34,000.

Suppose, however, the partnership's net income were $65,000, instead of $75,000. After the $36,000 in salaries, each partner is left with only $14,500 in net profits. Now Jones's situation is a little more complicated, because his share of net income doesn't cover the $15,000 balance in his drawing account. You can solve the problem in a three-part split transaction:

1. $14,500 assigned to Income/Jones:Capital. This increases his capital account by $14,500 and decreases the partnership's net income by the same amount.

2. - $15.000 assigned to /Jones:Capital. This decreases his capital account by $15,000.

3. $15,000 assigned to /Jones:Drawing. This increases his drawing account balance from -$15,000 to $0.00.

This transaction is shown in Figure 8.18. The net effect is to decrease partnership net income by $14,500, decrease Jones's capital account by $500, and return the balance in his drawing account to $0.00 for the beginning of the next accounting period.

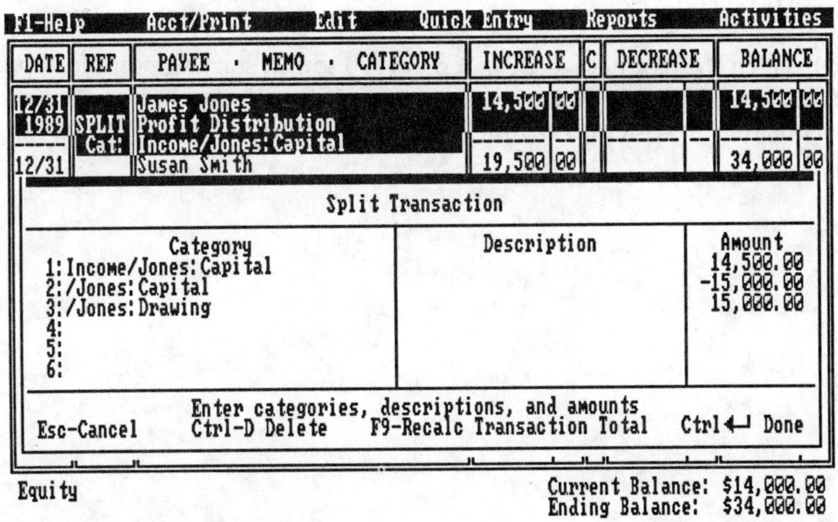

Figure 8.18. Distributing partnership income when the partner's share doesn't cover his drawing account.

In either example, the partnership has some decisions to make, because Smith and Jones's investments are no longer equal. Some partnerships pro rate net income based on capital invested. In that case Smith would get a larger share of the next period's profits. Alternatively, the partners could rebalance their investments—Smith would withdraw capital and/or Jones would make an additional contribution. But that's a business negotiation, not an accounting problem.

Conclusion

This chapter explained the basic concept of balance sheets and how to set them up. In formal business accounting, assets are recorded at original cost less depreciation. Most individuals want to keep track of their net worth on the basis of the market value of their assets. To create a market value balance sheet, you have to "cheat" the basic accounting equation, because assets change value without generating anything that one would ordinarily call "income" or "expenses."

Liabilities are more straightforward, because balances usually decline as you pay off the principal and they are not subject to market variations. Nevertheless, many individuals will want to treat loan payments as simple expenses and also periodically update the outstanding balances of the loans. Again, you have to "cheat" to do this.

The balance sheet or net worth statement is a sound starting point for financial record keeping. The next chapter moves forward to budgeting and taxes. Few people consider these items fun, but Quicken is well-equipped for the task.

9

Budgeting and Taxes

One of the main benefits of using Quicken is that the program can help you make tax planning, tax preparation, and budgeting easier, better organized and more accurate. Business budgeting may be more rigorous than most personal budgets, and business taxes may be more complex than personal taxes, but the basic strategies for keeping records with Quicken are the same.

For both budgeting and keeping tax records, the critical first step is to set up Quicken classifications—categories, subcategories, classes, and subclasses—that will produce the reports you need. In the case of tax records, of course, you also need to set up a system for keeping receipts and other paper records in case of an audit.

Cutting costs and reducing taxes are not necessarily ends in themselves. Cutting personal costs might require unacceptable changes in lifestyle. For a business, cuts can backfire if they reduce service or the quality of the product. Similarly, it would be foolish for either an individual or a business to make an investment that was otherwise unpromising just to reap tax benefits.

Your balance sheet or net worth statement may be a snapshot of the results of your personal or business financial life to date, but it doesn't tell you how you got there. To plan for the future you need to know where your money is going. Budgeting and tax planning work together to help you make rational financial decisions.

Obviously, your budget classifications must be consistent with your tax classifications. Since tax reporting requirements are predetermined, we'll begin there. Bear in mind, however, that Quicken allows you to budget only for Income and Expense categories and for transfers between accounts; you cannot budget for subcategories or classes. For example, if you set up a Utilities category with subcategories for Telephone, Gas, and Electricity, you can analyze your actual expenditures in as much detail as you want, but you can set up a budget for only the main category.

TAXES

Quicken has no provision for calculating your business or personal tax liability. The program does, however, allow you to designate categories as tax-related, and to produce a Personal Tax Summary of the transactions assigned to those categories. In a business, all transactions are tax-related, and the P&L Statement, the Cash Flow Report, or a Summary Report should provide the information you need.

The most important step in using Quicken for tax reporting is to make sure that your Quicken categories and classes match the lines on your tax forms. In general, the simplest course is to fill out your taxes from standard Quicken reports. If you file Schedule C—Profit or Loss from Business or Profession, for example, you will need such categories as Gross Receipts (Line 1a), Advertising (6), Dues and Publications (13), Office Expense (20), Repairs (23), and so on. Just check last year's returns and make sure you have the categories you need.

Keeping Tax Records

Quicken can produce reports based either on cash flow or on income and expenses, and it is critical to understand the difference when preparing tax reports. Cash flow reports measure inflows and outflows of cash, *regardless* of purpose. Purchase of capital equipment, for example, will appear as an outflow, even though the tax deductible expense does not occur until you depreciate the equipment. On the other hand, depreciation and other income and expense transactions in Other Asset and Other Liability accounts will not appear. Income and expense reports provide subtotals for all types of transactions, with transfers listed separately.

Quicken tends to assume that you will want to keep records on the basis of cash flow for personal finances and on the basis of income and expenses for business. (The Personal Cash Flow and Budget reports are cash flow reports; all Business reports except Cash Flow are income and expense reports.)

Tax reporting, however, must be categorized and based on income and expenses, so all transactions that affect your taxes must be assigned to Income or Expense categories. This does not create a problem if you use Quicken for simple bookkeeping. Your Quicken reports will provide the information you need at tax time. If your records include Other Asset and/or Other Liability accounts, however, Quicken record keeping can become more complex.

Let's return to the example of purchasing a computer for $5,000 and assigning the transaction to an Equipment Other Asset account. On a cash flow report, the purchase will show up as an outflow; on an income and expense report, it will show up as a transfer between two accounts—if it shows up at all (you can exclude transfers with the Options feature). The proceeds of a loan will show up as an inflow on a cash flow report, but as a transfer in an income and expense report.

No deductible expense is recorded until you enter a depreciation transaction in the Equipment Other Asset account, assigned to an Expense category. If you want to treat the purchase as an expense in the current tax year, which would be allowable in certain circumstances, you can either depreciate the computer completely this year or assign the original transaction to an Expense category. In either case, the expense would be reported as depreciation on your tax forms.

Other Liability accounts—typically loans—present a different set of questions at tax time. With few exceptions, loan payments consist of at least two parts: payments on principal and payments on interest. Payments on principal are not deductible. Interest generally is deductible for mortgages and business loans. For Federal income tax, interest on personal loans is 20 percent deductible in the 1989 tax year, 10 percent deductible in 1990, and nondeductible thereafter—although you may still be able to deduct personal interest for state or local taxes.

Mortgages often also include an escrow payment, which the lender eventually will use to pay your insurance and local property tax bills. The escrow payment is not deductible in itself, but the property tax payment is. The insurance payment is not deductible for personal property, but it is deductible for business property.

As explained in Chapter 5, you can record all of this information in Quicken as a split transaction each month, and in a formal accounting system, that is what you would do. For personal accounting or a small business, however, it may be far simpler to use Quicken to record income and expenses (the loan check is a payment to the bank assigned to a nontax Expense category) and to sort out the tax details from your statement from the lender. Or let your accountant do it.

You can keep Quicken records in as much detail as you want. In many cases, the simplest course is to use Quicken for simple bookkeeping and to do your tax accounting at the end of the quarter or the end of the year.

Tax Reports

Quicken includes only one report specifically designed for taxes, the Tax Summary on the Personal Reports submenu. This report lists individual transactions, subtotaled by tax-related Income and Expense categories. If you use this report for tracking your personal tax-related transactions, you will probably want to keep a copy with your permanent tax records.

The Personal Tax Summary may also be suitable for your small business if you designate all of your Income and Expense categories as tax-related. Alternatively, your P&L Statement will provide a summary of your income and expenses, without the detail of individual transactions.

You can also set up custom reports to provide exactly the tax information you want. Examples are given below.

The Tax Summary

The Tax Summary, selection 4 on the Personal Reports submenu, lists individual Income and Expense transactions in tax-related categories, grouped and subtotaled by category. If you designated all relevant categories as tax-related when you set them up—and recorded all relevant transactions—this report may provide all of the information to complete your tax return.

To create a Tax Summary, select 4. Tax Summary from the Personal Reports submenu. When the Tax Summary Report window (Figure 9.1) appears, enter a title and adjust the date range if you want, then press Ctrl-Enter to create the report. The result will look something like Figure 9.2.

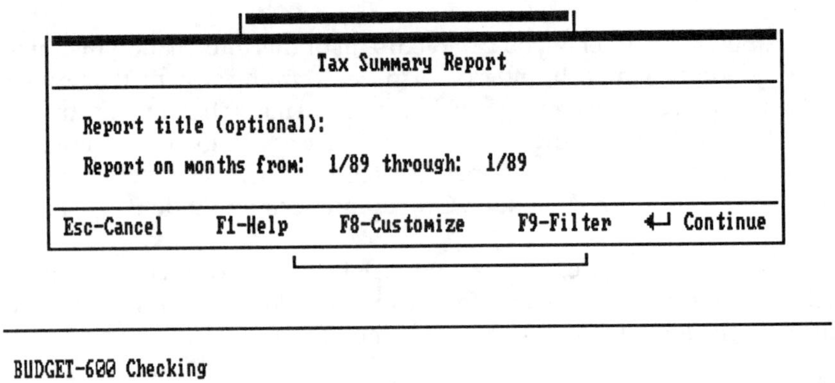

Figure 9.1. The Tax Summary Report window.

The Tax Summary is a variation of the Custom Transaction Report, subtotaled by category. You can easily reconfigure the report by selecting F8-Customize or F–9 Filter when the Tax Summary Report Window is displayed. If you want category

```
                            TAX SUMMARY REPORT
                        10/ 1/89 Through 10/31/89
All Accounts                                                         Page 1
11/ 8/89

 Date   Acct     Num        Payee          Memo        Category     Clr Amount
----- -------- ------ --------------- ---------- -------------- - ---------

               INCOME/EXPENSE
                 INCOME
                   Receipts
                   --------
10/ 1 AR       3452   Susan James Desi Yorx Brochu Receipts/James     1,322.31
10/ 7 AR       3455   Quiller Manufact Annual Repo Receipts/Quille    6,325.21
10/21 AR       3457   Food Processing  Quiller Art Receipts/Food        500.00
                                                                   ---------
                   Total Receipts                                   8,147.52
                                                                   ---------
                 TOTAL INCOME                                       8,147.52


                 EXPENSES
                   Auto
                   ----
10/ 1 Checking 1236   Branch Bank      Car Lease   Auto               -329.32
                                                                   ---------
                   Total Auto                                         -329.32

                   Office
                   ------
10/ 1 Checking 1235   Branch Bank      Computer Le Office             -236.25
10/ 3 Checking 1237 S Computer Emporiu Computer pa Office              -50.00
10/30 Checking 1249 S Computer Emporiu Computer pa Office              -50.00
                                                                   ---------
                   Total Office                                       -336.25

                   Payroll
                   -------
10/14 Checking 1241   John Jones                   Payroll            -698.32
10/14 Checking 1242   Susan Lampley                Payroll            -839.29
10/28 Checking 1246 S John Jones                   Payroll            -498.32
10/28 Checking 1247   Susan Lampley                Payroll            -839.28
                                                                   ---------
                   Total Payroll                                    -2,875.21
```

Figure 9.2. A Tax Summary Report.

totals without transaction detail, for example, you can adjust the Show totals only setting on the Report Options window from N(o) to Y(es). (To get to the Report Options window from the Tax Summary Report window, first select F8-Customize, then press F8 again to select Options.)

There are almost infinite possible variations of Quicken reports. Feel free to experiment until you find the combination of settings that works for you.

Business Tax Reports

For business tax reporting, the P&L Statement on the Business Reports submenu will usually provide the information you need. This report (Figure 9.3) shows the totals for each income and expense category.

```
                         PROFIT & LOSS STATEMENT
                        10/ 1/89 Through 10/31/89
All Accounts                                                          Page 1
11/ 8/89
                                                  10/ 1/89-
                   Category Description           10/31/89
                  ---------------------- --------------------
                  INCOME/EXPENSE
                    INCOME
                      Receipts                            8,147.52
                                                        ----------
                    TOTAL INCOME                          8,147.52

                    EXPENSES
                      Auto                                  329.32
                      Office                                336.25
                      Payroll                             2,875.21
                      Photo                                 329.32
                      Rent                                1,500.00
                      Repairs                             1,028.55
                      Utilities:
                        Electric               131.22
                        Telephone              436.22
                                           ----------
                      Total Utilities                       567.44
                      Expenses - Other                      200.00
                                                        ----------
                    TOTAL EXPENSES                        7,166.09

                                                        ----------
                  TOTAL INCOME/EXPENSE                      981.43
                                                        ==========
```

Figure 9.3. A P&L Statement.

To create a P&L Statement, select 1. P&L Statement from the Business Reports submenu. When the Tax Summary Report window appears enter a title and adjust the date range if you want, then press Ctrl-Enter to create the report.

The P&L Statement is a Summary Report with these settings. Rows are subtotaled by category, and columns are not subtotaled. You can adapt this report to your needs by selecting F8-Customize or F9-Filter when the Profit & Loss Statement Window appears.

Suppose, for example, you have both personal and business accounts in the same account group and want a quarterly P&L statement for only the business accounts. To create this report, press F8 to choose Customize. On the Create

Summary Report screen, change the Column headings setting to 6 (quarter) and the Use Current/All/Selected accounts setting to S(elected). When you complete the Create Report screen, the Select Accounts screen appears. Highlight each personal account, then press the space bar to exclude it. The result is a quarterly P&L Statement for transactions originating in your business accounts.

Perhaps you want to create a business tax report that lists individual transactions. This report will be similar to the Personal Tax Summary, except that you probably will not want to filter the report to include only tax-related categories. (For most businesses there is no point in designated categories, because all categories are tax-related.) You may also want to exclude transfers.

To create this report, select 4. Tax Summary from the Personal Reports submenu, then press F8 to select Customize; otherwise select 3. Transaction from the main Reports Menu. Either way, the Create Transaction Report screen appears. Subtotal by 9 (category) and select A(ll) accounts. Now press F8 to select Options. Set Report organization to 1 (income and expense), set Transfers to 2 (exclude all) and Show totals only to N(o).

For many businesses, an annual transaction report would be very unwieldy because of the number of transactions—and you might want monthly detail, anyway. You can create a monthly transaction report by entering the first and last days of the month on the Create Transaction Report screen, in the blanks labeled Restrict transactions from... through...

Quicken reports are extremely flexible—so much so that it is impossible to explore all of the possibilities here. Again, feel free to experiment.

ORGANIZING REPORTS BY TAX FORM

As suggested in the Quicken manual, you can refine your tax reporting by assigning transactions to classes corresponding to various IRS forms, and even subclasses corresponding to line numbers on each form. As the manual suggests, you could assign your income to, say, Salary/1040 or Salary/1040-7—the latter designating line 7 of Form 1040, for listing wages, salaries, tips, etc. This allows you to create summary reports with subtotals for each line of your tax forms—in the correct order, if you include line numbers in your classes.

For that matter, you can use the lines of the tax forms as your primary method of classifying transactions by category and subcategory. If you file Schedule C, for example, you could assign income to C:1a, indicating line 1a of Schedule C, advertising to C:6, and so forth. If you do this, you'll probably want to keep a list of your categories and subcategories handy when you record transactions with Quicken.

You can combine these two ideas by including tax form information in your basic category names, such as 1040-7 Salary, C-1a Income, C-6 Advertising, and so forth. Quicken reports will arrange your categories in the order they appear on the tax forms.

Before you go too far down this path, however, you should ask yourself whether it is less trouble to keep records this way *for the entire year* than it is to add up the results once a quarter or once a year—or to have your accountant do it. Maybe not.

Any well thought out system of classifying transactions in Quicken will provide exactly the information you need at tax time, and you will be spared the task of sorting through a shoe box full of rumpled receipts. The most critical decision comes when you begin keeping records with Quicken. Once you have set up a system of classifying transactions that meets your tax reporting requirements, Quicken's flexible reporting capability will allow you to produce reports in exactly the form you want.

BUDGETING

Formal business budgeting is more rigorous than household budgeting or budgeting for a small service business like those operated by many Quicken users. In a typical business the basic goal is unambiguous. There may be debate over what time period is most important, but in the long run the objective is to make money. In household budgeting—unless you are in financial trouble—financial objectives have to be weighed against lifestyle choices. Of course you want to increase net worth, but you may or may not be willing to give up dining out, to skip a vacation, or to drive the car an extra year to do it.

In business, managers prepare budgets. They may be subject to review and coordination with budgets for other parts of the company, but once the budgets are established, the managers are responsible for meeting them; their jobs may depend on it. Managers may not be allowed to shift money from one budget category to another. If an Expense category comes in under budget, the company will want to take the extra money to the bottom line, rather than use it to offset another expense. If a manager comes in over budget in a category, he or she may be faced with a decision to lay off employees or to play the old sausage game, as they call it in business school, by putting filler in the ground meat.

In addition, dozens—maybe hundreds—of budget ratios are published in various places for almost any conceivable kind of business. A manager can compare his budget with his competitors': what proportion goes to payroll, to overhead, to cost of goods; how are costs allocated among departments or divisions? If an individual company's ratios are out of line with the industry norm, that may be a sign of trouble—or a sign that the company is doing something right.

Personal accounting, on the other hand, is—and ought to be—less demanding. You don't have to account specifically for every dollar; your Miscellaneous Expense budget may be substantial. You *are* the boss, so you can shift money from one budget category to another. No one outside the family asks questions if you decide to buy a car instead of taking an expensive vacation, or vice versa.

In fact, some financial advisers explicitly recommend that you avoid wasting time on an elaborate household budget—that above all you keep your budgeting simple. There are two sound reasons for this. First, many would-be home accountants have abandoned their efforts because they set up systems that were more trouble than they were worth. Second, you may not have as much control over your personal budget as you think. If the price of natural gas goes up, for example, are you willing to turn down the thermostat five degrees, just because the increase busts your budget? And many first-time budgeters mistakenly believe that food is a flexible item, when in fact, reducing the family food budget significantly may require a lifestyle change comparable to one that would make an overweight person permanently slim. Everybody knows a dieter who has lost 150 pounds—the same 15 pounds 10 times over. An effort to cut your food budget is likely to have the same insignificant effect on your balance sheet. W.C. Fields once observed, "The cost of living has gone up a dollar a quart." One suspects he was going to pay the dollar, whether it was in his budget or not.

Still, all households should have at least a general idea where their money is going, and relatively small adjustments in unimportant areas can free funds for expenditures on higher priorities. As you begin using Quicken, over time you will get a good feel for your financial ebbs and flows, and your reports will warn you if you are beginning to slide into trouble.

Financial advisers do offer some personal budget ratios that are somewhat comparable those used in business:

- If you spend more than 30 percent of net income in cash or with checks that are uncategorized or assigned to a Miscellaneous Expense category, you may need to refine your records to budget adequately.

- *Save* at least 5 percent of net income; 10 percent is better. More conservative advisers recommend a minimum of 10 percent of gross income, with 15 percent of gross or 20 percent of net as an objective.

- Loan payments, other than mortgages, should not be more than 20 percent of net income—some say 15 percent. Think in terms of 10 percent if you are over 65. Mortgage payments should not be more than 30 percent of net. Total debt payments should not exceed 30 to 35 percent of *gross* income.

These rules of thumb can help you to avoid the predicament of one 39-year-old engineer who recently found his way into the financial press. The grim statistics: income $35,000, net assets $20,000, debts $82,000 (including $32,000 on 16 different credit cards), net worth -$62,000.

But you probably have a pretty good idea what your financial objectives are. Let's get down to the basics.

How Quicken Budgets Work

Quicken takes a very common sense approach to budgeting. Budget reports simply compare what you budgeted for each category with what you actually spent, then calculate the difference. That, of course, is just the way any personal or business budget works. There are, however, a few characteristics of Quicken budgets that you should consider as you set out.

You can set up budgets only for categories. You can report actual income and expenses in as much detail as you want, using subcategories, classes, and subclasses, but you cannot budget that way. For example, if you set up a Utilities category, with subcategories for Gas, Electricity, and Telephone, you can set up a Utilities budget, but you cannot establish budgets for each individual utility. If you want to set up a budget for, say Gas, you will have to set up a category for that expense.

For a business, this means that the accounts in your chart of accounts should probably be set up as categories, although you may want to use subcategories and classes to refine your reporting of actual activity. For a household, it means that you can establish a budget with broad strokes, without getting mired down in details you might want to record for nonbudgetary purposes.

You can set up fixed or variable monthly budgets for each category. If you set up a budget report for another period, such as a quarter, Quicken automatically adds up the monthly budget totals for the period and compares the result with actual activity. However, you cannot directly enter budget amounts for any period other than a month.

You can budget either by income and expenses or by cash flow. Again, Quicken's Personal Reports are generally oriented toward cash flow and Business Reports tend toward income and expenses. But there are many cases in which you might want to go the opposite way. A business, for example, will need to budget income and expenses, but it might also want to budget its cash. A business can be making a lot of money on paper and still not be able to pay the bills. Similarly, an individual who makes a lot of investments might want to operate the household on the basis of income and expenses, so that money flowing in and out of investments is not involved. If you are using only Bank accounts, Cash accounts, and Credit Card accounts, cash budgeting and income/expense budgeting come to about the same thing.

You can establish budgets for savings, investments, and debt reduction by setting up budgets for transfers. You can do this in either a cash budget or an income and expense budget. Together, these features allow you to set up a budget that fits the circumstances of your particular business or household.

Starting a Budget

For a business, budget categories tend to be predetermined by the budgeting process that goes on before you even begin using Quicken. Even if you are just starting a business, your budget categories will be largely determined by the chart of accounts you set up in consultation with your accountant or your tax reporting requirements.

Larger businesses usually identify income and spending accounts (categories in Quicken) by numbers. You can follow the same practice in Quicken, setting up such categories as 100 Gross Sales, 200 Rent, 210 Electricity, 220 Telephone, and so on—or whatever accounts your business normally uses. If you prefer, you can use simply the number as the category name, entering the purpose of the category as the description.

Middle managers, incidentally, can easily use Quicken to manage their departmental budgets, even though most don't write checks or manage checking accounts. One strategy is to set up a dummy Bank account and record sales and/or expenditures as they occur. The account balance will be meaningless, but your Quicken reports will keep you abreast of the status of your budget.

Another possibility for budgeting expenses is to set up a Bank account and "deposit" your total budget amount every month. Then you can record expenses as they occur. The declining balance in the dummy account will give you an idea of how much of your total budget is left. In this case, you can set up a separate Bank account for recording sales if your department is also expected to meet sales goals.

Smaller businesses—such as those in which an individual provides professional services—and individuals both have more latitude. Your Quicken categories do need to match your tax reporting needs; beyond that, the choices are yours.

You need to budget income, of course, so you will know how much you have to work with on the expense side. It may be helpful to establish budget priorities. In some areas, you have almost no flexibility—rent and mortgage payments, for example. Other categories, such as utilities, car expenses, and food may be slightly more flexible, but you're still pretty much locked into paying the bills. You need to know how much money these items require, but you may not need to budget such items in great detail, since they are hard to control anyway.

You may want to budget discretionary expenditures more closely, because this is where you can manage expenses most effectively. For example, you might set up separate categories for Entertainment, Hobbies, and Dining Out, rather than lumping all of these into a Miscellaneous category. If you entertain at home frequently, you may want to split that out from your basic grocery expenses. More detailed budgeting of discretionary expenses tells you exactly where your money is going, and it allows you to make choices about where you want to cut back.

Quicken always lists categories alphabetically. (Numbers are also listed in order, and they precede the alphabet.) As the Quicken manual suggests, you can group categories by assigning similar names, such as Ofc Rent, Ofc Electricity, Ofc Maintenance, and so forth.

You can also list your budget categories by assigning them numbers, as a business would. For example, income could be assigned to numbers between 100 and 199, inflexible expenses numbers between 200 and 299, and discretionary expenses numbers between 300 and 399. Category numbers should be spaced at intervals of, say, 10 to allow you to insert new categories later. This system has the effect of listing your categories in order of priority, so that you can look at categories near the bottom of the list when you need to cut back.

The Budget Reports

Quicken provides two predefined budget reports, the Personal Monthly Budget (selection 2 on the Personal Reports submenu) and the Budget Report (selection 5 on the main Reports Menu). The Monthly Budget Report is simply a variation of the Custom Budget Report, with certain selections already made.

The Monthly Budget Report

The Monthly Budget Report is the quickest way to set up a personal monthly budget. It allows you to set up a monthly cash flow budget for your Bank accounts, Cash accounts, and Credit Card accounts. It includes transfers to and from Other Asset accounts and Other Liability accounts, but not transfers among the cash accounts or changes in Other Assets or Other Liabilities.

You must set up your income and expense categories before you begin. To create a Personal Monthly Budget report, select 2. Monthly Budget from the Personal Reports submenu. When the Monthly Budget Report window appears, enter a report title and adjust the date range if you want. (Both are optional.) Now press F7 to select Edit Budget Amounts.

The Specify Budget Amounts Window (Figure 9.4) appears. (This step is required for your first budget report. Once the budget is set up, you can skip editing budget amounts by pressing Ctrl-Enter.)

Once you highlight a category, you have two options:

1. To establish a fixed monthly budget (the same amount every month), simply type a figure in the Budget Amount column and press Enter.

2. To establish a variable monthly budget, press Ctrl-e to select Edit Monthly Detail. The Monthly Budget window (Figure 9.5) appears. For each month, type an amount and press Enter. If you come to a point where the budget remains the same for several months, you can fill in the rest of the year by pressing F9

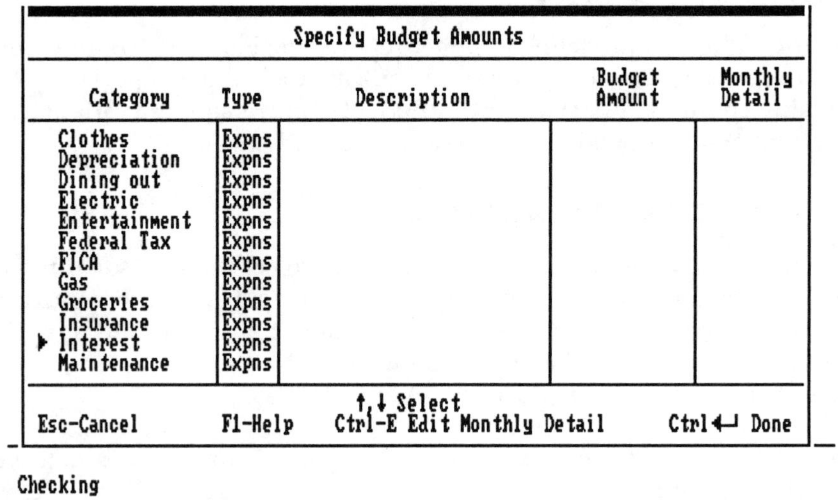

Figure 9.4. Specifying budget amounts.

to select Fill w/Amt. (This can save time even if you have to change the amounts for some later months.) When you have finished, press Ctrl-Enter to return to the Specify Budget Amounts window. Quicken enters the budget amount for the current month in the Budget Amount column. When you have finished your budget, press Ctrl-Enter to close the Specify Budget Amounts screen and return to the Monthly Budget Report window.

When you have set up your budget amounts, press Ctrl-Enter again to create the report. The report appears on the screen, and you can view it or print it as usual. The result should look something like Figure 9.6. A budget report usually will be wider than the screen. You can use the cursor control keys to move around the report, as described in the last chapter.

```
                     Specify Budget Amounts
          Monthly Budget For Category: Maintenance        Monthly
    Category                                              Detail
               Jan:
  Clothes      Feb:
  Depreciatio  Mar:
  Dining out   Apr:
  Gas          May:
  Groceries    Jun:
  Insurance    Jul:
  Interest     Aug:
▶ Maintenance  Sep:
  Medical      Oct:
  Miscellaneo  Nov:
  Mortgage     Dec:
  Maintenance
             Esc-Cancel    F9-Fill w/Amt    ↵ Continue

Checking
```

Figure 9.5. The Monthly Budget window.

The predefined Personal Budget is designed for household budgeting, and many Quicken users will find that it meets their needs without modification. You can of course, customize it to suit your own purposes, as explained in the next section.

Month

10/ 1/8

Selected Accounts
11/ 8/89

Category Description	10/ 1/89 Actual	- Budget	10/31/89 Diff	11/ 1/89 Actual	- Budg
INFLOWS					
Receipts	8,147.52	7,500.00	647.52	7,235.11	7,500
TOTAL INFLOWS	8,147.52	7,500.00	647.52	7,235.11	7,500
OUTFLOWS					
Auto	329.32	350.00	-20.68	0.00	350
Office	336.25	400.00	-63.75	0.00	400
Payroll	2,875.21	3,000.00	-124.79	0.00	3,000
Photo	329.32	350.00	-20.68	0.00	350
Rent	1,500.00	1,500.00	0.00	0.00	1,500
Repairs	1,028.55	500.00	528.55	0.00	500
Utilities	567.44	600.00	-32.56	0.00	600

↓ →

Selected Accounts (Filtered)
Esc-Create report F1-Help F8-Print

Figure 9.6. A Monthly Budget Report as it appears on the screen.

Custom Budgets

The procedures are essentially the same for setting up a Custom Budget Report and for modifying the predefined Personal Monthly Budget Report.

There are two ways to reach the Create Budget Report screen (Figure 9.7), the main screen for creating custom budgets, from the Reports Menu. The quickest is to select 5. Budget from the main Reports Menu. You can also select 2. Monthly Budget from the Personal Report submenu, and then press F8 to select Customize when the Monthly Budget Report window appears. In addition to providing blanks for a report title and date range, the Create Budget Report window allows you to choose the periods for your budget report and to select which accounts will be included (Current/All Selected).

```
                         Create Budget Report

  Report title (optional):

  Restrict to transactions from:  1/ 1/89 through:  6/30/89

  Column headings (across the top): 1
       1. None                       5. Month
       2. Week                       6. Quarter
       3. Two Weeks                  7. Half Year
       4. Half Month                 8. Year

  Use Current/All/Selected accounts (C/A/S): A

 Esc-Cancel   F7-Budget Amts   F8-Options   F9-Filter   ↵ Continue


BUDGET-Checking
```

Figure 9.7. The Create Budget Report screen.

From the Create Report screen, you can select F8-Options to set report organization (income and expense or cash flow). On the Report Options screen, you can also specify whether transfers will be included in the report (Include All/Exclude All/Include only transfers to accounts outside this report). You can also select F-9 Filter to filter report transactions.

The Personal Monthly Budget report, for example, is just a Custom Budget Report with the following settings. On the Create Report screen, it is subtotaled by 5 (month) for S(elected) accounts (Bank, Cash, and Credit Card). On the Report Options screen, the settings are: Report organization, 2 (cash flow); for Transfers, 3 (include only transfers to accounts outside this report). The report is not filtered.

Together, these options allow you to create almost any type of budget report you might need. Once you have designed your budget, press F7 to set monthly amounts for each category. Again, to set up a variable monthly budget, select a category, then press Ctrl-e to enter varying amounts for each month.

Budgeting Savings

Financial advisers are unanimous in recommending that you make room for savings in your personal budget. When you press F7 to select Budget Amts from the Create Budget Report screen, you will notice that your Quicken accounts are listed along with your Income and Expense categories. You can budget changes in your account balances just as you budget income and expenses.

If you propose to add $500 a month to your Money Market account, for example, you can enter 500 in the Budget Amount column of the Specify Budget Amounts screen. Similarly, you can budget a reduction in a Credit Card account by entering a figure in the same column.

Playing 'What If?'

The whole purpose of a budget, of course, is to map your financial strategy. Suppose you run a business with budgeted sales of $25,000 per month. A schematic budget might look like Figure 9.8 on the Specify Budget Amounts screen. A monthly budget report (before you begin recording income and expenses) might look like Figure 9.9.

Specify Budget Amounts

Category	Type	Description	Budget Amount	Monthly Detail
100 Sales	Inc		17,500.00	
200 Salaries	Expns		13,600.00	
210 Rent	Expns		2,500.00	
220 Telephone	Expns		125.00	
230 Electricity	Expns		235.00	
240 Supplies	Expns		500.00	
250 Repairs	Expns		250.00	
255 Travel	Expns		250.00	
▶ 260 FICA	Expns		950.00	
270 Depreciatio	Expns		200.00	
280 Comp Lease	Expns		455.00	
290 Insurance	Expns			

Esc-Cancel   F1-Help   ↑,↓ Select   Ctrl-E Edit Monthly Detail   Ctrl↵ Done

BUDGET-600 Checking

Figure 9.8. Setting up a budget for a small business.

BUDGET REPORT BY MONTH
1/ 1/89 Through 1/31/89

BUDGET-All Accounts   Page 1
6/30/89

Category Description	1/ 1/89 Actual	- Budget	1/31/89 Diff
INCOME/EXPENSE			
INCOME			
100 Sales	0.00	17,500.00	-17,500.00
TOTAL INCOME	0.00	17,500.00	-17,500.00
EXPENSES			
200 Salaries	0.00	13,600.00	-13,600.00
210 Rent	0.00	2,500.00	-2,500.00
220 Telephone	0.00	125.00	-125.00
230 Electricity	0.00	235.00	-235.00
240 Supplies	0.00	500.00	-500.00
250 Repairs	0.00	250.00	-250.00
255 Travel	0.00	250.00	-250.00
260 FICA	0.00	950.00	-950.00
270 Depreciatio	0.00	200.00	-200.00
280 Comp Lease	0.00	455.00	-455.00
TOTAL EXPENSES	0.00	19,065.00	-19,065.00
TOTAL INCOME/EXPENSE	0.00	-1,565.00	1,565.00

Figure 9.9. A monthly budget report (before income and expenses are recorded).

According to the budget, you should be clearing nearly $6,000 a month. But sales have been hovering between $17,000 and $18,000; you're not quite breaking even, despite a three-month sales campaign. New accounts are coming in, but old ones are turning over just as quickly. You will have to raise the bridge or lower the river.

First, you go to the Specify Budget Amounts screen and enter a more realistic sales figure, say $17,500. When you plug in this figure and create a new budget report, you find that you're losing more than $1,500 a month, when your business plan says you should be making $6,000, and even a marginal return on investment requires a profit of $3,000.

Maybe you can sell your way out of the ditch. You go to the budget, select 100 Sales, then press Ctrl-e to edit monthly detail. You budget $18,000 for February, $18,500 for March, $19,000 for April, and so on. If nothing else changed, you would reach the $3,000 profit figure in about nine months. But increasing sales increases expenses. The business makes more long distance phone calls. You add a new computer to the Comp Lease category. The cost of Supplies increases. You add these amounts on the budget.

Now you create a new budget report. The totals for September still show a profit of only $1,500. Not good enough. You whack away at relatively discretionary expenses, such as Supplies and Travel. You're still not satisfied. The only solution is to reduce staff, cutting the budget for 200 Salaries, 260 FICA, and perhaps several other lines.

Now the budget works, and Quicken has made most of the calculations for you.

Conclusion

Budget and tax decisions can be tough, but Quicken makes the calculations behind those judgments much easier. Many people will need to take these strategies a step further, to cover investments, rental real estate, accounts receivable and payable, and much more, as explained in the following chapters.

10

Investments and Rental Properties

Classes are one of Quicken's most flexible and most useful features. While Quicken categories correspond to the income and expense accounts for a business or household budget, classes are generally intended to designate who, where, or the accounting period related to a transaction. They are, as the Quicken manual says, a "'second dimension' that is unrelated" to the category. This means that you can put classes to work to sort transactions in ways totally separate from your categories. You can also use them to sort information within categories to create very detailed reports of your financial activity.

This chapter explores two such uses—managing investments and rental properties. As you will see, you can use classes for a wide range of purposes. Your imagination is about the only limitation.

Managing Investments

Quicken has no special provision for recording investments in stocks, bonds, retirement plans, annuities, and so on. However, the people at Intuit, the company that publishes Quicken, have come up with an ingenious system for using classes to manage your investments.

The first step in setting up an investment management system is to create an Other Asset account for recording your holdings. You can set up separate accounts for liquid investments and nonliquid investments. Liquid investments are those you can cash in on short notice, such as stocks, bonds, T bills, mutual funds, publicly traded real estate investment trusts (REITs), and precious metals. Nonliquid investments lock your money up for extended periods. In most cases you *could* get your money out in an emergency, but you might have to pay a substantial penalty in taxes and/or fees. Examples include certificates of deposit; various retirement plans, such as IRAs, Keoghs, 401Ks, 403Ks, and annuities; limited partnerships; oil and gas deals; cash value life insurance policies (whole life policies and their variations; term policies have no cash value and are not investments); and rental real estate.

When you make an investment, you will generally want to record it as a transfer to an Other Asset account; an investment is not an expense but, one hopes, a transfer of funds to a more productive investment. You will also need tax-related Income categories for recording dividends and/or interest.

You might start out with Other Asset accounts called Liquid and Nonliquid, plus Income categories for investment interest and dividends. You can set up that part of the system as it suits you. The critical point is to use classes to record investment transactions.

The next sections offer ways of tracking stocks, bonds, and other investments.

Tracking Securities

When you invest in stocks, there are a number of things you need to keep track of:

- Original purchase price, including commissions. The purchase of each lot must be recorded separately, even if you make several purchases of a particular stock, because your capital gains (or losses) will depend on which particular shares you sell.

- Sales price, with commissions deducted, when you sell.

- Capital gains (or losses). Even though the tax reform of 1986 eliminates the preferred tax rate for long-term gains, you still have to report long-term and short-term gains (or losses) on Schedule D, Capital Gains and Losses. Any asset you acquired before January 1, 1988, has acquired long-term status, since the holding period for those investments is only six months. For investments made after that date, the holding period is one year. Your broker will report the gross proceeds of sales to the IRS on form 1099-B.

- Fluctuations in the market price of your investments. You might want to assign changes in securities prices to a nontax-related Income category called Unrealized Gains, but the main purpose here is to keep your balance sheet accurate. If you revalue your stocks, you should update the prices for all of them at the same time—on a monthly basis, for example. Otherwise, your Balance Sheet, net worth, or Account Balances reports for your investments will be meaningless. What would the report mean, for example, if you had revalued half of your stocks before the crash of 1987 and half after? You might have come out all right, or you might have lost your shirt; the report wouldn't tell you.

- Dividends and interest are usually treated as ordinary income, to be reported on Schedule B, Interest and Dividend Income. You can record them in Quicken as you would any other income, but you may need to adapt your entries on the category line to meet the reporting requirements.

- Stock splits and stock dividends. These transactions usually affect neither the basis in the investment nor count as income for tax purposes.

Buying, Revaluing, and Selling Stocks and Bonds

If you invest in stocks and bonds, you need to keep your Quicken records in a manner consistent with IRS Schedule D, Capital Gains and Losses. This form requires the following information (the form's column designations and descriptions are transcribed here):

(a) Description (Example, 100 shares 7% preferred of "Z" Co.)

(b) Date acquired (Mo., day, yr.)

(c) Date sold (Mo., day, yr.)

(d) Sales price

(e) Cost or other basis

(f) LOSS if (e) is more than (d), subtract (d) from (e)

(g) GAIN if (d) is more than (e), subtract (e) from (d)

It's actually quite simple. For tax purposes, commissions and option premiums are added to the purchase price, or basis. They're not tax deductible when you make the purchase, but when you claim your gain (or loss), they're part of the original cost of the investment. When you sell, the sale commission may be either added to the basis or deducted from the selling price, depending on how your broker reports the transaction to the IRS on Form 1099-B. In effect, you deduct both commissions when you sell the stock. The example given here is for a stock, but you would keep track of bonds the same way, except that you would assign transactions to a class called Bonds.

NOTE: If you are just beginning to use Quicken and want to record a security purchased before the current year, record the original cost as a transaction dated when you purchased the security or on the last day of the previous year. (In the latter case, note the purchase date on the memo line.) This will eliminate the purchase from your transaction records for the current year. However, when you want complete reports of your stock holdings, you will have to make sure that the report date range extends back to your earliest purchase (except for Balance Sheets or Account Balances Reports).

Suppose that on January 15 you buy 100 shares of XYZ stock at 25, with a $62 commission. The total cost is $2,562. At the end of February, the stock has risen to $30, and by June it has risen another $2. Finally, you sell on September 15 at $40 with an $82 commission, leaving you with $3,918.

To set up an account for your investment portfolio, first set up an Other Asset account called Liquid for recording liquid investments and classes called Stocks, XYZ, Buy, Revalue, and Sell. You will also need an Income category called Unrl (unrealized) for recording changes in price before you sell. (You have to keep the name of this category short, because of limited space on the category line.) This should be a non tax-related category. In fact, you might want to exclude it from all of your Quicken reports, since the gains will be only on paper. This income will not show up in a Cash Flow Report, anyway, because it will be recorded in the Other Asset account.

Now you are ready to begin recording your actual transactions. Suppose you buy the XYZ stock through your brokerage account at your investment firm, and the purchase price is automatically deducted. You can record the purchase in the Register of either your Brokerage Bank account or your Liquid Other Asset account:

1. Enter the name of the asset, such as XYZ Common Stock in the payee blank.

2. Enter the full cost of the trade, including commissions, in the amount column (as a Payment in the Bank account or as an Increase in the Other Asset account).

3. For a memo, enter a description of the transaction, such as 100 shares @ $25.

4. If you are recording the trade in the Bank account, make this entry on the category line (Quicken will supply the brackets automatically):

   ```
   [Liquid]/Stocks:XYZ:Buy
   ```

   In the Other Asset account, the entry would be:

   ```
   [Brokerage]/Stocks:XYZ:Buy
   ```

NOTE: If you later buy another lot of XYZ stock, you will need to record the purchase and revaluations separately from your original purchase, so you can calculate capital gains (or losses) properly when you sell. You could, for example, use XYZ-1 and XYZ-2 as subclasses. When you sell, the report from your broker will indicate precisely which shares were sold.

At the end of February, you can record the stock's rise from $25 to $30 (100 shares x $5) by recording a $500 Increase in the Register of your Liquid Other Asset account. For the payee, enter the stock name again, and add a descriptive note on the memo line, such as Revalue 100 to $30. On the category line, make this entry:

```
Unrl/Stocks:XYZ:Revalue
```

In June, when the stock price has increases another $2, you can repeat the last procedure to add another Increase of $200 to bring your total investment to $3,200.

NOTE: Again, it is important to update the value of all of your investments at the same time, so you won't end up with a hodgepodge of values at different times. A transaction group, as explained in Chapter 5, will greatly simplify the task.

Finally, when it comes time to sell the stock on September 15, you need to revalue the stock to the sales price, so that the sale will return the balance for XYZ stock to zero. The correct sales price depends on how your broker fills out IRS Form 1099–B. (Ask if you aren't sure.) There are two possibilities:

- If the broker reports the *net* amount of the sale, after commissions, the final commission is deducted from the sales price in Column d of IRS Schedule D, Capital Gains, and Losses. In this case, update the value of the stock to reflect that figure—the amount you actually receive after commissions. In the example, you would enter an increase of $656 to bring the value of the stock up to $3,918—$4,000 less the $82 commission.

- If your broker reports the *gross* amount of the sale, before commissions, the IRS requires you to report that figure as the sales price. The commission is added to the cost or basis, as if it were part of the original cost of the stock. In this case, you would revalue the stock by $738 to bring the total to $4,000, recorded as a split transaction, as shown in Figure 10.1. The commission is assigned to Unrl/Stocks:XYZ:Buy to increase the basis of the stock, as required on Schedule D.

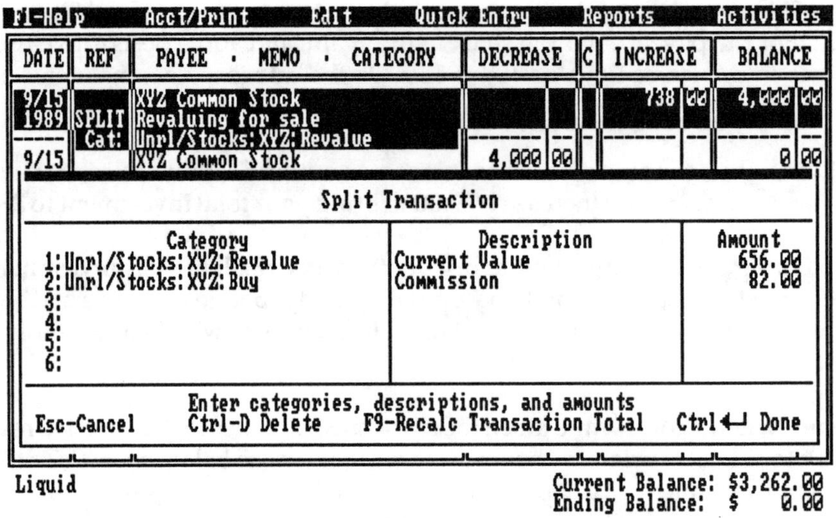

Figure 10.1. Updating the price of a stock before a sale.

Now that you have updated the value of the stock to the sale price, you can record the actual sale. The method also depends on how your broker reports the transaction on Form 1099-B. Again, there are two possibilities:

- If the broker reports the *net* sales price, after commissions, record the net price in the Decrease column of the Liquid Other Asset Register. The category line should contain this entry: [Brokerage]/Stocks:XYZ:Sell. This transfers the proceeds of the sale ($3,918) to the Brokerage account and reduces the value of the stock to zero in the Liquid Other Asset account.

- If the broker reports the *gross* sales price, record the sale as a split transaction, as shown in Figure 10.2. In this case, the gross amount of the sale ($4,000) is entered in the Decrease column of the Register. The net price, after commissions, is transferred to your Brokerage account. The commission ($82) is assigned to Unrl/Stocks:XYZ:Sell. Thus, the sales commission has increased the basis and is included in the sales price, whereas it is excluded from both in the previous example. The result is a wash—the total capital gain remains unchanged.

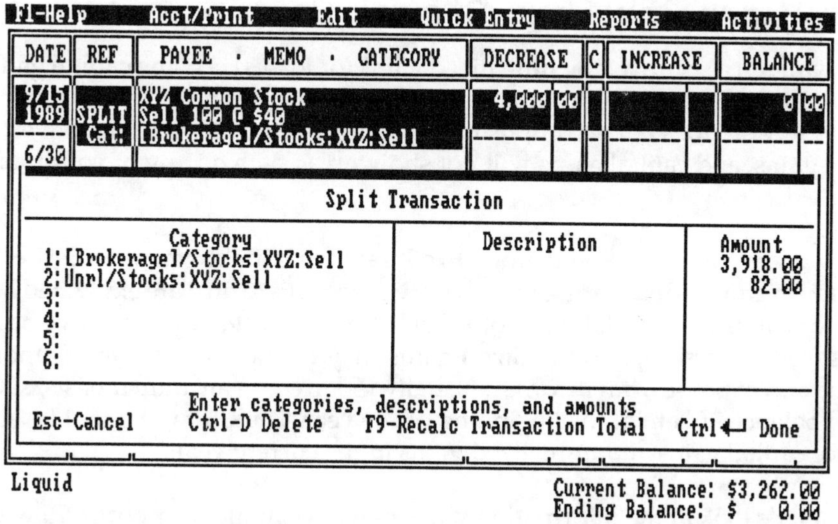

Figure 10.2 Recording the gross amount of a stock sale.

After recording the sale, enter asterisks (*) in the C(leared) column of all XYZ transactions. This allows you to keep a permanent record of the transactions, but you can exclude stocks you no longer own from Quicken reports by filtering them to include only transactions whose cleared status is blank.

All of this works beautifully until the end of the year arrives. The problem—not insurmountable—is that most people keep records on an annual basis, whether by calendar year or fiscal year. Quicken reports tend to cover transactions from the beginning of the calendar year to the current date, unless you specify otherwise.

Your portfolio, however, probably includes some securities that you bought before the beginning of the current year and some you will keep past the beginning of the next. This means that you must bring forward uncleared transactions, when you use the Copy/Shrink option on the account Group Activities submenu to start a new year, as explained in Chapter 13. In addition, when you create Quicken reports on your portfolio, you must make certain that the date range extends back to the earliest transactions in your portfolio (except balance sheets or Account Balances Reports).

As suggested earlier, you also have to be careful about handling unrealized gains and capital gains. This is the topic of the next section.

Unrealized Gains and Capital Gains

When you sell a security, any unrealized gains (or losses) become capital gains (or losses), and you have to report the result on Schedule D. The method described in the last section does not accomplish that—unrealized gains are not converted to capital gains, and capital gains will not show up as such on any of your Quicken reports.

However, you can convert unrealized gains to capital gains, with the latter reported in an appropriate Income category. Two ways to do it are explained below. The problem is that capital gains often offset unrealized gains that have built up over several years. These unrealized gains may be included on your reports of income and expenses, but income is usually reported on an annual basis, starting with a balance of zero at the beginning of the year. Thus, you may not be able to balance capital gains and unrealized gains in the current year.

First let's look at the information you can report about your portfolio without converting unrealized gains to capital gains.

Reporting on Your Portfolio

There are a number of reports you can use to analyze activity in your Liquid Other Asset account. The Personal Itemized Categories Report, the Custom Transaction Report, and the Custom Summary Report are possibilities. These can provide summaries of all of the transactions in your portfolio for a given period, subtotaled either by security or by time period. The Account Balances or Balance Sheet Report is probably the most useful, because it allows you to summarize your current situation by both class and category.

The system described above uses a system of classes and subclasses to categorize securities transactions. Securities transactions are classified by type (stocks, bonds), company (XYZ in the example), and type of transaction (buy, sell, revalue).

Categories, usually the main method of classifying transactions in Quicken, play a secondary role. The reason for this is that many of the transactions are transfers, and you cannot subcatgorize a transaction assigned to another account on the category line.

What you need is an Account Balances Report subtotaled by class. To create this report, first, choose 6. Account Balances from the Reports Menu. To include classes, choose S(elected) on the Use Accounts line on the Create Account Balance Report screen. When the Select Accounts window appears, press F9 twice to exclude all accounts, then select your Liquid Other Assets account and press the space bar twice to select Detail. On the Create Report screen, you can also choose report intervals if you want a monthly or quarterly report, rather than a current date "snapshot" of your portfolio.

A simplified example of the result, showing only the XYZ transactions, is shown in Figure 10.3. In a more complete report, each security would be listed in similar fashion. This shows that the basis or cost of the stock was $2,644 (the subtotal for Buy), that it was sold for $4,000 (the subtotal for Sell), and that the capital gain was $1,356 (the subtotal for Revalue). (This is the gross sales price example; if your broker reported the net sale price on Form 1099-B, both the basis and the sales price would be $82 lower, but the gain would still be $1,356.)

```
                          ACCOUNT BALANCES REPORT

                              As of 12/31/89
INVEST-Selected Accounts
7/30/89
                                                    12/31/89
        Account                                      Balance
 --------------------------------   ------------------------------------------
 Total Cash and Bank Accounts                                           11,956.

 Other Assets
   Liquid
     Stocks:
       XYZ:
         Buy                              2,644.00
         Revalue                          1,356.00
         Sell                            -4,000.00
                                        ----------
       TOTAL XYZ                                          0.00
                                                    ----------
     Total Stocks                                                  0.00
                                                                          ↑↓ →
INVEST-Selected Accounts                                              (Filtered)
Esc-Create report                 F1-Help                               F8-Print
```

Figure 10.3. A simple Account Balances Report of stock transactions.

Meanwhile, reports that include your unrealized gain Income category can help you keep tabs on how your investments are doing. Just bear in mind that actual capital gains are also included. Thus, this system provides the information you need for capital gains reporting, even though it does not report capital gains as such. The next section explains how to record capital gains so they will appear in your income reports.

Reporting Capital Gains

You can record capital gains (or losses) when you sell securities by adding two offsetting transactions to the Split Transaction window, but you will still need the cost and sales price figures, which will not show up on an income report. If you use this method, you should select categories to filter your unrealized gains Income category out of reports of Income and Expenses.

In the XYZ example, the gain was $1,356. This can be entered as shown on lines 3 and 4 of the Split Transaction window in Figure 10.4, assigned to Unrl:XYZ and Cap Gains:Short:XYZ. Notice that these transactions are assigned to categories and subcategories, instead of classes and subclasses. There are two reasons. First, we want these transactions to show up on routine reports of income and expenses (a cash flow report will not help in identifying capital gains). Second, we do not need—in fact do not want—these transactions to appear in reports on the Liquid Other Asset account.

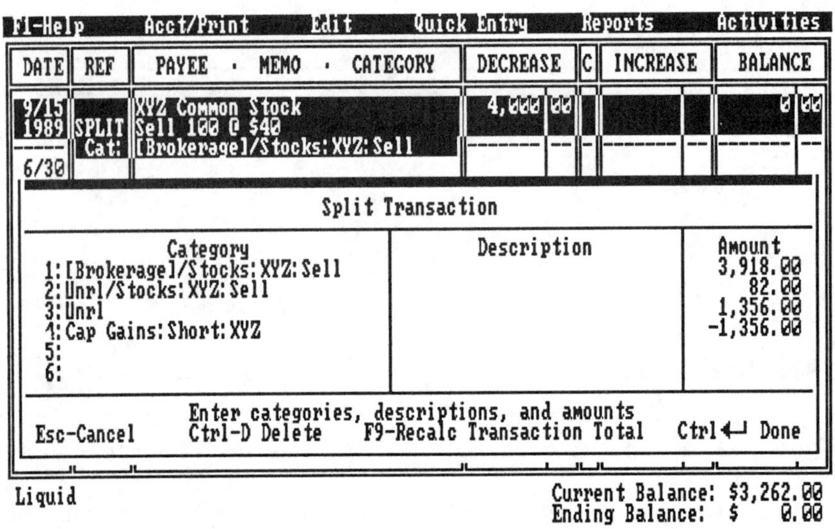

Figure 10.4. Recording a transaction to report capital gains.

When you record this transaction, the balance of the unrealized gains Income category *decreases* by $1,365. The amount is entered as a positive number because the main transaction is in the Decrease column of the Other Asset account. The Cap Gains Income balance *increases*, by the same amount, entered as a negative number.

If this is confusing, it might be easier to record the entire transaction in the Brokerage Bank account. There, the first transaction split would assigned to [Liquid]/Stocks:XYZ:Sell, and the signs on the last two splits would be reversed, because the Brokerage account deposit *increases* the balance of that asset.

This method sacrifices the unrealized gains Income category, because the decrease is not recorded the same way as the increases. In any case, any report of unrealized gains would now be meaningless unless all of your capital gains were for investments bought and sold in the current tax year, because the capital gain occurs in the current year, but unrealized gains may have built up for several. The simplest solution is to filter unrealized gains out of your income and expense reports.

Once you satisfy that simple filtering requirement, a predefined Business P&L Statement will show you your capital gains. To create the report, select 1. P&L Statement from the Business Reports submenu, then follow these steps:

1. Press F9 to filter the report and change Select Categories to Y(es) on the Filter Transactions screen, then press Ctrl-Enter. The Select Categories screen appears.

2. Highlight Unrl, the unrealized gains category, and press the space bar to exclude it, then press Ctrl-Enter to return to the Profit & Loss Statement window.

3. Enter a report title if you want, and adjust the report period if necessary, then press Ctrl-Enter again to create the report.

The Income portion of the report is shown in Figure 10.5. This example is schematic, but it shows a short-term capital gain for XYZ and total capital gains. If you had recorded long-term gains, those would be included. This report calculates the amount you must report on Schedule D. You will also need a report that includes the cost or basis of the investment and the sale price.

```
                    PROFIT & LOSS STATEMENT

                    1/ 1/89 Through 12/31/89
     INVEST-All Accounts
     6/30/89
                                          1/ 1/89-
      Category Description               12/31/89
     ___________________________  ___________________________
     INCOME/EXPENSE
       INCOME
         Cap Gains:
           Short:
             XYZ                  1,356.00
                                  ________
             Total Short                    1,356.00
                                            ________
           Total Cap Gains                            1,356.00
                                                      ________
         TOTAL INCOME                                 1,356.00

                                                      ________

INVEST-All Accounts                                           (Filtered)
Esc-Create report              F1-Help                          F8-Print
```

Figure 10.5. Reporting capital gains income on a Profit & Loss Statement.

Reporting Dividends and Interest

Interest and dividends are generally treated as ordinary income and reported on Schedule B, Interest and Dividend Income. No special tactics are required to record this income with Quicken, other than to identify the payer. If you receive dividends or interest through a brokerage, the form asks you to identify the firm as the payer, but you might still want to identify the specific investment for your own records. The various versions of IRS Form 1099 you receive are the key to reporting dividends and interest correctly on your tax returns.

Interest and dividends can be recorded as simple deposits in the account where you deposit the check, whether it's an account at your bank or at your brokerage. (For clean-cut record keeping, you should deposit the check, rather than cashing it or making a deposit with cash back. That way, your bank records will match your Quicken records, and there will be no confusion about how much you actually received.)

You must also report nontaxable interest on tax exempt state and local bonds on Form 1040, even though it does not affect your taxable income. You don't have to report interest on IRAs, even on the Tax-Exempt interest line of 1040, until you begin withdrawing funds.

> **NOTE:** Distributions from partnerships and S corporations are reported on Schedule E, Supplemental Income Schedule. Capital gains distributions from mutual funds are generally reported as long-term gains on Schedule D, Capital Gains and Losses. Form 1099 will indicate how to report the income; if you have doubts, consult a financial adviser.

Categories and subcategories are the easiest way to classify dividends and interest payments. In the case of interest payments, you will need separate Income and Expense categories, such as Int Inc and Int Exp to distinguish between interest income and interest you pay.

Suppose, for example, that you receive $250 in dividends on your stock in XYZ Co. through a brokerage called Security Investments, $150 in interest on Acme corporate bonds through Jones Securities, and a direct check for $200 on Elm City municipal bonds. You could record these transactions as ordinary deposits in the appropriate bank or brokerage account, with the entries shown in Table 10.1. If you received all of these payments as deposits in your brokerage account at Security Investments, you could record the deposit as a split transaction in your Brokerage Bank account as shown in Figure 10.6.

Table 10.1. Entries for recording dividends and interest with Quicken.

Deposit:	$250.00
Payee:	Security Investments
Memo:	2nd quarter dividends, XYZ
Category:	Div:Security:XYZ
Deposit:	$150.00
Payee:	Jones Securities
Memo:	1st half interest, Acme
Category:	Int Inc:Jones:Acme
Deposit:	$200.00
Payee:	Elm City Municipals
Memo:	1st half interest, Elm City Munis
Category:	Int Nontax:Elm City

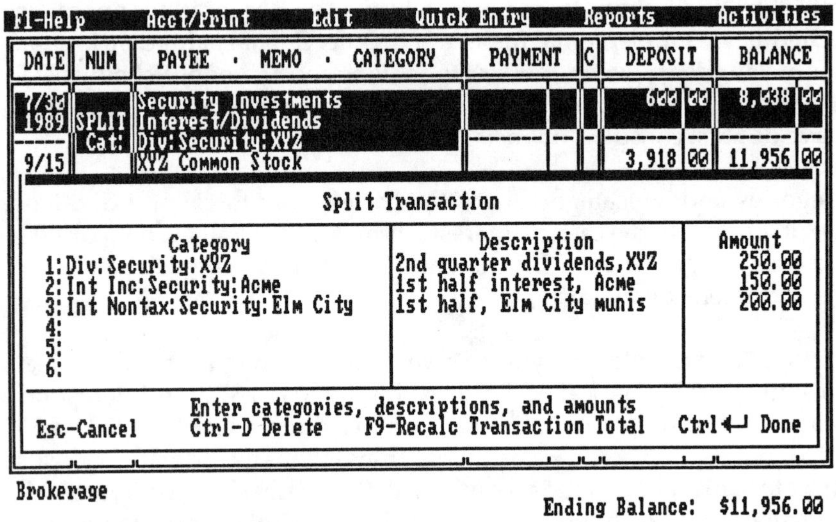

Figure 10.6. Recording dividends and interest paid through a brokerage house as a split transaction.

Your dividends and interest will show up like any other income on your reports on income and expenses or cash flow. At tax time, you will need to check your records against the various versions IRS Form 1099 or equivalent statements from your brokerage.

Stock Splits and Stock Dividends

Sometimes a company splits its stock to make its shares more marketable. Stockholders might receive three shares for every two, or two for one. Companies sometimes also issue stock dividends, giving stockholders, say, one new share for every 10 they own.

Stock splits and the most common form of stock dividends usually have no tax implications at all; they are not income nor do they affect your cost or basis in your original investment. If you own 100 shares out of 1 million in a company, that's the same proportion as 200 shares out of 2 million. (Certain less common types of stock dividends are taxable as income, but the rules are too complicated to go into here. Check with your broker or financial adviser.)

Nevertheless, you do need to record the split to be able to calculate the current value of your stock and to figure your capital gain when you sell. The simplest solution is to edit the memo in your original purchase to reflect the split. In the XYZ example, the memo might now read:

```
100 @ $25; split 2-1 8/20/89.
```

If you need more room, you can split the transaction and record additional information in the Split Transaction window. You should also indicate the current number of shares whenever you update the value of your stock. If you bought more than one lot of a particular stock, splits and stock dividends should be recorded separately for each lot.

A Final Note on Securities Transactions

There are, of course, many other types of investment transactions, such as short sales, options, and commodities transactions. The tax rules for reporting many of these are quite complex. However, in general you should be able to use the same basic strategies just described to record any of these transactions with Quicken. In most cases, statements from your broker will provide the information you need to record these transactions.

In a short sale, for example, you borrow stocks from your broker, and the transaction is not completed for tax purposes until you buy stocks to replace the broker's. This can be recorded exactly like the purchase and sale of a stock, with revaluations in between. The only difference is that the sale leaves a negative balance for the stock in your Liquid Other Assets account, and the purchase completes the transaction and returns the balance to 0.

Options give the purchase the right to buy or sell stock at a certain price within a certain period. The underlying securities are seldom actually traded. Instead, the investor usually buys or sells an offsetting option to satisfy his or her obligation. This can be recorded like any other securities exchange, yielding a capital gain or loss. If you allow an option to expire unexercised, treat it as a sale for 0 on the expiration date.

Managing Rental Properties

The "tax simplification" of 1986 did not make it any easier for landlords to complete their tax returns accurately—particularly in the areas of depreciation, dealing with "passive" investments, and rental losses. Once you determine what information you require, however, you can set up a Quicken system for recording real estate transactions to provide exactly the reports you need.

To manage real estate with Quicken, you will need a Bank account for paying expenses and an Other Asset account for recording your basis in the properties, including improvements (which increase the value or extend the life of the property, as opposed to routine repairs). You can also keep on the current value of the properties. You will probably also need an Other Liability account for keeping track of mortgages.

The system suggested here uses classes to calculate subtotals for each property in the Other Asset and Other Liability accounts. These might be street names, such as Jones, Elm, and Watauga. If you prefer, however, you can set up separate accounts for each property. You will also need categories for the relevant lines on IRS Schedule E, Supplemental Income Schedule. These include an Income category for recording rents and Expense categories for advertising, repairs, and so forth.

Categories, subcategories, classes, and subclasses will be subtotaled in alphabetical order on your Quicken reports. In the following examples, we want cost, accumulated depreciation, and improvements to appear in that order on the balance sheet, so the following subclass names are assigned: Cost, Dep, and Improve.

If you are keeping track only of current income and expenses, you can omit the Other Asset and Other Liability accounts. However, when you sell a property, you will have to come to grips with the original cost or basis, capital improvements, and accumulated depreciation to figure your capital gain or loss.

Setting Up the Accounts

First, set up an Other Asset account called Real Estate and an Other Liability account called Mortgages. The opening balances should be 0.00. If you buy a rental property in the current year, the initial transactions are simply treated as transfers among your Other Liability, Bank, and Other Asset accounts. If you own other rental properties, you can use classes to keep separate records for each.

Suppose you buy a rental property on Watauga Street for $100,000, taking out a mortgage for $80,000. The loan is a transfer of $80,000 from your Mortgages Other Liability account to your Bank account. This increases the balances in both accounts by $80,000. If you record the transaction in the Bank account, the category entry might be [Mortgages]/Watauga. In the Mortgages account, it would appear as [Checking]/Watauga. When you pay for the house, the transaction is a transfer to the Mortgages Other Asset account. The category entry might be [Real Estate]/ Watauga:Cost.

The cost is your basis in the house. It will decrease as you claim depreciation and increase if you make permanent improvements that increase the value of the house or extend its life. When you sell, the basis is the amount you deduct from the sale price (less sale expenses) to determine your capital gain.

Appreciation (or decline in market value) has no effect on your basis. If you want to keep track of changes in market value in order to establish your net worth (as explained below) you might want to add an additional subcategory called Basis. Then you can assign transactions to /Watauga:Basis:Cost, /Watauga:Basis:Dep (for accumulated depreciation), and /Watauga:Basis:Improve (for improvements). That way, your Quicken balance sheet will calculate your basis for you. Alternatively, you can omit the Basis subclass and total Cost, Dep, and Improve yourself whenever you need to know your current basis.

Getting Started with Existing Properties

Setting up your Other Asset and Other Liability accounts is not quite as simple if you owned rental properties before the tax year in which you begin using Quicken, but it's still a manageable chore.

Suppose you paid $150,000 for a duplex on Elm Street and $90,000 for a single-family unit on Jones Street. The outstanding mortgage balances are $110,000 and $65,000, respectively, and in previous years you have claimed depreciation of $20,000 and $8,000. (These examples, of course, are schematic. Many variables affect actual depreciation and loan amortization.)

You can set up a Real Estate Other Asset account and a Mortgages Other Liability account with opening balances of 0.00. Ideally, you should set up these accounts at the beginning of a tax year, and the opening balances should be dated 1/1. If you begin using Quicken midyear, you can transfer your paper records to Quicken. Alternatively, you can piece together your paper records and your Quicken records for the first year; your Quicken records should be complete thereafter.

Since you did not purchase the properties in the current tax year, the initial transactions in these accounts should appear only on your balance sheet, not on reports of income and expenses. If you use cash flow reports, this will not be a problem, because Other Asset and Other Liability transactions will not appear unless they are transfers to Bank, Cash, or Credit Card accounts. If you use income and expense reports, there are several tactics for taking the initial transactions "off budget":

- Date the transactions on the last day of the previous year.

- Assign them to a dummy category, such as None, then filter your reports to exclude that category.

- If you routinely assign all of your other transactions to categories, leave these transactions uncategorized, then filter Not categorized out of your reports.

Reporting income and expenses will not be a problem after the first year, since these totals begin anew at the beginning of each year. Your Balance Sheets and Account Balances Reports with summarize all of your real estate activity to date.

Establishing Cost and Basis

You have already set up a Real Estate Other Asset account with an opening balance of 0.00, preferably dated at the beginning of the year. You may want to delete the opening balance from the Register. (Otherwise it will show up as "Other" on your reports). The next step is to enter the original cost of the buildings.

The original prices were $150,000 and $90,000. You can record these balances as increases in the Real Estate Other Asset Register. Make your own choice for a date, enter the address in the payee blank, and the amount in the increase column. In the memo blank, make a notation such as Original cost 5/1/85. (You will need to report the purchase date on your tax forms when you sell.) Finally, on the category line, assign the transaction to /Elm:Cost or /Jones:Cost. This assigns the original cost to a class and a subclass. You can either leave the category blank or use a dummy category, such as None/Elm:Cost.

The balance in your Real Estate Other Asset account is now $240,000. However, you have already claimed $28,000 in depreciation for previous years. (Remember that you can depreciate only buildings, not land.) This decreases your basis in the property. Most likely, you will want to record previous depreciation through the end of the previous year, since you have not yet claimed this year's depreciation as a tax deduction.

Previous depreciation is recorded for each property as a decrease in the Register. Enter the address on the payee line, then record the accumulated depreciation in the decrease column. In this case, you would enter 20000 for the Elm Street duplex and 8000 for the Jones Street house. On the memo line enter a notation such as Acc Dep through 12/31/88. On the category line assign the transactions to /Elm:Dep and to

/Jones:Dep. (If you prefer to use a dummy category, you can enter None/Elm:Dep and None/Jones:Dep). You can use the same method as before for keeping the transaction out of your records of income and expenses for the current year.

If you have made permanent improvements to the properties, you will also need to add their cost to your initial basis. The cost of improvements are entered in the increase column of the Real Estate Other Asset Register, but otherwise the procedure is the same as for recording accumulated depreciation. In this case, the transactions can be assigned to /Elm:Improve and /Jones:Improve.

> **NOTE:** If you plan to keep track of your properties current market value to measure your net worth, you can add a Basis subclass for recording cost, accumulated depreciation, and improvements in this fashion: /Elm:Basis:Dep and so forth. Otherwise, you can calculate the basis by totaling the balances in these subclasses.

Establishing the basis of your properties is the first step in setting up your balance sheet. It should also include the outstanding balances of your mortgages, as explained next.

Setting Up a Mortgages Account

In the example we've been using, the duplex on Elm Street has an outstanding mortgage balance of $110,000 and the house on Jones has a balance of $65,000. Establishing opening mortgage balances is easier than establishing your initial basis, because accumulated depreciation and improvements do not come into play.

Ideally, you should begin keeping your records at the beginning of the tax year, although you can piece together your paper records and your Quicken records. Also, you can use the methods described earlier to exclude the initial transactions from your current Quicken transaction-based reports.

The first step is to set up the Mortgages Other Liability account with an opening balance of 0.00. You can delete the opening balance from the Register so it won't appear in your reports. Recording the actual outstanding loan balances is simply a matter of recording increases in the Other Liabilities Register. (In this case, the entries are 110000 for Elm Street and 65000 for Jones.) Note the date of the balances on the memo line: Balance 12/31/88, for example. Finally, on the category line, assign each transaction to a class designating the property (/Elm and /Jones.)

You don't need subclasses if there is only one mortgage on each property. If you have second mortgages, however, you can use subclasses to designate separate mortgages: /Elm:1st and /Elm:2nd. If you are using a dummy category to exclude these transactions from current transactions reports, you could designate the dummy category, such as None/Elm.

The balance in the Mortgages Other Asset account is now $175,000, and it will decline each time you make a payment. (Only the payment on principal reduces outstanding principal; payment for taxes, insurance, and interest are simple expenses, and can be deducted in the current year.)

At this point, you are ready to begin recording routine income and expenses. First, let's take a look at a balance sheet.

A First Balance Sheet

Suppose you have recorded opening balances for the Elm Street duplex, as of December 31, and have bought the Watauga property on January 1. You can create a balance sheet for your real estate holdings, subtotaled by class.

To create the report, select 6. Account Balances from the Reports Menu, enter a report title if you want, then select 1. None for the report interval. Make sure the Selected accounts blank is set for S(elected). Press Ctrl-Enter to call up the Select accounts window. Exclude all accounts except Real Estate and Mortgages. The setting for these accounts should be Detail. (Highlight the account and press the space bar once.) Finally, press Ctrl-Enter to create the report.

The result should look like Figure 10.7. Notice that subtotals are given by Cost, Dep, and Total for each property. Since no improvements have been made, this represents the total basis of each. Outstanding loans total $255,000, leaving an Overall Total of $57,000.

```
                        ACCOUNT BALANCES REPORT
                            As of 1/ 3/89
RENTALS-Selected Accounts                                              Page 1
6/30/89
                                              1/ 3/89
              Account                         Balance
        -------------------------  ------------------------------------
        ASSETS
          Other Assets
            Real Estate
              Elm:
                Cost                  150,000.00
                Dep                   -20,000.00
                                    ------------
              Total Elm                             130,000.00
              Jones:
                Cost                   90,000.00
                Dep                    -8,000.00
                                    ------------
              Total Jones                            82,000.00
              Watauga:
                Cost                  100,000.00
                                    ------------
              Total Watauga                         100,000.00
                                                  ------------
            Total Real Estate                                    312,000.00
                                                                ------------
          Total Other Assets                                     312,000.00

                                                                ------------
        TOTAL ASSETS                                             312,000.00

        LIABILITIES
          Other Liabilities
            Mortgages
              Elm                                   110,000.00
              Jones                                  65,000.00
              Watauga                                80,000.00
                                                  ------------
            Total Mortgages                                      255,000.00
                                                                ------------
          Total Other Liabilities                                255,000.00

                                                                ------------
        TOTAL LIABILITIES                                        255,000.00

                                                                ------------
        OVERALL TOTAL                                             57,000.00
                                                                ============
```

Figure 10.7. A Balance Sheet summarizing real estate investments.

This report may have little to do with the actual value of the real estate, since it is based on original cost less depreciation, rather than market value. Adjusting for market value is explained later.

Recording Income and Expenses

IRS Schedule E, Supplemental Income Schedule (Figure 10.8), is the guide for keeping the books on rental properties. It requires you to report rental income and expenses for each property. Most rental income and expenses are recorded as simple deposits and payments in the Bank account you use for managing your rental properties. Once the transactions are recorded, you can create a Summary Report that provides exactly the information you need to file your tax return.

The basic Quicken strategy is to set up Income and Expense categories matching those on Schedule E. You might set up an Income category called Rent, for example, and Expense categories for Insurance, Repairs, Taxes, Utilities, and so on. If you want more detailed reports, you can break the main categories into subcategories, such as Repairs:Painting and Repairs:Plumbing.

For more than one rental property, you can use classes to identify each. In the examples here, these are /Watauga, /Elm, and /Jones. For properties with more than one unit, you can set up subclasses for each. For the Elm Street duplex, for example, the subclasses might be /Elm:East and /Elm:West.

If you set up an elaborate system of classifying transactions, remember that the maximum entry on the category line of a Quicken transaction is 31 characters, so you will have to keep your category and class names short. With a little planning, you can record all of your transactions in the detail you want.

Once you have set up categories and classes, recording income and expenses is simply a matter of recording transactions in your Bank account Register. If you receive $700 for each side of the Elm Street duplex, for example, you could record the deposit $1,400 as a split transaction, with $700 assigned to Rent/Elm:East and $700 to Rent/Elm:West. A $100 plumbing repair might be assigned to Repairs:Plumbing/Elm. And if you pay $250 to a lawyer to straighten out a liability claim at Jones, you could assign the transaction to Legal/Jones.

We haven't recorded the mortgage payments yet, and that can be a bit more complex.

SCHEDULE E (Form 1040)
Department of the Treasury
Internal Revenue Service

Supplemental Income Schedule

(From rents, royalties, partnerships, estates, trusts, REMICs, etc.)
▶ Attach to Form 1040, Form 1041, or Form 1041S.
▶ See Instructions for Schedule E (Form 1040).

OMB No. 1545-0074
1988
Attachment Sequence No. **13**

Name(s) as shown on Form 1040 | **Your social security number**

Part I Rental and Royalty Income or (Loss) **Caution:** Your rental loss may be limited. See Instructions.

1 In the space provided below, show the kind and location of each rental property.	2 For each property listed, did you or a member of your family use for personal purposes any of the properties for more than the greater of 14 days or 10% of the total days rented at fair rental value during the tax year?	Yes	No	3 For each rental real estate property listed, did you actively participate in the operation of the activity during the tax year? (See Instructions.)	Yes	No
Property A	▶			▶		
Property B	▶			▶		
Property C	▶			▶		

Rental and Royalty Income		Properties A	Properties B	Properties C	Totals (Add columns A, B, and C)	
4 Rents received					4	
5 Royalties received					5	
Rental and Royalty Expenses						
6 Advertising	6					
7 Auto and travel	7					
8 Cleaning and maintenance	8					
9 Commissions	9					
10 Insurance	10					
11 Legal and other professional fees	11					
12 Mortgage interest paid to financial institutions (see Instructions)	12				12	
13 Other interest	13					
14 Repairs	14					
15 Supplies	15					
16 Taxes (Do **not** include windfall profit tax here. See Part V, line 40.)	16					
17 Utilities	17					
18 Wages and salaries	18					
19 Other (list) ▶						
20 Total expenses other than depreciation and depletion. Add lines 6 through 19	20				20	
21 Depreciation expense (see Instructions), or depletion (see Publication 535)	21				21	
22 Total. Add lines 20 and 21	22					
23 Income or (loss) from rental or royalty properties. Subtract line 22 from line 4 (rents) or 5 (royalties)	23					
24 Deductible rental loss. **Caution:** Your rental loss on line 23 may be limited. See Instructions to determine if you must file **Form 8582,** Passive Activity Loss Limitations	24					

25 **Profits.** Add rental and royalty profits from line 23, and enter the total profits here	25	
26 **Losses.** Add royalty losses from line 23 and rental losses from line 24, and enter the total (losses) here	26	( )
27 Combine amounts on lines 25 and 26, and enter the net profit or (loss) here	27	
28 Net farm rental profit or (loss) from Form 4835. (Also complete Part VI, line 43.)	28	
29 Total rental or royalty income or (loss). Combine amounts on lines 27 and 28, and enter the total here. If Parts II, III, IV, and V on page 2 do not apply to you, enter the amount from line 29 on Form 1040, line 17. Otherwise, include the amount from line 29 in line 42 on page 2 of Schedule E	29	

For Paperwork Reduction Act Notice, see Form 1040 Instructions. **Schedule E (Form 1040) 1987**

Figure 10.8. Schedule E, Supplemental Income Schedule.

Mortgage Payments

Mortgage payments consist of at least two parts, principal and interest. They may also include payments for insurance and property taxes. Even if the payments consist only of principal and interest, the amount for each changes every month as you pay off the mortgage.

Strictly speaking, the payment on principal is not an expense, but a reduction of a liability, and it is not tax deductible; the interest payment is a simple expense, and is deductible. This means that you will have to calculate the totals separately when you file taxes. However, the lender will provide a statement with this information at the end of the year. Thus, if you use Quicken primarily to manage flow, you can assign the entire payment to an Expense category and use the lender's statement for tax reporting.

If you prefer to keep track of payments on principal and interest as you go along, you can record the mortgage payment as a split transaction, part assigned to an Interest Expense category, and part treated as a transfer to your Mortgages Other Liability account. If the mortgage payment on the Watauga house is $705, in a given month $664.25 might be assigned to Interest/Watauga and $40.75 to [Mortgages]/ Watauga. Since principal and interest payments vary each month, you may find it convenient to pull out your payment schedules at the beginning of the year and record the entire year's payments as postdated checks.

Mortgage payments often include payments for insurance and real estate taxes. The lender puts these payments in an escrow account and pays the bills when they are due. The lender will provide an annual summary. To record escrow payments in Quicken, you will need to set up an Escrow Other Asset account. (That way, cash flow reports will show the outflow when you make the payment, not when the lender pays the bills.) Then you can record a mortgage payment as a split transaction, with an expense assigned to an Interest category and transfers to Escrow and Mortgages. When you receive your statement from the lender, you can record the insurance and tax payments in your Escrow account.

Reporting Income and Expenses

A simple Business P&L Statement for January for the properties on Watauga, Jones, and Elm might look like Figure 10.9. It includes the totals you need for tax reporting. Unlike a Cash Flow Report, the P&L Statement excludes transactions irrelevant to taxes, such as payments on mortgage principal and investments in long-term improvements that have to be depreciated. You might, however, want to use a Cash Flow Report to determine how the three properties are affecting your bank accounts.

```
                         PROFIT & LOSS STATEMENT
                         1/ 1/89 Through 1/31/89
RENTALS-All Accounts                                                  Page 1
7/30/89
                                               1/ 1/89-
            Category Description               1/31/89
           ---------------------- --------------------
           INCOME/EXPENSE
             INCOME
               Rent                                 3,050.00
                                                  ----------
             TOTAL INCOME                           3,050.00

             EXPENSES
               Interest                             2,090.88
               Legal                                  250.00
               Repairs:
                 Painting                2,300.00
                 Plumbing                  100.00
                                       ----------
               Total Repairs                        2,400.00
                                                  ----------
             TOTAL EXPENSES                         4,740.88

                                                  ----------
           TOTAL INCOME/EXPENSE                    -1,690.88
                                                  ==========
```

Figure 10.9. A P&L Statement for January.

The P&L Statement does not break down income and expenses by property, as required by Schedule E, since in provides subtotals by category, not by class. To obtain that information, you need a Summary Report that subtotals by both categories (income and expenses) and classes (individual properties).

Since the P&L Statement is a variation of a Summary Report, you can reach the Create Summary Report screen by pressing F8-Customize when the Profit & Loss Statement window is displayed. You can also call up the Summary Report screen by selecting 4. Summary from the Reports Menu. Once there, select 1. Category for Row headings and 10. Class for Column headings. To get a clean income and expense report, without transfers, press F8 to select Customize, then exclude all transfers. Finally, return to the Create Summary Report screen and press Ctrl-Enter to create the report. The result is shown in Figure 10.10. As you can see, it matches the requirements of Schedule E almost exactly. At tax time, you can create a similar report for the entire year and copy the numbers onto the form.

Real Estate Summary
1/ 1/89 Through 1/31/89

RENTALS-All Accounts
7/30/89

Category Description	Elm	Jones	Watauga	OVERALL TOTAL
INCOME/EXPENSE				
INCOME				
Rent	1,400.00	750.00	900.00	3,050.00
TOTAL INCOME	1,400.00	750.00	900.00	3,050.00
EXPENSES				
Interest	922.40	504.23	664.25	2,090.88
Legal	0.00	250.00	0.00	250.00
Repairs:				
Painting	0.00	0.00	2,300.00	2,300.00
Plumbing	100.00	0.00	0.00	100.00
Total Repairs	100.00	0.00	2,300.00	2,400.00
TOTAL EXPENSES	1,022.40	754.23	2,964.25	4,740.88
TOTAL INCOME/EXPENSE	377.60	-4.23	-2,064.25	-1,690.88

Figure 10.10. A Summary Report of income and expense by property.

DEDUCTING DEPRECIATION

Deducting depreciation on rental real estate allows you to amortize the property's original cost over an extended period. It has nothing to do with the actual value of the property, which is probably increasing, rather than "depreciating." Depreciation reduces your basis in the property, so your capital gain will be higher when you sell. Since capital gains are no longer taxed at a preferential rate, this means that a depreciation deduction is really more of a tax deferment than a write-off.

Under the 1986 tax law, residential real estate placed in service after December 31, 1986, is depreciated by the straight-line method over 27.5 years; straight-line depreciation for commercial real estate placed in service since then is spread over 31.5 years. During the first year, depreciation is prorated for the period you owned it. For property placed in service before 1987 and property placed in service during the current year, the depreciation rules are too complicated to go into here. See an adviser or consult a tax manual, such as *J.K. Lasser's Your Income Tax.*

Depreciation is recorded at the end of an accounting period—a month, quarter, or year. When you record depreciation in Quicken, you should assign the transaction to a Depreciation Expense category, so it will show up on your P&L Statement or Summary Report. (Depreciation will never show up on a Cash Flow Report, because it is recorded in an Other Asset account.) You will also need to reduce your basis in the property by the amount of the depreciation.

If you bought the house on Watauga for $100,000 in January 1989, for example, the first year's depreciation might be about $3,000, depending on the value of its lot. (Remember, land is not depreciable.) To record this depreciation at the end of the year, go to the Real Estate Other Asset account Register, and record a Decrease of $3,000 dated December 31 assigned to Depreciation/Watauga:Dep.

Three thousand dollars is added to the Depreciation Expense category on your P&L Statement or Summary Report, and your tax basis is the Watauga house is decreased by the same amount. Your basis in the Watauga house now looks like this on a detailed Account Balances Report:

```
Watauga:
  Cost                    100,000.00
  Dep                      -3,000.00
                          ----------
Total Watauga              97,000.00
```

This has nothing to do with the actual value of the house. For purposes of determining net worth, you may want to add appreciation.

A Note on Appreciation

Appreciation has nothing whatever to do with your record keeping for tax purposes, and you probably do not want to count it as income in your Quicken reports. Nevertheless the market value of your real estate is the figure your bank will want when you apply for a loan to buy a new property, and it's a useful gauge for assessing the return on your investment for each property.

On December 31, the house on Watauga may be worth $110,000, having increased in value by 10 percent in the course of the year. Your balance sheet, however, lists its value—basis, actually—at $97,000. You can record the appreciation using the same method described earlier for revaluing securities investments. In this case, the house has appreciated not $10,000 but $13,000 over its "book value." This would be your taxable capital gain (supposing you could get $110,000 for the house after commissions and other expenses) if you sold the house at the end of the year.

To include the appreciation in your Quicken records—after you record the depreciation—you can enter a transaction in your Real Estate Other Asset account Register. In this case, on December 31, you would enter an Increase for $13,000, assigned on the category line to Apprec/Watauga:Revalue, where Apprec is an Income category. Now the asset part of your Watauga balance sheet looks like this:

```
Watauga:
  Cost                   100,000.00
  Dep                     -3,000.00
  Revalue                 13,000.00
                         ----------
Total Watauga            110,000.00
```

Your basis is still $97,000 ($100,000 cost - $3,000 depreciation). If you want, you can create an additional subcategory for Basis, as described earlier. You would then assign the original purchase price to [Real Estate]/Watauga:Basis:Cost and depreciation to Depreciation/Watauga:Basis:Dep. Now the asset part of your Watauga balance sheet looks like this:

```
Watauga:
  Basis:
    Cost                 100,000.00
    Dep                   -3,000.00
                         ----------
  Total Basis             97,000.00
  Revalue                 13,000.00
                         ----------
Total Watauga            110,000.00
```

Now you have your basis in the property, its current value, and the amount on which you would pay capital gains if you sold it. However, Quicken reports will tend to treat the transaction assigned to Revalue as income. This amount will not show up on cash flow reports, because it occurs in an Other Asset account. If you do not want appreciation to appear on income and expense reports, you can filter your reports to exclude Revalue.

MAJOR IMPROVEMENTS

Routine repairs, such as fixing plumbing leaks and repainting, are treated as expenses. However, permanent improvements must be depreciated. These include improvements that enhance the value of the property, such as kitchen remodeling, adding central air, or the addition of a room. Routine repairs, such as painting and wallpapering, may also have to be depreciated if they are part of a major renovation. Major replacements, such as replacing roof shingles or a furnace, should also be depreciated.

Major improvements increase your basis in the property. When you sell the property, however, you will have to list both the cost and improvements to the property, so you will need a separate class for improvements. Suppose you add central air to the Watauga Street house for $5,000. If you are not recording appreciation, you could record this transaction in your Checking Bank account like this:

```
Payee: Acorn Air & Heating
Payment: 5000
Memo: Add Central Air
Category: [Real Estate]/Watauga:Improve
```

Now the asset part of your Watauga balance sheet (assuming you have not begun depreciating the improvement) looks like this:

```
Watauga:
  Cost                   100,000.00
  Dep                     -3,000.00
  Improve                  5,000.00
                         ___________
Total Watauga            102,000.00
```

If you are recording appreciation, using a Basis subclass, and calculate that the addition of air conditioning adds $4,000 to the market value of the house, the same report looks like this:

```
Watauga:
  Basis:
    Cost                  100,000.00
    Dep                    -3,000.00
    Improve                 5,000.00
                          ----------
  Total Basis             102,000.00
  Revalue                  12,000.00
                          ----------
Total Watauga             114,000.00
```

When you sell the property, you subtract the basis from the selling price to determine your capital gain.

Selling Investment Real Estate

When you sell a rental property you will probably realize a taxable capital gain. (Even if you lose money, the calculation is basically the same.) Table 10.2 is a worksheet for calculating your capital gain (or loss).

Table 10.2. A worksheet for calculating the capital gain (or loss) on the sale of a rental property.

Selling price	________
Less selling expenses (Commissions, fixup costs, etc.)	________
Amount realized	________
Cost or unadjusted basis	________
Improvements	________
Less Depreciation	________
Adjusted basis	________
Net profit (or loss) (Amount realized less adjusted basis)	________

Suppose you sell the Watauga house for $125,000 after three years. The cost was $100,000; improvements total $5,000; and depreciation amounts to $9,298. The sales commission was $7,500, leaving an amount realized of $117,500. The remaining balance on the mortgage is $78.682.

The asset part of your Watauga balance sheet provides all of the information you need.

CONCLUSION

This chapter described how to record securities and real estate investments with Quicken. These are the most important business transactions many people make. The next chapter gets down to the nitty gritty of using Quicken for a small business.

11

Accounts Payable and Receivable

Most small businesses need to keep track of accounts payable and accounts receivable. If you provide professional services and bill your clients, for example, you will need to keep track of how much you are owed, and by whom. Even if you use an accountant for your financial reports and taxes, you will still need to record payables and receivables correctly to provide the information the accountant needs. A business that neither extends nor uses credit might be an exception, but even such a business might want to keep track of bills coming due—in effect, accounts payable.

Quicken handles accounts receivable and accounts payable easily. This chapter explains the special techniques you will need, whether your business keeps records on a cash basis or on an accrual basis.

Cash Accounting versus Accrual Accounting

Many small businesses use cash accounting. In cash accounting, income and expenses are recorded when money changes hands, and keeping business books is not much different from personal record keeping. You can simply assign transactions to Income and Expense categories as you receive money and make payments. For example, if you bill a company for $500 in consulting services, you do not record any income until you get the check. Similarly, if you have an account with the local office supplies company, which bills you 30 days net, the expense does not occur until you pay the bill.

Recording accounts payable on a cash basis with Quicken is easy. Just record postdated checks dated when bills are due. The Business A/P by Vendor report will provide accounts payable by vendor and by month, but no expense is reported until the date of the check. You can also use custom reports to report accounts payable exactly the way you want.

Accounts receivable can be a little trickier in a cash accounting system, because you need to record the transaction in receivables when it occurs, but you must not recognize income until payment is received. Using a Cash Flow Report instead of a P&L Statement will solve this problem for many businesses. Another possibility, described below, is a two-step procedure that assigns an invoice or bill to a dummy Income category when it is issued, then transfers it to a real Income category when payment is received. You can exclude the dummy category from your reports to avoid confusion about actual income.

Larger businesses—and all C corporations (regular corporations)—use accrual accounting. In accrual accounting the income is recorded when it is earned, and expenses are recorded when they are incurred—regardless of when payment is actually made. Cash transactions are recorded just as they are in a cash system, because the transaction and payment occur simultaneously. When you receive or issue a bill, however, you need to record the income or expense on the date of the transaction. You also need to record the payment when it occurs.

Accounts payable and receivable are actually easier to record with Quicken on an accrual basis than in a cash system. When you incur an expense, you just record it in an Other Liability account, assigned to an Expense category. (You can also record a postdated check if you want to use Billminder. It won't interfere with your reports.) When you issue a bill, you record it in your accounts receivable Other Asset account, assigned to an Income category. In either case, when payment is made, you record it as a transfer between AR or AP and a Bank account.

Whichever method you use, your bookkeeping is partly for the purpose of managing your business and partly for filing tax returns, so the IRS has something to say about which method you use. The Tax Reform Act of 1986 requires accrual accounting for C corporations, partnerships that have C Corporations as partners, tax shelters, and some other organizations. Other businesses in which inventory plays a prominent role also must record sales and inventory purchases on an accrual basis, but they may keep the rest of their records on a cash basis. This means that inventory purchases accrue when merchandise is received and sales income accrues on the date of sale, regardless of when payment is made. Other types of transactions—rent, payroll, and fees for services, for example—may be recorded on a cash basis.

Accounts Payable

Recording accounts payable on a cash basis is one of Quicken's strongest suits. When a bill arrives, all you have to do is to record the transaction as a postdated check. Quicken automatically records it in the Register. Quicken's Billminder feature will remind you when to make the payment. The program can then produce reports of accounts payable in whatever detail you require.

On an accrual basis, you will need to record the bill and your payment as separate transactions. The expense occurs when you owe the money. The payment is not an expense, but a reduction in your accounts payable liability. The simpler version—cash basis accounts payable—comes first.

Cash Accounts Payable

In a cash-based accounting system, recording accounts payable is simply a matter of recording your bills as postdated checks. You can use this method even if you write checks by hand, rather than printing Quicken checks. Expenses are recorded when payments are actually made, so you don't have to make any special provision for timing expenses.

Suppose you receive an invoice for $256.32 for supplies from the Computer Emporium, dated June 13. The payment will be past due July 13, so you decide to write the check on July 12. If you print Quicken checks, all you have to do is to write a check, dated on that date, on the Write/Print Checks screen. When you print the check, Quicken automatically removes it from the Write/Print Checks screen and from accounts payable reports based on checks.

To record a postdated handwritten check, write the check as usual on the Write/Print Checks screen, entering the date you intend to pay the bill. When you actually write a check by hand, go to the Register, find the postdated transaction, and enter the check number in the NUM column, replacing the five asterisks (*****) entered there. (The asterisks appear automatically in the Register when you write a check on the Write/Print Checks screen.) Finally, press Ctrl-Enter to record the changes. This removes the check from the unprinted check list, so it will no longer appear in your accounts payable reports.

In addition, you can record other expected expenses as postdated checks, even if you do not receive a bill or invoice. Examples include rent, payroll, payments for FICA and federal withholding tax for employees, quarterly income tax, and sales tax. You can save considerable time by setting up transaction groups for recording routine transactions, as explained in Chapter 6.

In a cash accounting system, this method gives you access to a range of Quicken reports for analyzing accounts payable. Just set the date range to exclude transactions that have already occurred. In an accrual system, you need a system for timing expenses correctly.

Accrual Accounts Payable

In an accrual accounting system, expenses are recognized in your P&L Statement when they are incurred regardless of when payment is actually made. When you pay, the transaction should be included in your Cash Flow Reports, but not in your P&L Statement.

The Quicken manual suggests using classes to designate the time period when expenses occurred. When you write a check on July 15 for an bill dated June 20, for example, you can assign the transaction to, say, Utilities:Electric/June89. If you use this method, you must assign *every* Income and Expense transaction in all accounts to a time period class. Otherwise, your reports won't make any sense. You can create a Summary Report or customized P&L Statement with categories listed down the side (rows) and classes across the top (columns). This works, but it can become cumbersome, particularly if you want to use classes for other purposes. Here's another way.

Accounts payable is a liability, and you can record payables in an Other Liability account. Expenses will be reported on your P&L Statement and Summary Reports when they are incurred, and your Cash Flow Reports will reflect expenses when they are paid. You can still postdate checks to keep track of payables by due date and to use Billminder.

The first step is to set up an Other Liability account, called, say, Payables or AP (you can't name the account A/P, because you can't use slashes in account names), for recording incurred expenses. When an invoice arrives, record it both in Payables and as a postdated check. To record the invoice and payment for the June 13 invoice of $256.32 for supplies, for example, follow these steps:

1. Go to the Payables Other Liability Register and enter an Increase of $256.32, dated 6/13/89 and assigned on the category line to Supplies. You can add a class to identify a vendor or job. The expense is now recorded and will be included in your P&L Statement, but it will not be reported in a Cash Flow Report.

2. Go to the Write/Print Checks screen of your checking account, write a check postdated for the day you plan to pay the invoice. Assign the transaction to [Payables] on the category line. Use the same class designation as you did in the payables account.

Now you have recorded two separate transactions. The first adds $256.32 to the total in your Supplies Expense category and increases the balance in Payables Other Liability account. The second remains on the unprinted check list until you print the check. When you print the check, the balances in both the Bank account and Payables are reduced by $256.32, and the postdated check is removed from the from the list of checks to print. Now the transaction will be included in your P&L Statement on the invoice date and in your Cash Flow Reports on the date of the check.

Reporting Accounts Payable

There are many potential ways to create reports of accounts payable. If you record amounts payable as postdated checks, you can use Quicken's predefined Business A/P by Vendor report to report total accounts payable by payee. If the report covers more than one month, it will show monthly subtotals for each vendor. You can also marshal the flexibility of other reports to meet your exact needs.

You should be careful about dating A/P reports correctly, especially if you have recorded amounts you will owe over an extended period. If it's April, for example, you may not want to include December's rent in your current accounts payable.

The A/P by Vendor Report

The predefined A/P by Vendor Report provides monthly subtotals for checks payable to each payee, overall totals for each payee, overall totals for each month, and a grand total of all unprinted checks. You can use this report in either an accrual or a cash-based system. The only requirement is that you enter *all* transactions you want to include in the report as postdated checks in your Bank accounts. Postdated transactions recorded only in the Register will not be included unless you enter an asterisk (*) in the NUM column to transfer checks to the Write/Print Checks screen. If you enter postdated checks for amounts for which you do not receive bills, such as rent and payroll, this report will also provide a monthly forecast of cash requirements.

Since the report subtotals by payee, it is critical that you record transactions consistently. If you have an employee named John R. Jones, for example, Quicken will provide separate subtotals if you sometimes write his paycheck to John Jones and sometimes to John R. Jones. Memorized transactions or transaction groups are highly recommended to ensure consistency.

To create an A/P by Vendor report, select 3. A/P by Vendor from the Business submenu of the Reports Menu. A window appears, labeled A/P (Unprinted Checks) by Vendor. Enter a title if you want. If you want to modify the predefined report, you can select F8-Customize or F9-Filter to change the report settings. (See Chapter 7 for details on customizing reports.) Finally, press Ctrl-Enter to create the report. The result should look something like Figure 11.1. You have the usual options for printing the report.

A/P (UNPRINTED CHECKS) BY VENDOR

8/ 1/89 Through 9/30/89

AR-All Accounts
7/30/89

Payee	8/89	9/89	OVERALL TOTAL
Bell Telephone	-463.22	-246.32	-709.54
Branch Bank	-236.25	-236.25	-472.50
Computer Emporium	-48.92	0.00	-48.92
John Jones	-1,264.50	-1,264.50	-2,529.00
Jones Office Supply	-19.36	0.00	-19.36
New Jersey Power	-231.36	-323.13	-554.49
Yorx Management	-1,500.00	-1,500.00	-3,000.00
OVERALL TOTAL	-3,763.61	-3,570.20	-7,333.81

AR-All Accounts (Filtered)
Esc-Create report F1-Help F8-Print

Figure 11.1. The A/P by Vendor Report.

The A/P by Vendor Report is easily customized. The basic report is a variation of the Custom Summary Report subtotaled by payee for row headings and by month for column headings. It is filtered to include only unprinted checks. If you use classes to identify vendors, for example, you can subtotal row headings by class instead of payee. Or you could create a weekly report by changing the setting for column headings to week. Again, see Chapter 7 for details on customizing reports.

Accounts Payable by Time Period

You can also use Transaction Reports to show individual payable items subtotaled by time period—anticipated payments for each week or month, for example. This report lists individual transactions and forecasts your cash requirements for the time periods included in the report, but does not subtotal by vendor or payee.

To create the report, first record payable items as postdated checks as usual, then select 3. Transaction from the Custom Reports section of the Reports Menu. When the Create Transaction Report screen appears, enter a title if you want and date range for the period you want to cover. In the Subtotal by: blank, select the period for which you want subtotals, such as 2. Week or 5. Month. If you have postdated transactions in non-Bank accounts, choose S(elected), then select all of your Bank accounts on the Select accounts window. If you don't have postdated transactions elsewhere, you can select A(ll) to include all accounts. Finally, if you have recorded postdated transactions that are not unprinted checks, select F9-Filter, then restrict the report to Unprinted checks only.

When you have finished, press Ctrl-Enter as many times as required (it depends on which window is currently displayed) to create the report. The result looks something like Figure 11.2. Note that this report takes your current balance forward. Since the report does not include deposits, your bank balance is likely to turn negative for later periods. You have the usual options for printing the report.

TRANSACTION REPORT BY WEEK
8/ 1/89 Through 9/30/89

AR-Selected Accounts — Page 1
7/30/89

Date	Acct	Num	Payee	Memo	Category	Clr	Amount
		BALANCE	7/31/89				8,267.68
8/ 1	Checking	*****	Yorx Management	August Rent	[Payables]/Yorx		-1,500.00
8/ 1	Payables		Yorx Management	August Rent	[Checking]/Yorx		1,500.00
8/ 1	Payables		Yorx Management	August Rent	Rent		-1,500.00
		TOTAL	8/ 1/89 - 8/ 5/89				-1,500.00
		BALANCE	8/ 5/89				6,767.68
8/ 6	Checking	*****	Jones Office Sup	Inv. #329	Office		-19.36
8/12	Checking	*****	Bell Telephone		Utilities:Telep		-463.22
8/12	Checking	*****	New Jersey Power		Utilities:Elect		-231.36
		TOTAL	8/ 6/89 - 8/12/89				-713.94
		BALANCE	8/12/89				6,053.74

Figure 11.2. Reporting accounts payable by week.

Reporting from an A/P Other Liability Account

If you set up an Other Liability account for recording accounts payable on an accrual basis, you can still use all of the reporting methods described above, as long as you record prospective payments as postdated checks. Since the A/P by Vendor Report includes *only* unprinted checks, it doesn't matter that you have also recorded the same expenses in your Other Liability account. Nor will your unprinted checks interfere with other Quicken reports, although you do have to be careful about setting date ranges to get the exact results you want on Balance Sheet or Account Balances Reports.

In addition, when you use an Other Liability account for accounts payable, you have access to the full range of Quicken reports for transactions in that account. Examples include Balance Sheets that include payables and receivables; P&L Statements that recognize income and expenses when they are incurred, rather than when they are received; and Cash Flow Reports that show cash transactions when they occur, rather than when income and expenses are recorded.

If you use an accrual accounting system, you may find that using the Other Liability account method of recording accounts payable gives you more flexibility and fuller reporting than using classes, such as /Jan89 to assign transactions to particular accounting periods. It's up to you.

Accounts Receivable

Recording accounts receivable with Quicken is fairly straightforward. The basic strategy is to set up an accounts receivable Other Asset account that works like a Credit Card account in reverse. With a Credit Card account, a purchase increases the balance; your payment to the credit card company decreases it. In accounts receivable, an invoice or bill increases the Other Asset account balance; a customer's payment decreases it.

In the method described below, and in the Quicken manual, invoices or bills are dated—and income recorded—on the date issued. Payments are recorded as transfers from an Other Asset account to a Bank account, generating cash flow, but no income.

This system times income correctly for accrual accounting, and the P&L Statement and other reports will be accurate. Income is recorded when the bill is sent, cash flow when payment is received.

For cash accounting, however, you need to record income when payment is received. For many businesses, a Cash Flow Report will solve this problem, since it reports inflows and outflows when cash actually changes hands. This works well, provided all actual income and expenses are in cash and you do not have other inflows and outflows. Depreciation of equipment, for example, will not appear in a Cash Flow Report, but the purchase of equipment, which may not be an expense for tax purposes, will. Loans are another potential problem. The proceeds of a loan will appear as an inflow of cash, although it is not income, and payments on principal will appear as outflows, although they are not expenses for tax purposes.

If Cash Flow Reports do not meet your needs for reporting income and expenses, one option, described later in Another Approach to Cash Basis Receivables, is to adapt your record keeping to record income when cash is received. Then you should be able to use the P&L Statement.

Aging receivables is another consideration. Using the method described here, you can age receivables by invoice date, but not by due date. This should not be a problem if you offer all customers the same terms, such as 30 days net, but it may be if customers have varying payment schedules.

If the methods described here don't meet your needs, a final possibility is to set up a separate account group for recording receivables, so you can handle them independently of other records. (You could enter invoices by their due date for more accurate aging, for example.) This approach will require you to enter some of the same transactions twice in Quicken, but it will still allow you to produce the reports you need with less trouble than keeping the same records on paper.

Quicken's A/R by Customer Report (Figure 11.3) summarizes uncleared transactions in Other Asset accounts, subtotaled by payee (customer) and by month. It also lists overall totals by payee and by month. Only uncleared transactions are included in the totals.

A/R BY CUSTOMER

10/ 1/89 Through 12/31/89

AR
7/30/89

Payee	10/89	11/89	12/89	OVERALL TOTAL
Advent Stereo	0.00	732.23	0.00	732.23
Arizona Symphony	0.00	2,345.00	0.00	2,345.00
Calabrisi Restaurant	0.00	1,500.00	1,032.12	2,532.12
Food Processing Magazine	500.00	0.00	0.00	500.00
Fred Marquhardt & Assoc.	0.00	0.00	750.00	750.00
Quiller Manufacturing	6,325.21	1,000.00	5,000.00	12,325.21
Smith Olds & Co.	0.00	0.00	4,325.00	4,325.00
Stone & Co.	0.00	762.65	500.00	1,262.65
Susan James Design	1,322.31	0.00	0.00	1,322.31
Willer & Rockett	0.00	895.23	0.00	895.23
OVERALL TOTAL	8,147.52	7,235.11	11,607.12	26,989.75

AR (Filtered)
Esc-Create report F1-Help F8-Print

Figure 11.3. The A/R by Customer Report.

Recording Invoices or Bills

You can keep track of invoices either by the "balance forward" method or the "open items" method. The first maintains a running balance for each customer. It is generally recommended for businesses that receive payments mostly for multiple invoices. The second tracks payments of individual invoices and is appropriate when most invoices are paid individually. You may want to consult with your accountant before choosing.

For the purposes of entering invoices and payments the two methods differ only in detail. If you use the balance forward method, you should set up a class, such as /Jones or /Ripkin, for each customer, so you can create reports with subtotals for each. If you have more than one customer with the same name and want them listed in alphabetical order, enter the last name first (/Jones, J., for example). If you use the open item method, you must mark both the invoice and payment as cleared when you receive payments. This allows you to filter reports to exclude bills that have already been paid. Even if you use this method, you may still want to use classes to identify customers if you want, for example, to itemize outstanding invoices by customer.

NOTE: If you use classes only in accounts receivable, they will not interfere with your other Quicken reports. However, if you use classes differently elsewhere and make multiple-account reports that include receivables, you may get odd results. One solution is to organize global reports by category, omitting class detail. You can also experiment with subtotaling your accounts receivable by payee, rather than using classes. All Transaction Reports and Summary Reports (including A/R by customer) can be subtotaled by payee.

Before you begin recording invoices, set up an Other Asset account named Receivables or AR. (You cannot name it A/R, because you cannot use slashes in account names.) You will also need one or more Income categories, such as Sales or Receipts. You can also use subcategories if you want. Finally, set up a class for each customer if you use the balance forward method. (This is optional but may still be useful if you use the open item method.) New classes can be added "on the fly" while you are entering invoices.

Memorized transactions are highly recommended to ensure consistent entries in the payee blank, especially if you do not use classes. The predefined A/R by Customer report subtotals transactions by payee, and you will get erratic results if there are even slight variations in the way you enter each customer's name.

When you are ready to begin entering invoices, go to the Register of the Receivables Other Asset account. Each invoice is an ordinary Quicken transaction. If the customer will pay in installments, enter a separate transaction for each. Use split transactions if an invoice includes several items you want to record separately.

For each invoice, make these entries:

1. The *issue date* of the invoice in the Date column.

2. The invoice number in the NUM column.

3. The customer's name the Payee column. (To repeat, it is critical to enter each customer's name consistently if you plan to use the A/R by Customer Report or other reports subtotaled by payee.)

4. The amount of the invoice in the Increase column. (You can enter an amount in the Decrease column if you are crediting the customer for return.)

5. Whatever description you want for a memo (including the invoice number if your invoice numbers are more than five digits long.)

6. In the category blank, enter your Income category name. (Split the transaction if the invoice includes more than one item you want to record separately). If you use the balance forward method, add the customer's class designation, such as /Jones. (Optional in the open item method.) The result might look like Receipts/Jones or Sales:Shipping/Funderburk.

When the transaction is completed, press Ctrl-Enter to record it.

Recording Payments

When a customer or client pays a bill or invoice, the transaction reduces the balance in accounts receivable and increases in your Bank account. Because this is a *transfer*, you cannot assign the payment to an Income category. In an accrual system, the income occurs when the invoice is issued. In either an accrual or a cash system, payments will be correctly timed as Inflows FROM Receivables in your Cash Flow Reports. (For an alternate method, see Another Approach to Cash Basis Receivables below.)

Recording a payment is essentially the same for the balance forward and open item methods. In the balance forward method, you identify customers by classes, and you do not clear paid items. In the open item method, classes are optional, and you mark both the payment and the invoice(s) it covers as cleared by typing an asterisk in the C(leared) column.

You can record a payment as either a deposit in a Bank account or as a decrease in your accounts receivable Other Asset account. On the category line, assign the transfer to the corresponding account and a customer class, if you use classes to identify customers. In the Bank account, the entry might be [AR]/Jones, for example; in receivables it might appear as [Checking]/Jones. In the Memo line, you can include the numbers and dates of the invoices covered by the payment and other descriptive information. If you use the open item method, enter an asterisk (*) in the C(leared) column to indicate the bill has been paid; leave this column blank if you use the balance forward method. When you've finished, press Ctrl-Enter to record the transaction.

If you use the open item method, you now need to clear the original invoice. This will allow you to exclude all paid bills from your accounts receivable reports by filtering out cleared transactions. To do this, highlight the invoice in the Register and type an asterisk (*) in the C(leared) column. You may also want to enter the payment date on the memo line to keep track of customer payment history. When finished, press Ctrl-Enter to record the changes.

Another Approach to Cash Basis Receivables

If you keep books on a cash basis and the Cash Flow Report doesn't meet your income reporting needs, you will need to adopt a different approach to managing accounts receivable. One solution, suggested earlier, is to keep receivables in a separate account group. Here's another.

The basic accounting equation (Net Worth = Assets - Liabilities) won't let you record a new asset—a new invoice receivable, for example—without specifying where it came from. In the case of cash basis accounts receivable, however, you want to record the invoice when you issue it, but you don't want to record the income until the invoice is paid.

The alternative is to set up a dummy nontax income category—such as AR (you can't use a / in a category name)—for accounts receivable, then recording the payment in a three-part split transaction that transfers the income from the dummy category to a "real" income category. You'll probably want to exclude your AR category from most reports.

When you record the invoice in the Register of your accounts receivable Other Asset account, assign the transaction to your AR income category. If you want, you can add a class, such as /Jones, to designate the customer or client. The category line might look like this: AR/Jones. This increases the balance in receivables and the AR category, which you will not include in reports of income and expenses.

When you receive payment, you need to record a transfer from accounts receivable to a Bank account, to *increase* your real (taxable) Income category balance by the amount of the payment, and to *decrease* the balance in your AR Income category by the same amount. Because the last two items cancel each other out, the total amount of the transaction—the transfer to the Bank account—equals the payment received.

Suppose you send a bill for $100 to a client named R.D. Farnsworth and record it in your accounts receivable Other Asset account, assigned to AR/Farnsworth on the category line. You can record the payment as a split transaction, as shown in Figure 11.4.

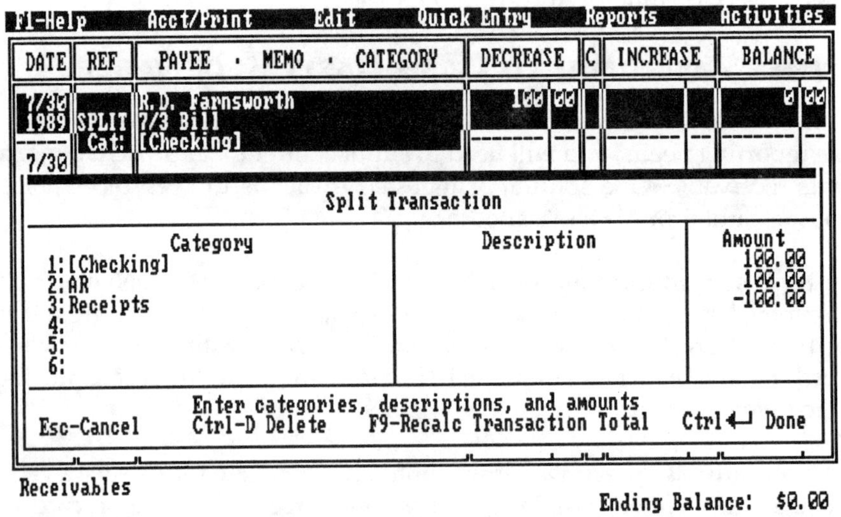

Figure 11.4. A sneaky way of recording cash-basis income in accounts receivable.

Remember that the entire transaction is recorded in the Decrease column of the Register. Note that the transfer to Checking is 100.00, because it *decreases* the balance in accounts receivable. The income entries may be confusing at first. The AR entry is also 100.00, because a *decrease* in an Other Asset account also *decreases* the balance in the Income category it is assigned to. But the Receipts entry is *minus* 100.00; it is a negative decrease—which amounts to an increase—in accounts receivable, so it *increases* the balance in the Receipts Income category.

If the Farnsworth bill and payment were the only transactions recorded, the Checking Bank account and the Receipts Income category would both have balances of $100.00. The balance in the AR Income category would be $0.00—the original bill added $100.00, and the payment subtracted the same amount. Both the bill and the payment should be marked as cleared with asterisks in the C(leared) column, because they no longer belong in your reports of accounts receivable. That way, you can filter cleared transactions out of your reports.

This method allows you to keep accounts receivable with income correctly timed on a cash basis *and* to use the P&L Statement and other reports based on income and expenses.

Reporting Accounts Receivable

Quicken's predefined A/R by Customer (designed for open item record keeping) report provides one easy option for reporting accounts receivable. There are also many ways you can design custom reports of receivables. If there's a way to classify a transaction—by payee, category, class, or date—you can use it as the basis for a Quicken report. It isn't possible to describe all of the possibilities, but some examples follow.

The A/R by Customer Report

The A/R by Customer Report, shown in Figure 11.3, is designed for open item records. You must mark payments and related invoices as cleared for it to produce meaningful results. The report summarizes unpaid invoices by payee (customer) and by month of issue. If it's June for example, and a customer still hasn't paid invoices issued in April, they're overdue if you allow customers 30 days to pay. The right column shows the total each customer owes; the bottom row provides totals for unpaid invoices issued each month. The figure at the bottom right corner is the total amount you are owed.

The time period for the report is predefined as from January 1 of the current year to the end of the current month, and the report is filtered to include only uncleared transactions. The basic report is also predefined to include *all* Other Asset accounts. If you use Other Asset accounts for other purposes, such as keeping track of real estate or depreciable equipment, be sure to exclude the unrelated accounts when the Select Accounts window appears.

You can modify most of the report's settings to suit your needs, but once you have set up your Receivables Other Asset account and recorded your invoices and payments, creating a basic A/R by Customer takes only seconds.

To create the report, select 2. Business Reports from the Reports Menu, then 4. A/R by Customer from the Business submenu. When the A/R by Customer window appears, enter a report title if you want, then press Enter to continue. If you do not enter a title, the report will be named A/R by Customer. Next, the Select Accounts window appears (Figure 11.5). To eliminate unrelated accounts (such as the Equipment account in the illustration), highlight each, then press the space bar to exclude it. (If you change your mind, repeat the procedure to change the setting in the right column back to Include.) Finally, press Enter to create the report. When it appears on the screen, you can press F8 to print it, as usual.

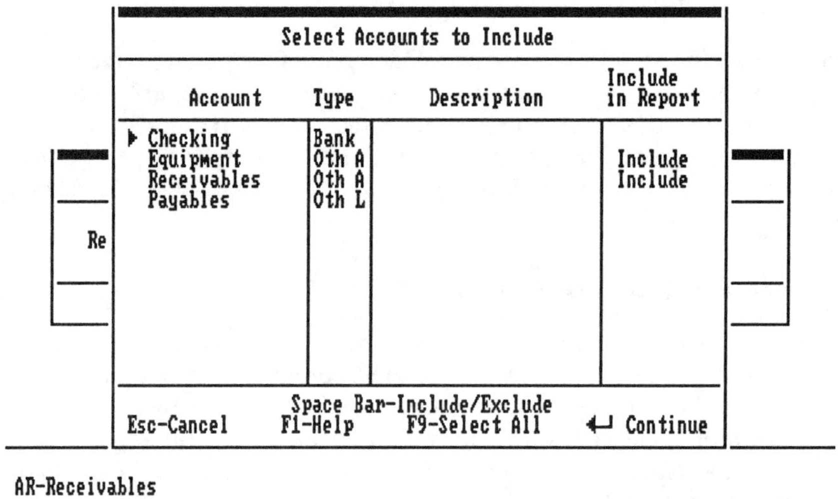

Figure 11.5. The Select Accounts window for the A/R by Customer Report.

You can create a similar report of only overdue accounts by customizing the A/R by Customer report. When the A/R title window appears, press F8 (Customize), then set the ending date to the current date less the number of days you allow customers to pay.

The A/R report is simply a Summary Report that subtotals rows by payee and columns by month. The report is also filtered to include only uncleared transactions; on the Filter Report Transactions screen (F9), the Cleared blanks are set to include blank only; "*" and "X" are set to N(o).

There are other ways you might want to customize the A/R by Customer Report. (See Chapter 7 for details on creating custom reports.) If you use classes to identify customers, for example, you would want to change the Row headings entry to class. You are generally free to change any the report settings. One exception is report organization (income and expense) on the Report Options window (F8). Since invoices are recorded as income transactions in an Other Asset account, all would be excluded if you changed the basis to cash flow.

More Detailed Open Item Reporting

You may need a more detailed report of unpaid items than the monthly totals in the A/R by Customer Report. You can easily create custom Transaction Reports that itemize individual unpaid invoices, subtotaled by week or by customer.

Before beginning, make sure that the current account is your accounts receivable Other Asset account. To report unpaid receivables by week, select 3. Transaction from the Reports Menu. On the Create Transaction Report screen, set the date range to cover the entire range of invoices, and subtotal by 2 (week). Next, press F9 to filter the report, and restrict the report to uncleared transactions. (On the Cleared status line, the entries should be: Y(es) for blank, N(o) for "*" and "X".) Press Ctrl-Enter twice to generate the report. The result will look like Figure 11.6.

```
                          TRANSACTION REPORT BY WEEK
                          10/ 1/89 Through 12/31/89
AR                                                                Page 1
12/31/89

 Date   Num         Payee              Memo          Category     Clr  Amount
----- ------ ------------------- ------------- ----------------- - ----------

10/ 1 3452   Susan James Design  Yorx Brochure Receipts/James        1,322.31
10/ 7 3455   Quiller Manufacturi Annual Report Receipts/Quiller      6,325.21
                                                                   ----------
             TOTAL 10/ 1/89 - 10/ 7/89                               7,647.52

                                                                   ----------
             TOTAL 10/ 8/89 - 10/14/89                                   0.00

10/21 3457   Food Processing Mag Quiller Articl Receipts/Food          500.00
                                                                   ----------
             TOTAL 10/15/89 - 10/21/89                                 500.00

                                                                   ----------
             TOTAL 10/22/89 - 10/28/89                                   0.00

11/ 2 3460   Stone & Co.         Festival Broch Receipts/Stone         762.65
                                                                   ----------
             TOTAL 10/29/89 - 11/ 4/89                                 762.65

11/ 8  3465  Willer & Rockett    Advent recepti Receipts/Willer        895.23
                                                                   ----------
             TOTAL 11/ 5/89 - 11/11/89                                 895.23

11/12 3469   Advent Stereo       Nakamichi Ad  Receipts/Advent         732.23
11/17 3471   Calabrisi Restauran Design Logo   Receipts/Calabris     1,500.00
                                                                   ----------
             TOTAL 11/12/89 - 11/18/89                               2,232.23

11/21 3479   Arizona Symphony    Spring Brochur Receipts/Arizona     2,345.00
                                                                   ----------
             TOTAL 11/19/89 - 11/25/89                               2,345.00

11/30 3482   Quiller Manufacturi New Product Br Receipts/Quiller     1,000.00
12/ 1 3590   Quiller Manufacturi Retainer      Receipts/Quiller      5,000.00
12/ 1 3591   Calabrisi Restauran New ad        Receipts/Calabris       632.12
                                                                   ----------
             TOTAL 11/26/89 - 12/ 2/89                               6,632.12
```

Figure 11.6. A custom Transaction Report showing unpaid invoices subtotaled by week.

There are many possible variations. For a report of only overdue bills, for example, count back the number of days you allow for customers to pay, and set that date as the closing date of the date range. If it's June 30, for example, enter 6/1 as the closing date. You could also count back 60 days for a report of bills more than 30 days overdue.

```
                      TRANSACTION REPORT BY PAYEE
                       10/ 1/89 Through 12/31/89
AR                                                                  Page 1
7/30/89

 Date   Num        Payee              Memo          Category      Clr  Amount
----- ------ ------------------- ------------- ---------------- - ----------


11/12 3469   Advent Stereo       Nakamichi Ad  Receipts                732.23
                                                                   ----------
             Total Advent Stereo                                       732.23


11/21 3479   Arizona Symphony    Spring Brochur Receipts             2,345.00
                                                                   ----------
             Total Arizona Symphony                                  2,345.00


11/17 3471   Calabrisi Restauran Design Logo   Receipts              1,500.00
12/ 1 3591   Calabrisi Restauran New ad        Receipts                632.12
12/20 3495   Calabrisi Restauran Redesign Ad   Receipts                400.00
                                                                   ----------
             Total Calabrisi Restaurant                              2,532.12


10/21 3457   Food Processing Mag Quiller Articl Receipts               500.00
                                                                   ----------
             Total Food Processing Magazine                            500.00


12/16 3594   Fred Marquhardt & A Consultation  Receipts                750.00
                                                                   ----------
             Total Fred Marquhardt & Assoc.                            750.00


10/ 7 3455   Quiller Manufacturi Annual Report  Receipts             6,325.21
11/30 3482   Quiller Manufacturi New Product Br Receipts             1,000.00
12/ 1 3590   Quiller Manufacturi Retainer       Receipts             5,000.00
                                                                   ----------
             Total Quiller Manufacturing                            12,325.21


12/ 3 3592   Smith Olds & Co.    Annual Report  Receipts             4,325.00
                                                                   ----------
             Total Smith Olds & Co.                                  4,325.00


11/ 2 3460   Stone & Co.         Festival Broch Receipts               762.65
12/10 3593   Stone & Co.         Industrial Hyg Receipts               500.00
                                                                   ----------
             Total Stone & Co.                                       1,262.65
```

Figure 11.7. An itemized list of amounts receivable, subtotaled by customer.

The procedure for creating a report subtotaled by customer is identical, except that on the Create Transaction Report screen, the entry for Subtotal by: is 11 (payee). If you use classes to identify customers, you can subtotal by 10 (class) instead. This has the advantage of eliminating the risk of erratic entries on the payee line of your transactions. Each customer's invoices are listed in chronological order. Again, you can list only overdue invoices by setting the end of the date range on the last day for which bills are now due. The result is shown in Figure 11.7.

REPORTING BY BALANCE FORWARD

When you use the balance forward method of tracking accounts receivable, you are not concerned with individual invoices, only with the balance each customer owes. If you use this method, it is recommended that you use classes to identify customers. You could subtotal by payee, but you run the risk of inconsistent entries.

The report suggested in the Quicken manual is a custom Summary Report like the one shown in Figure 11.8. The right column of the report shows each customer's outstanding balance and, at the bottom, the total amount you are owed. The monthly figures really don't mean much, since they reflect only the difference between how much each customer paid and how much he was billed. (Suppose, for example, that in June a customer pays his May bill of $500 and you issue a new bill for $600. The June subtotal will be $100.) You can easily eliminate the extraneous monthly figures by electing not to subtotal by columns.

SUMMARY REPORT BY MONTH
10/ 1/89 Through 12/31/89

AR Page 1
7/30/89

Class Description	10/89	11/89	12/89	OVERALL TOTAL
Advent	0.00	0.00	0.00	0.00
Arizona	0.00	2,345.00	0.00	2,345.00
Calabrisi	0.00	1,500.00	1,032.12	2,532.12
Food	500.00	0.00	-500.00	0.00
James	1,322.31	0.00	-1,322.31	0.00
Marquhardt	0.00	0.00	750.00	750.00
Quiller	6,325.21	1,000.00	-2,825.21	4,500.00
Smith	0.00	0.00	4,325.00	4,325.00
Stone	0.00	762.65	500.00	1,262.65
Willer	0.00	895.23	0.00	895.23
OVERALL TOTAL	8,147.52	6,502.88	1,959.60	16,610.00

Figure 11.8. A custom Summary Report showing receivables by customer (designated by class).

This report, in fact, is identical to A/R by Customer except that it is not filtered to exclude cleared items and that it is subtotaled by class instead of payee. (The second difference is minor, since classes here are merely another means of identifying payees.) In any case, the report is easy to create. Your accounts receivable Other Asset account should be the current account.

To create the report, select 4. Summary from the Reports Menu. When the Create Summary screen appears, select 2 (class) for row headings. For column headings, enter 5 (month) to create the report shown in Figure 11.8 or 1 (don't subtotal) to eliminate the monthly totals. On the bottom line of the screen, restrict the report to the C(urrent) account, then press Ctrl-Enter to create the report.

You can also report of balances by customer with a detailed Account Balances Report. If you want, you can show each customer's balance at the end of each month. (See Figure 11.9). To create this report, select 6. Account Balances from the Reports Menu. On the next screen, set Use Current/All/Selected accounts to S(elected). If you want monthly balances also set Report at intervals to 5 (month).

ACCOUNT BALANCES REPORT BY MONTH
As of 12/31/89

AR Page 1
7/30/89

Account	10/ 1/89 Balance	10/31/89 Balance	11/30/89 Balance
ASSETS			
Other Assets			
AR			
Advent	0.00	0.00	0.00
Arizona	0.00	0.00	2,345.00
Calabrisi	0.00	0.00	1,500.00
Food	0.00	500.00	500.00
James	1,322.31	1,322.31	1,322.31
Marquhardt	0.00	0.00	0.00
Quiller	0.00	6,325.21	7,325.21
Smith	0.00	0.00	0.00
Stone	0.00	0.00	762.65
Willer	0.00	0.00	895.23
TOTAL AR	1,322.31	8,147.52	14,650.40
Total Other Assets	1,322.31	8,147.52	14,650.40
TOTAL ASSETS	1,322.31	8,147.52	14,650.40
LIABILITIES	0.00	0.00	0.00
OVERALL TOTAL	1,322.31	8,147.52	14,650.40

Figure 11.9. An account balance report showing each customer's balance by month.

When you press Ctrl-Enter to complete the screen, the Select Accounts window appears. Press F9 until no accounts are included, then highlight receivables and press the space bar twice. The entry in the right column should be Detail, and the rest of the column should be blank. Finally, press Enter to create the report.

Even though you are not concerned with individual invoices if you use the balance forward method, you are still concerned with overdue bills. A detailed monthly Account Balances Report is quite useful for this purpose.

Customer Billing and Overdue Bills

Many businesses—including professionals like attorneys, psychologists, and consultants—present their customers or clients with monthly itemized statements. A typical example is similar to a credit card bill, with an opening balance, transactions during the month, and a closing balance. You can, of course, keep this information on paper and enter only monthly totals in Quicken. However, if you record transactions as you go along, Quicken can help with your billing. You can also check your reports to identify unpaid bills.

Quicken makes no special provision for statement reports, but you can get the information you need by creating two reports: (1) A detailed monthly Account Balances Report and (2) A Transaction Report for the month, subtotaled by customer (class). A comparison of the two will quickly turn up any customers who haven't made payments during the current month. (If you just want to see who hasn't paid, you can filter the Transaction Report to restrict it to payments.)

The detailed monthly Account Balances Report is described in the last section and shown in Figure 11.9. Figure 11.10 shows a Transaction Report for a month, subtotaled by customer. Before creating the Transaction Report, make sure your accounts receivable Other Asset account is the current account, then select 3. Transaction from the Reports Menu. On the Create Transaction Report screen, set the date range to cover the statement period (e.g., 10/1/89 to 10/31/89). Subtotal by 10 (class), and restrict the report to the C(urrent) account. Press Ctrl-Enter to create the report.

```
                              December
                      12/ 1/89 Through 12/31/89
AR                                                                  Page 1
7/30/89

 Date   Num         Payee              Memo          Category      Clr Amount
----- ------ ------------------ ------------- ------------------ - ---------


12/ 1 3591   Calabrisi Restauran New ad        Receipts/Calabrisi       632.12
12/16 3471   Calabrisi Restauran               Receipts/Quiller   * -1,500.00
12/20 3495   Calabrisi Restauran Redesign Ad   Receipts/Calabrisi       400.00
                                                                    ---------
             Total Calabrisi Restaurant                                -467.88


12/27 3457   Food Processing Mag               [Checking]/Food    *    -500.00
                                                                    ---------
             Total Food Processing Magazine                            -500.00


12/16 3594   Fred Marquhardt & A Consultation  Receipts/Marquhard       750.00
                                                                    ---------
             Total Fred Marquhardt & Assoc.                             750.00


12/ 1 3590   Quiller Manufacturi Retainer      Receipts/Quiller       5,000.00
12/14 3455   Quiller Manufacturi               [Checking]/Quiller * -6,325.21
                                                                    ---------
             Total Quiller Manufacturing                             -1,325.21


12/ 3 3592   Smith Olds & Co.    Annual Report Receipts/Smith         4,325.00
                                                                    ---------
             Total Smith Olds & Co.                                  4,325.00


12/10 3593   Stone & Co.         Industrial Hyg Receipts/Stone          500.00
                                                                    ---------
             Total Stone & Co.                                          500.00


12/11 3452   Susan James Design                [Checking]/James   * -1,322.31
                                                                    ---------
             Total Susan James Design                                -1,322.31
                                                                    ---------
             OVERALL TOTAL                                            1,959.60
                                                                    =========
```

Figure 11.10. A Transaction Report showing customer activity for the month.

If you just want to report payments to identify overdue bills, your can filter the report by pressing F9 when the Create Transaction Report screen is displayed. Set the Payments/Deposits/Unprinted checks entry to P(ayment), then press Ctrl-Enter twice to create the report.

There is no way to print a statement with a beginning balance, transactions during the period, and ending balance directly with Quicken. However, you can print the Transaction Report to disk and complete your statements with your word processor or Lotus 1-2-3. To do this, display your Transaction Report on the screen, then press F8 to print. When the Print Report Screen appears, select 4. Disk (ASCII file) to create a word processor file or 5. Disk (1-2-3 file) to create a Lotus file.

CONCLUSION

This chapter covered the basic steps for recording and reporting accounts payable and accounts receivable. Particularly in the case of reports, you may want to adapt the methods suggested here to your own needs. Whatever method you use, it is a good idea to experiment with reports before you commit to a method of recording accounts payable and accounts receivable to make sure it works for you. Above all, be consistent.

Quicken can also help you record payroll, job cost, and cost of goods sold. This is covered in the next chapter.

12

More Business Uses

Different types of businesses have different accounting needs. Some have payrolls; others need to keep track of income and expenses by job or project; some have to manage inventory. This chapter explains how to adapt Quicken for these purposes. Many businesses may have other specialized needs. Once you understand the examples here and in the preceding chapters, you should be able to adapt Quicken to almost any small business accounting need.

PAYROLL

Managing payroll is one of the most complex bookkeeping tasks a small business faces. A single payroll check involves at least five transactions: gross pay, federal withholding, Social Security tax (FICA), the employer's FICA contribution, and state withholding. It may also include deductions for medical insurance or other company sponsored programs, as well as withholding for other types of taxes. Your reporting system must provide subtotals for each employee and, in some cases, by tax reporting period.

Quicken cannot calculate wages for hourly employees or deductions for taxes and other items (although the pop-up calculator can make this task much easier). However, you can set up a transaction group to streamline recording entries and print paychecks on Quicken checks. A fairly simple Summary Report will provide most of the information you need for tax reporting.

A paycheck is recorded as a split transaction. The employer's primary expense is gross pay—the amount of the check before deductions. The employer also incurs an expense for the business's FICA contribution. These are assigned to Expense categories. Taxes and other amounts withheld are treated as transfers to Other Liability accounts, because the employer must pay these amounts on the employee's behalf.

In addition to a business checking account, you will need a Payroll Expense category with at least two subcategories—Gross for gross pay and FICA for the company's FICA contribution. You can add subcategories for Regular pay and OT (overtime). You may also want subcategories for other company-paid benefits, such as Medical. Here is a sampling of Other Liability accounts you will need:

Payroll-FWH	Federal income tax withheld
Payroll-FICA	Social Security tax withheld
Payroll-SWH	State income tax withheld

You may also need Other Liability accounts for local taxes, company-sponsored programs, and any other deductions withheld from your employees' checks.

Setting Up Payroll

Once you have set up categories and the Other Liability accounts, you are ready to produce your first payroll. Figure 12.1 shows a typical payroll check, recorded as a split transaction. Notice that gross pay and the company's FICA contribution are positive amounts assigned to Expense categories. Federal, state, and FICA withholding are negative amounts assigned to Other Liability accounts. (The [Payroll-FICA] entry reflects both withholding and the employer's contribution. You can enter these items separately if you prefer.)

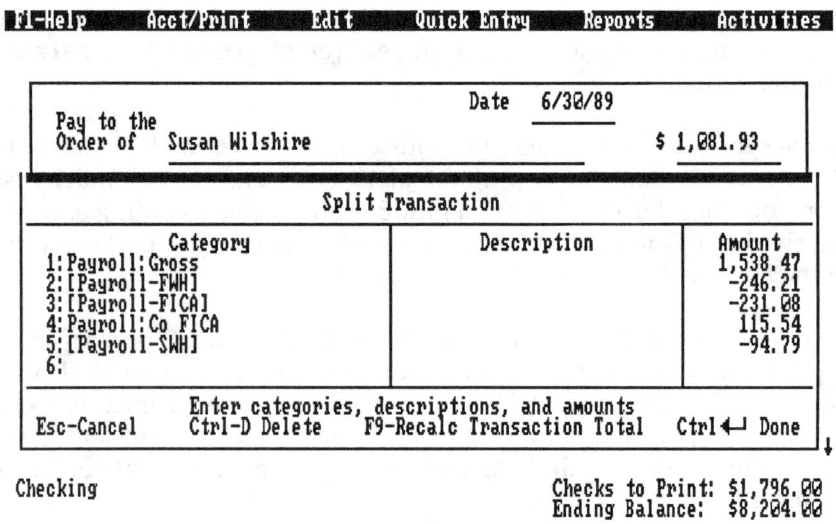

Figure 12.1. The Split Transaction window for a typical payroll check.

The first time you do a payroll with Quicken, you can set up a transaction group, so that you have to enter only dates and amounts in the future. The categories in the split should be the same for all employees. When you are setting up your system, your work will go faster if you memorize a template for the items in the Split Transaction window before starting to write checks.

To set up your payroll transaction group, go to the Write/Print Checks screen for your business checking account (or the Register, if you write paychecks by hand). Then follow these steps:

1. Press End to go to the blank transaction at the end of the unprinted checks list (or Register), then press Ctrl-s to split the transaction.

2. Enter the Expense categories and Other Liability transfer accounts in the category column of the Split Transaction window, but do not enter amounts. Press Ctrl-Enter to close the window, then Ctrl-m to memorize the template.

3. Enter the first employee's name in the payee blank. Also enter any amounts that are constant for all pay periods, including amounts in the Split Transaction window. (For salaried employees the entire transaction may be the same every pay period.) Press Ctrl-m to memorize the transaction. Complete the first paycheck as usual and record it.

4. For the next employee, press Ctrl-t to call up the Memorized Transactions List and select the template. (It's the one with a blank in the description column.) Repeat the procedure until you have finished the payroll.

5. Press F4 to call up the Quick Entry Menu, then select 6. Set Up Transaction Group. Select the first <unused> group, name the group Payroll, set the Frequency for your pay period interval, enter the date for your next payroll, and record the transaction group.

Now you can do your payroll by pressing F4 to call up the Quick Entry Menu, selecting 5. Execute Transaction Group and filling in the blank amounts for each employee on the Split Transaction window.

Paying Payroll Taxes and Other Deductions

When you withhold pay for taxes or any other purpose, the amount is assigned to an Other Liability account, because the company must make a payment on the employee's behalf. When you make the payment, assign the transaction to the relevant Other Liability account. When you submit withheld taxes to the IRS, for example, you would assign the check to [Payroll-FWH] on the category line. There is no need for any further classification.

Payroll Reports

A simple custom Summary Report will provide most of the information you need for filing your own income taxes and filling out the various forms required for submitting withheld taxes. This is a Summary Report by Payee with the date range set for the reporting period.

Before creating this report, first make sure that the Bank account on which you write payroll checks is the current account, then select 4. Summary from the Reports Menu. When the Create Summary Report screen appears, enter the report period (e.g., 1/1/89 to 3/30/89 for the first quarter) for the blanks labeled: Restrict to transactions from/to. Enter 1 (category) for Row headings and 11 (payee) for Column headings. On the last line of the screen, enter C(urrent) for selected accounts. Now press F9 to filter the report and enter Payroll.. in the Category matches blank.

NOTE: The two periods in the Payroll.. filter set up a wildcard search. The report will include all transactions assigned to Payroll and its subcategories and all transfers to accounts that begin with Payroll, including Payroll-FWH, Payroll-SWH, and so on.

Payroll
1/ 1/89 Through 12/31/89

PAYROLL-Checking Page 1
7/30/89

Category Description	Loren Thomas	Susan Wilshire	OVERALL TOTAL
INCOME/EXPENSE			
EXPENSES			
Payroll:			
Co FICA	1,982.50	3,004.04	4,986.54
Gross	26,399.74	40,000.00	66,399.74
Total Payroll	28,382.24	43,004.04	71,386.28
TOTAL EXPENSES	28,382.24	43,004.04	71,386.28
TOTAL INCOME/EXPENSE	-28,382.24	-43,004.04	-71,386.28
TRANSFERS			
FROM Payroll-FICA	3,965.26	6,008.08	9,973.34
FROM Payroll-FWH	4,224.74	6,401.46	10,626.20
FROM Payroll-SWH	1,626.82	2,464.54	4,091.36
TOTAL TRANSFERS	9,816.82	14,874.08	24,690.90
OVERALL TOTAL	-18,565.42	-28,129.96	-46,695.38

Figure 12.2. An annual Summary Report showing each employee's gross pay, federal withholding, Social Security withholding, and state withholding.

This report provides most of the information you need to pay your payroll taxes, to fill out employees' W-2 forms, and to complete other tax forms. Figure 12.2 shows an annual Summary Report for two employees. Under Payroll:Gross, you can see each employee's total earnings. If you have employees who earn more than the Social Security cap, you can monitor this figure during the year with year-to-date reports to determine when to stop withholding FICA. Under Transfers, FROM Payroll-FICA shows Social Security tax withheld for each employee; FROM Payroll-FWH shows federal income tax withheld; and FROM Payroll-SWH shows state income tax withheld. You can also produce quarterly or monthly reports by setting appropriate date ranges.

Some tax forms require you to report payroll data by pay period. To obtain this information, you can create a similar Summary Report subtotaled by your pay interval rather than payee. For example, the setting for Column headings might be 3. Two Weeks or 4. Half Month.

Occasionally, you may have to make a manual calculation or design a different custom report, but this system will provide most of the payroll information you need for filing taxes.

Job Reports

Many businesses need to keep track of income and expenses by job, customer or client, department, property, or another classification. In Quicken, classes are the key to keeping this kind of record. Classes allow you to produce reports that break down income and expenses in this fashion and still produce general reports, subtotaled by category, that do not include unnecessary detail.

To create a job report, set up Income and Expense categories as usual, then set up classes for each job or other classification for which you want detailed records. A contractor, for example, might assign numbers to jobs. A class might be named /Job 321 with a description such as Jones kitchen. Or an attorney might set up a class named /Jones with a description such as Jones v. Wade.

When you incur an expense or receive a payment, simply assign the transaction to a category and class. If the contractor pays a plumber $300 to work on the Jones kitchen project, for example, he or she might assign the expense to Plumbing/Job 321 on the category line of the transaction. If the plumber submits a bill for $650 for work on the Jones kitchen and the Smith bathroom, the contractor can split the transaction with, say, $300 assigned to Plumbing/Job 321 and $350 assigned to Plumbing/Job 325.

Once you have assigned income and expenses to categories and classes, you can produce a variety of reports detailing that information by job or class. Here are some examples:

- The predefined Business Job/Project Report (option 5 on the Business Reports submenu) details income and expenses by class.

- A custom Summary Report can summarize expenses by class by month or other time period.

- A custom Transaction Report can list individual transactions subtotaled by class.

- You can filter any of the above to produce a report on an individual job or class.

The predefined Job/Project Report (Figure 12.3) is simply a custom Summary Report. Row headings are set to 1 (category); column headings are set to 10 (class); and A(ll) accounts are selected. On the Report Options screen, Report organization is set to 1 (income and expense) and all transfers are included.

JOB/PROJECT REPORT

1/ 1/89 Through 12/31/89

JOBS-Checking
7/30/89

Category Description	Jones Kitchen	Smith Bath	OVERALL TOTAL
INCOME/EXPENSE			
EXPENSES			
Labor	-765.32	-326.65	-1,091.97
Materials	-1,326.23	-632.12	-1,958.35
Painting	-236.00	-432.00	-668.00
Plumbing	-300.00	-350.00	-650.00
TOTAL EXPENSES	-2,627.55	-1,740.77	-4,368.32
TOTAL INCOME/EXPENSE	2,627.55	1,740.77	4,368.32

JOBS-Checking (Filtered)
Esc-Create report F1-Help F8-Print

Figure 12.3.The predefined Job/Project Report.

To create this report, select 5. Job/Project Report from the Business Report submenu. When the Job/Project Report window appears, enter a title and date range if you want, then press Ctrl-Enter to create the report.

You may need to customize this report if your accounts include transactions, categories, and/or classes, you do not want to include for example:

- If your account includes transactions that do not relate to the projects being reported on, you can filter the report to select categories and/or classes. You can also filter by classes to limit the report to a particular project or group of projects.

- To eliminate transactions not assigned to classes, enter two periods (..) in the category matches blank on the Filter Report Transactions screen.

- If all transactions are through a single Bank account or an accounts payable Other Asset account, restrict the report to that account.

- If you sometimes pay cash and sometimes run bills through payable, select your Bank account and the A/P account and exclude transfers from the report. (Otherwise a bill will appear both as an expense when you enter it in A/P and again as a transfer when you pay the bill.)

To customize the report, when the Job/Project Report window appears, press F8 to call up the Create Summary Report screen. You can change the basic report settings on this screen. From here, press F9 to filter the report or F8 to reset report options.

Other Reports

You can marshal Quicken's custom reporting features to produce nearly any type of job report you need. Here are some examples:

- To summarize job expenses by month, create a Custom Summary Report with 2 (class) for row headings and 5 (month) for column headings, then filter the report to include only Payments. Base the report on your checking Bank account if you pay cash or your accounts payable Other Liability account if invoices go through A/P. If you sometimes pay cash and sometimes accept credit, select both accounts—but exclude all transfers from the report, so checks assigned to A/P are not included.

- To list individual transactions by job or class, create a Custom Transaction Report subtotaled by 10 (class). Include all accounts in which relevant transactions occur. Again, you may want to exclude transfers to avoid reporting transactions both in A/P when you receive them and in checking when you pay.

- To create any report for an individual job or class, filter the report for class matches or to select classes.

These are only a few of the job or project reports you can create. Experiment until you get exactly the results you want.

NOTE: If some transactions in the accounts reported on are not assigned to classes, you can restrict the report to those that are by entering two periods (..) in the class matches blank on the Filter Report Transactions screen.

INVENTORY

Although Quicken is not designed as an inventory management program, it can handle inventory transactions for many small businesses. Most small businesses take physical inventory, often only once a year. Quicken can handle these transactions quite easily. If you sell relatively few large items, you can use Quicken for perpetual inventory, keeping track of each inventory purchase and sale.

Regardless of which method you use, the basic formula for calculating cost of goods sold is:

  Beginning inventory
+ Purchases (less returns and
    items withdrawn for personal use)
+ Shipping

  Inventory to be accounted for
- Ending inventory

  Cost of goods sold

Remember that the IRS requires businesses for which inventory is a significant factor to account for inventory and sales by the accrual method. This means that inventory purchases are recorded when goods are received, even if you pay sometime later. Businesses that buy items for each particular job can treat such purchases as simple expenses.

Physical Inventory

If you take physical inventory, recording inventory transactions in Quicken is fairly simple. Inventory purchases are treated as transfers to an Inventory Other Asset account from your checking account or your accounts payable Other Liability account. Then when you take inventory, you will enter a balance adjustment in your Inventory account, assigned to an Expense category for cost of goods sold.

This system does not keep track of items actually in inventory, and you will not be able to determine actual net sales accurately until you take inventory. Nevertheless, it fits the inventory system used by many small businesses.

Before beginning, in addition to your checking Bank account, you should have set up an accounts payable Other Liability account (unless you always pay upon receipt, in which your can record inventory purchases in your checking account); an Inventory Other Asset account; and Expense categories for COG (for cost of goods) with subcategories for Goods and Shipping.

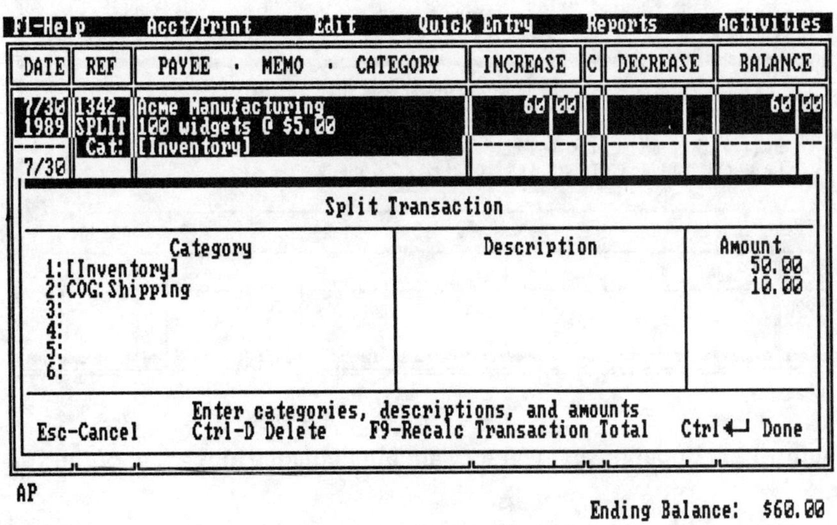

Figure 12.4. Recording an inventory purchase as a split transaction.

Suppose, for example, you receive a shipment of 100 widgets at $5 apiece, plus $10 shipping. Record the shipment as a split transaction in accounts payable, with $50 assigned to [Inventory] and $10 assigned to COG:Shipping, as shown in Figure 12.4. This increases the balances by $50 in the Inventory account by $10 in COG:Shipping.

When you take inventory, you can record actual inventory as a balance adjustment in the Inventory account. Suppose you have $10,000 in inventory at the beginning of the year, and purchase $20,000 in inventory during the year. The balance in the Inventory account is $30,000. When you take physical inventory on December 31 (or at the end of an interim accounting period), you find that actual inventory is $12,000.

To record this transaction, go to the Register of your Inventory Other Asset account and press F6 to pull down the Activities menu, then select 2. Update Balance. On the Update account Balance Screen, update the balance to $12,000 and assign the transaction to COG:Goods (Figure 12.5).

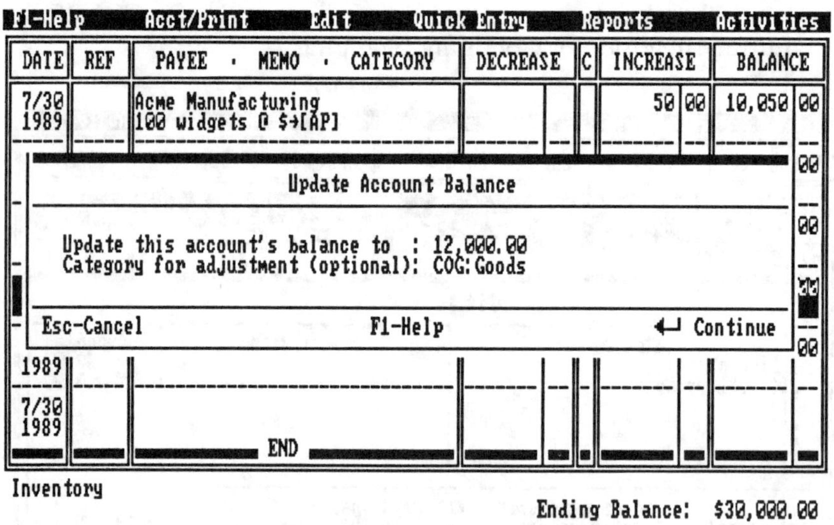

Figure 12.5. Updating an Inventory account balance at the end of the year.

Meanwhile, you may have paid $2,500 for shipping. The calculation for cost of goods sold looks like this:

$10,000	Beginning inventory
+20,000	Purchases
+ 2,500	Shipping
32,500	Inventory to be accounted for
- 12,000	Ending inventory
$20,500	Cost of goods sold

A Summary Report will show $18,000 for COG:Goods, $2,500 for COG:Shipping, and $20,000 in transfers to Inventory. If you need a report of inventory balances, you can get the figures you need with an account Balances Report for Inventory on January 1 and December 31.

Perpetual Inventory

Quicken is not suitable for keeping perpetual inventory for a business, such as a hardware store or a book store, that keeps large stocks of hundreds of items. But if your business makes relatively few, relatively large sales, and has a fairly limited number of items in inventory, you can keep perpetual inventory by a method similar to the one described for securities investments in Chapter 10.

In this case, purchase of inventory is treated as a transfer from accounts payable (or a Bank account) to inventory. When you sell the item, the transaction is recorded as a split transaction with the total amount assigned to an Income category, such as Sales; a reduction in Inventory; and an offsetting increase in cost of goods sold.

To use this system you will need an accounts payable Other Liability account; an Inventory Other Asset account; an Expense category called COG with subcategories for Goods and Shipping; a Sales Income account; perhaps an Other Liability account for Sales Tax (a liability to be paid later); and a class for each type of item you keep in inventory.

Suppose for example, you buy a refrigerator for $500 plus $45 shipping. You can record the purchase as a split transaction in accounts payable as shown in Figure 12.6, using a class to designate the item being added to inventory. Accounts payable and Inventory each increase by $500, and COG:Shipping increases by $45.

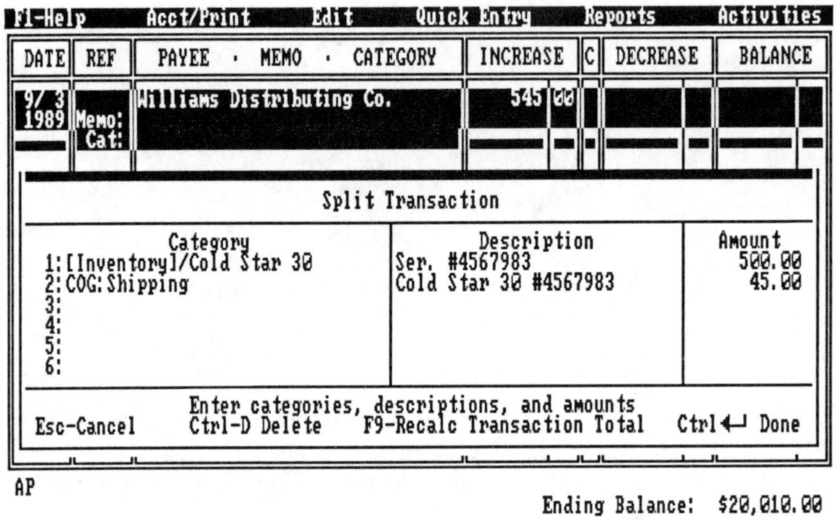

Figure 12.6. Recording an inventory purchase in accounts payable.

Now you sell the refrigerator for $750, plus $37.50 sales tax and record the sale as a split transaction in a Cash account, as shown in Figure 12.7. (Record the deposit as a transfer from Cash to Checking.) Here, $750 is assigned to the Sales Income account and $37.50 to the Sales Tax Other Liability account. The $500 decrease in Inventory is offset by the increase in the COG Expense account. The Inventory transaction is recorded as a positive amount, because an increase in one asset (the Cash account) decreases another (Inventory). The COG expense is negative because it is, in effect, a negative deposit in the Cash account.

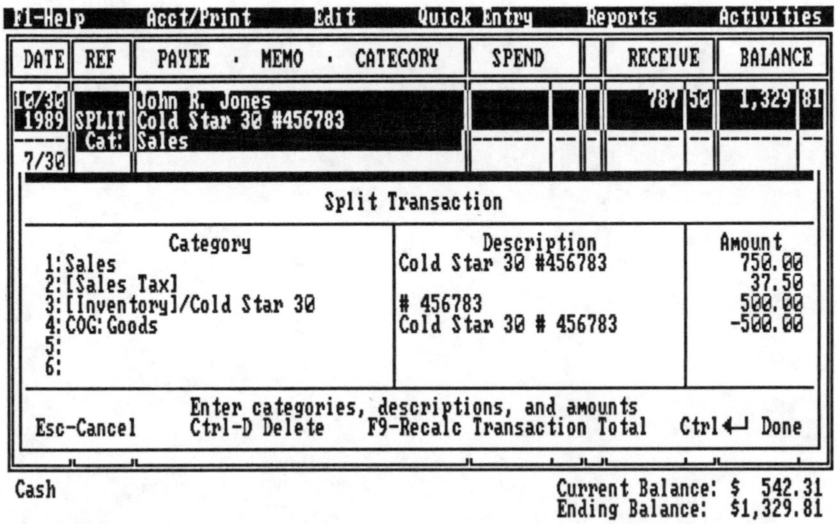

Figure 12.7. Recording a sale with the perpetual inventory system.

After completing the transaction in the Cash account, go to the Inventory account and place asterisks in the C(leared) column of both the purchase and sale transactions for the refrigerator.

At the end of the year (or other accounting period) a Summary Report will show expenses for COG:Goods and COG:Shipping. The total for COG is the cost of goods sold for the year. The report will also show inventory purchases as transfers to Inventory, a figure you will need for your tax return. The Inventory balance at the end of the year should equal ending inventory; an Account Balances Report for January 1 provides beginning inventory.

To get a report of inventory in stock, create a custom Transaction Report on your Inventory account, subtotaled by class and filtered to exclude cleared transactions.

Conclusion

The last two chapters provided only a sampling of possible business applications for Quicken. As these examples show, the program is very flexible. Once you understand how categories, classes, and reports work, you should be able to adapt the examples here to your own business.

13

HOUSEKEEPING

The Change Setting Menu is Quicken's housekeeping department. It provides the tools for setting up and managing account groups, setting up Quicken for your monitor and printer, establishing passwords, and customizing certain Quicken features, such as whether confirmation is required when you record a transaction.

In most cases, Quicken will work properly with your monitor without adjustment. Quicken will also run most parallel printers in their normal mode, even if you do not select a printer setting. However, you will need to set up Quicken for your printer if you want to use special features, such as compressed type or letter-quality mode, or if you have a serial printer or laser printer.

The remaining settings govern details of the way Quicken operates. You should probably use the program for a while before changing these settings.

To call up the Change Settings Menu, select 5. Change Settings from the Main Menu. The options on the Change Settings Menu (Figure 13.1) are largely self-explanatory. Account Group Activities allows you to set up, select, back up, and copy account groups. The next two selections govern your monitor display. Printer Settings allows you to set up as many as three printers—or to set up one printer three different ways. The Password option allows you to designate a password to control access to your records or to prevent unauthorized changes in records for "closed" accounting periods. Finally, Other Settings controls the way Quicken performs certain tasks.

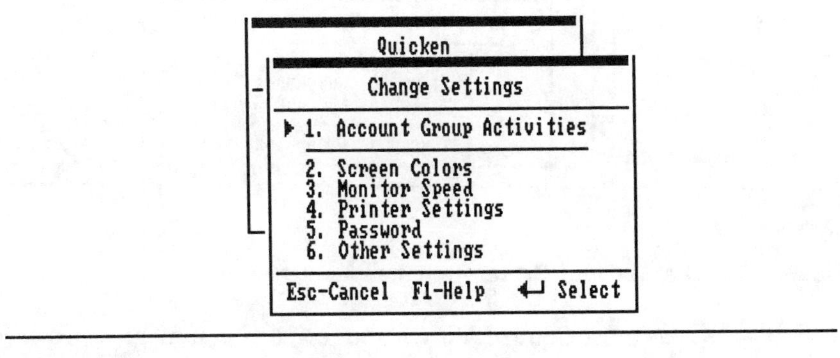

Figure 13.1. The Change Settings Menu.

Account Group Activities

As you learned in Chapter 2, your Quicken accounts form an account group. When you begin using Quicken, the program automatically sets up an account group called QDATA. Many users do not need more than one group. However, you might need two—or several—if you want to keep your personal finances separate from your business records or keep books for more than one company.

Even if you use only one account group, Account Group Activities provides several useful tools for managing it. It's always a good idea, for example, to back up your data in case disaster befalls your data disk or your computer. In addition, at the end of the year, you will probably want to "shrink" your account group to start the new year. This option allows you to bring forward only uncleared transactions into the new year.

To call up the Account Group Activities Menu, select 5. Change Settings from the Main Menu, then 1. Account Group Activities from the Change Settings Menu. The Account Group Activities Menu (Figure 13.2) offers five options, described below.

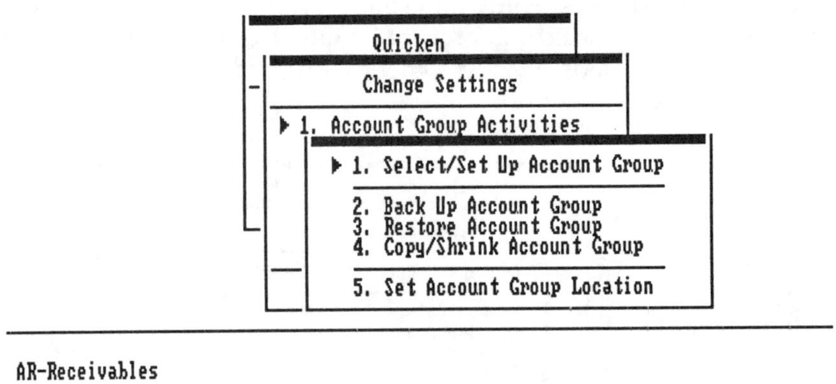

Figure 13.2. The Account Group Activities Menu.

1. **Select/Set Up Account Group.** Allows you to set up a new group, select a group to use (if you have more than one), or rename or delete a group.

2. **Back Up Account Group.** Creates a backup copy of your account group on a floppy disk.

3. **Restore Account Group.** Restores an account group from a backup copy.

4. **Copy/Shrink Account Group.** Copies an account group. You can also "shrink" a group, carrying forward only the transactions you choose.

5. **Set Account Group Location.** Allows you to set up or use an account group in a different directory or drive.

The following sections discuss these options in sequence. Finally, there is one other procedure that fits into this general category but does not appear on the Account Group Activities: copying from one account to another.

SELECT/SET UP ACCOUNT GROUP

When you select the first option on the Account Group Activities Menu, the Select/Set Up Account Group screen (Figure 13.3) appears. This screen allows you to set up a new account group, select a group to use (if you have several), rename a group, or change directories.

```
                    Select/Set Up Account Group
                    
                     Current Directory: B:
                           (58K free)
                                       Next Check       Next
   Account Group       Date     Size    To Print      Group Due

   <Setup New Grp>
 ▶ AR                7/30/89      6K  Tue   8/ 1/89
   BALANCE           7/ 1/89      3K
   BUDGET            6/30/89      2K
   FRED              7/30/89      1K
   INVENTOR          7/30/89      4K
   INVEST            7/30/89      3K
   JOBS              7/30/89      1K

            Ctrl-D Delete   Ctrl-E Edit   ↑,↓ Select
 Esc-Cancel      F1-Help      F9-Set Directory            ↵ Use
```

AR-Receivables

Figure 13.3. The Select/Set Up Account Group screen.

To begin any of these procedures, choose 1. Select/Set Up Account Group from the Change Settings Menu. When the screen appears, highlight an account group to work with or <Setup New Grp> to create a new group.

Once the Select/Set Up screen is displayed, you can change to a different drive or directory before proceeding with any of the following activities. To change directories, press F9 (Set Directory). A window will appear asking you to Enter new pathname: Type the path for the drive or directory you want to use, using DOS conventions, and press Enter. The Select/Set Up screen will reappear, this time listing the account groups in the directory or drive you specified. From there, all procedures are the same as described below.

SETTING UP A NEW ACCOUNT GROUP

Setting up a new account group is similar to setting up a new account. To begin, call up the Select/Set Up screen and press Home to highlight <Setup New Grp>. When you press Enter, the Create an Account Group window (Figure 13.4) appears.

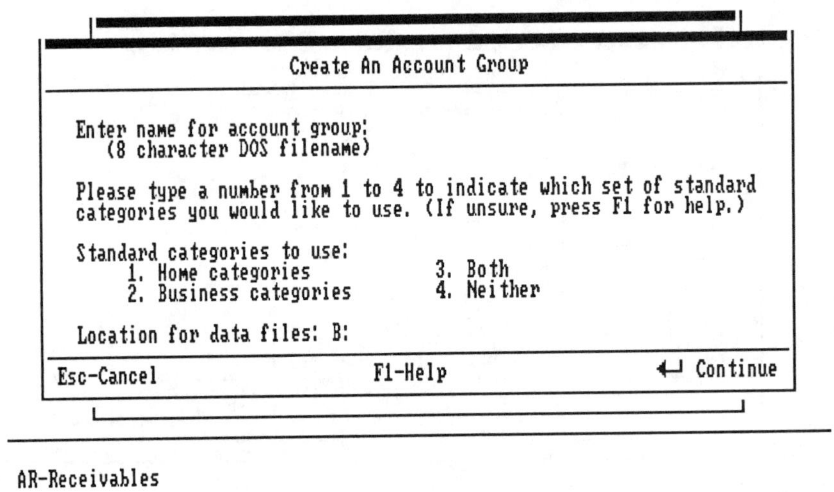

Figure 13.4. The Create An Account Group window.

In this window, the prompt Enter name for account group allows you to give the new group any DOS file name of up to eight characters. (Press F1 for help on the rules.) Do not use an extension (e.g. filename.ext); Quicken provides its own.

In the blank labeled Standard categories to use you can choose to use Quicken's predefined Home Categories, Business Categories, both, or neither. (See Chapter 3 for more information on predefined Categories.)

The Location for data files entry is usually C:\QUICKEN3\ for hard disks or B: for floppy drives. Just press Enter to store your new group along with your existing ones. If you prefer, you can type a new path, using DOS conventions (press F1 for instructions).

When you press Enter to complete the window, the Select/Set Up screen reappears, with your new account group listed in alphabetical order. You can now select it—or any other group—to work with, as explained in the next section.

Selecting an Account Group

Selecting an account group to work with is almost the same as selecting an account on the Select Accounts screen. You simply call up the Select/Set Up screen, highlight the account group you want to use, then press Enter. The Select Accounts screen for the group you have selected will appear.

Renaming an Account Group

You can rename (edit) or delete any account displayed on the Select/Set Up screen. Again, the procedure is almost the same as working with accounts on the Select Accounts screen.

To rename (edit) the highlighted account group, highlight the group you want to rename, then press Ctrl-e (for edit). A window appears asking you to Enter New Account Group Name. Type a new DOS file name of up to eight characters and press Enter.

When you have finished, the Select/Set Up Account Group window reappears, with the new name of the account group listed in its proper alphabetical spot. You have merely renamed the group; nothing else has changed.

DELETING AN ACCOUNT GROUP

Deleting an account group is risky. You will permanently erase all information—including transactions, categories, and classes—pertaining to the group. Nevertheless, you may have set up a group to experiment with when you began using Quicken that you no longer want. Or if you have a hard disk, you may occasionally want to back up old records on floppy disks and clear them from your hard disk.

To delete an account group, highlight it on the Select/Set Up screen, then press Ctrl-d. A window appears with this warning:

```
CAUTION! Permanently removing this account group.
```

Type yes to confirm (a " y " is not sufficient), then press Enter. (There is little danger of deleting a group accidentally. If you do anything else at this point, Quicken will cancel the procedure and return your to the Select/Set Up screen.) Quicken will delete the account group. The group, and the information in it, is irretrievable.

BACK UP ACCOUNT GROUP

Backing up your Quicken records on a regular basis can save you from disaster if something goes wrong with your computer or the disk you use to store your main records is damaged. If you have a hard disk, you should back up your records on a floppy disk, in case the entire hard disk should fail. If you have a floppy drive system, use a separate floppy disk for your backup.

Each account group must be backed up separately. It is recommended that you back up *all* groups at least once a month—and more often if you use Quicken frequently. The first time you back up your Quicken records, you will need a blank, formatted data disk for storing your backups. There after, you can update your files on the same disk.

To back up an account group, select 2. Back Up Account Group from the Account Group Activities Menu. A window will appear, directing you where to put your backup disk. This will usually be drive A whether you have a hard disk or a floppy disk system, but you can specify another drive. On the next screen, labeled Select Account Group to Back Up, highlight a group, then press Enter.

In a few seconds, you will see this message:

```
Account Group backed up successfully.
```

Press Enter to return to the Select Account Group screen. At this point you can select another account group to back up, or press Esc to return to the Account Group Activities Menu.

There are also two ways to back up the account group you are currently using without going to the Account Group Activities Menu:

1. From the Write/Print Checks screen or Register, press F2 to pull down the Acct/Print menu, then select 4. Back Up All Accounts. Now you follow the prompts to complete the procedure, which is very similar to the one described here.

2. At the Main Menu, press Ctrl-b (for back up) or Ctrl-e (for back up and exit), then follow the prompts. This is equivalent to the option on the Acct/Print menu.

Restore Account Group

If you use floppy disks, you can simply start using your backup disk if your original disk is damaged. (Back up your backup disk first! The same problem may reoccur.) You will not need to use the Restore Account Group Option.

If your hard disk fails, however, you can use this option to restore your groups after you reinstall the Quicken program on your hard disk.

To restore a backup account group, select 3. Back Up Account Group from the Account Activities Menu. The Select Account Group screen appears. Highlight the group you want to store and press Enter. Follow the prompts to insert your backup disk in the drive indicated (or designate another drive and insert the disk there), then press Enter.

In a few seconds, this message will appear:

```
Account Group restored successfully.
```

When you press Enter, the Select Account Group screen reappears. You can now restore another group or press Esc to return to the Account Activities Menu.

Copy/Shrink Account Group

Quicken allows you to copy all or part of an account group to a new file. Quicken will copy accounts, memorized transactions, transaction groups, categories, and classes. Also included in the new group will be the transactions you specify by date range and/or cleared status). The old account group remains intact.

There are several reasons you might want to do this. At the beginning of a new fiscal year, for example, you will probably want to copy your account group to a new file, so you can leave behind old transactions that have already cleared. You can also make more room on a nearly-full floppy data disk by "shrinking" your account group file. (Be forewarned, however, that your Quicken reports will not be accurate for periods before the "shrinkage." It is best to do this at the end of a fiscal period, such as a quarter. You may want to overlap by several months.) Another reason to copy information is to set up a new account group using established memorized transactions, transaction groups, categories, and classes.

Before you begin, make sure the account group you want to copy or shrink is active. When you select 4. Copy/Shrink Account Group from the Account Group Activities Menu, the Copy Account Group window appears (Figure 13.5). You can copy all, some, or none of the transactions in the original group.

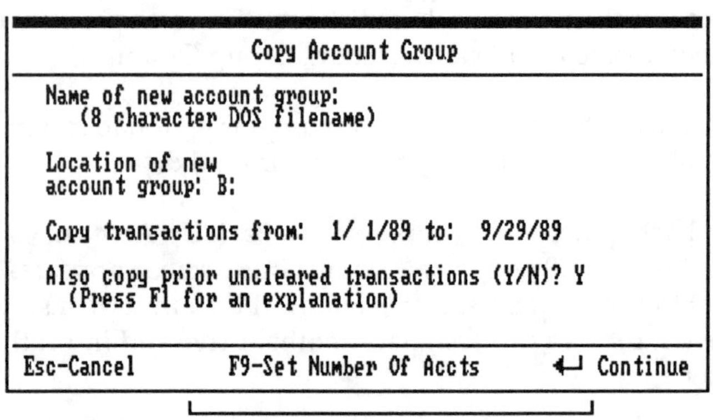

Figure 13.5. The Copy Account Group window.

In the Copy transactions from/to blanks, you can specify a date range. Quicken will copy all of the transactions in this range, regardless of whether they are cleared. You may want to overlap the two groups, so you can check old records while you are using the new one.

On the last line, Also copy prior uncleared transactions, you have the option of copying uncleared transactions recorded before the beginning of the date range you have specified. You should set this to Y(es) if you use the reconciliation feature for Bank accounts or Credit Card accounts or if you use Other Asset accounts and Other Liability accounts for any purpose. If neither applies, the setting should be N(o).

At the bottom of the screen is another option: F9-Set Number of Accts. Normally, an account group can contain up to 64 accounts. To change this limit, press F9 and enter a new number in the window that appears. The maximum is 255.

To copy or shrink the group to a new file, select 4. Copy/Shrink Account Group from the Account Group Activities Menu. When the Copy Account Group window appears, enter a DOS file name of up to eight characters in the first blank, specify a drive or directory for the location of the new group, and set a date range for transactions to be copied. Finally, specify Y(es) or N(o) to indicate whether you want to include previously dated uncleared transactions. (See explanation above.)

When you press Ctrl-Enter to complete the screen, it will take Quicken a few seconds to copy the account group. (If you have a floppy drive system, Quicken will ask: Copy to a different disk? Type 1 for No, 2 for Yes.) When copying is finished, Quicken will tell you,

```
Account Group copied successfully.
```

Press Esc to return to the Account Group Activities Menu.

Set Account Group Location

Most users store all of there Quicken files in once place—typically drive B: for a floppy drive system or C:\QUICKEN3 for a hard disk. If you store Quicken data in more than one directory or drive, the program automatically looks for data in the last one you used. On the Account Group Activities Menu, 5. Account Group Location allows you to tell Quicken to look for a group in another directory or drive. That location will remain active until you change it again.

To switch to a different directory or disk drive, select 5. Set Account Group Location from the Account Group Activities Menu. Enter a new path, such as A: to specify floppy drive A or C:\directory for a hard disk, then press Enter. The Account Group Activities Menu reappears, but Quicken is now directed to the new location. Repeat the process to return to your original data location.

Copying From One Account Group to Another

On rare occasions you may want to copy transactions from one account group to another. While the Export and Import options on the Acct/Print pull-down menu are meant primarily for transferring information to and from other programs, you can also use it to transfer information between account groups. You can also use this method to copy transactions from one account to another within the same group if, for example, you discover that you have just entered 25 transactions in the wrong Account. (Make sure to delete the transactions from the first group; otherwise, they will be recorded twice.)

Before copying transactions, you should make sure that they are compatible with the account group you are copying them to. Copying transactions that are transfers between accounts can be tricky. In a transfer transaction, the corresponding account is enclosed in brackets on the category line (e.g., [Checking]). The brackets do not survive the copying procedure, so the corresponding account looks like a category (e.g., Checking) when you copy the transaction. If the receiving account group includes an appropriate transfer account, you can select it from the Category List. If the transfer account does not exist, however, you will have to assign the transaction to a category, then go back and edit it to assign it to a transfer account.

Different groups may not have the same Category and Class Lists, but that is generally not a problem. If Quicken does not recognize a category or class in the receiving account group, you have the usual option of adding the classification to the list or selecting from the list. The latter option also allows you to set up new categories or classes in the receiving account group.

Before beginning the copying procedure, make sure you are in the account you want to copy transactions from and go to the Register or the Write/Print Checks screen. To execute the transfer, press F2 to pull down the Acct/Print menu and select 5. Export. In the Export Transactions window, enter a file name and a date range for the transfer. (If you have floppy drive system, specify the drive of your data disk in this format: B:filename. If you have a hard disk, Quicken will put the new file at the same location as your Quicken program unless you specify otherwise.) When you complete the Export Transactions window, Quicken creates the file. Note its name.

Now you are ready to import the information from the file just created. To do this, go to the Register or Write/Print Checks screen of the account to receive the data (switch account groups via the Change Settings Menu if necessary), pull down the Acct/Print menu, and select 6. Import. An Import window appears (Figure 13.6). Enter the name of the file you just created. (Include the directory or drive if it is different from the location of your Quicken program.) Leave the next entry set to Y(es) if you want to include transfers, or change it to N(o) if you do not.

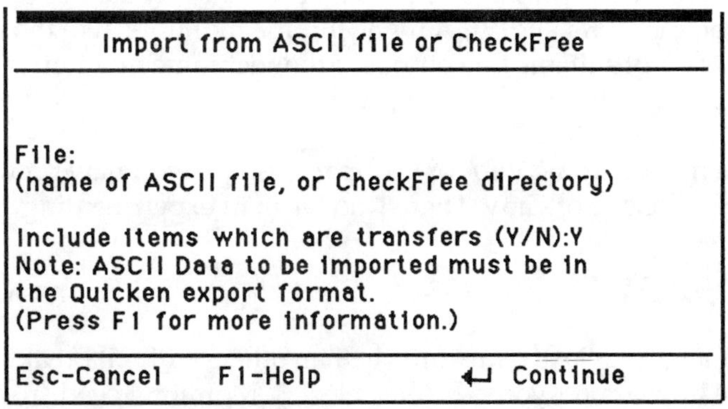

Figure 13.6. The Import file window.

When you complete the Import window, Quicken begins importing the data. If the program encounters a category or class that is not on the lists of the new account group, you will have the usual opportunity to add it to the list or select from the list. When all of the transactions have been imported you will see this message:

```
Successfully imported X item(s).
```

When you press Enter to continue, the Register of the receiving account appears.

Screen Colors

Quicken automatically adapts to most monitors, but you can adapt it to your personal preference or make a correction if necessary. To change the colors or shades of your monitor display, select 2. Screen colors from the Change Settings Menu. A window labeled Change Color Scheme appears. This menu offers five options:

1. **Monochrome**.For one-color monitors that cannot display shades of gray, like the TTL monitors that were standard on the original IBM PC.

2. **Navy/Azure.** For color monitors, the choice between Navy/Azure and White/Navy is a matter of personal preference.

3. **White/Navy**. White on navy background.

4. **Red/Gray**. Helpful for color blind users with color monitors.

5. **Shades of Gray.** For monochrome monitors that can display shades of gray, including Compaq monitors and VGA monochrome monitors, like those for the IBM PS/2 series. Not suitable for composite monochrome monitors, which have lower resolution.

Even if you have a monochrome VGA or Compaq monitor, you may prefer the monochrome setting to Shades of Gray. There's no harm in experimenting.

Monitor Speed

Some monitors can change displays more quickly than others without breaking up the image. If "snow" appears on your screen, select 3. Monitor Speed from the Change Settings Menu, then select 1. Slow. The second option, 2. Fast changes the speed back to fast.

Printer Settings

Quicken will run most parallel printers without modification. However, you can set up the program to take advantage of your printer's special features, and in some cases—including all serial printers—printer setup is required.

When you select 4. Printer Settings from the Change Settings Menu, a window allows you to select 1. Check Printer Settings, 2. Report Printer Settings, or 3. Alternate Report Settings. You can set up three different printers or one printer three different ways. You might, for example, set up the Check Printer for letter quality print, the Report Printer for draft, and the Alternate Report Printer for condensed type.

The Printer List

When you select one of the three options on the Printer Settings submenu, the Printer List appears (Figure 13.7). You can use the cursor control keys to explore the list (there are several additional screens of options).

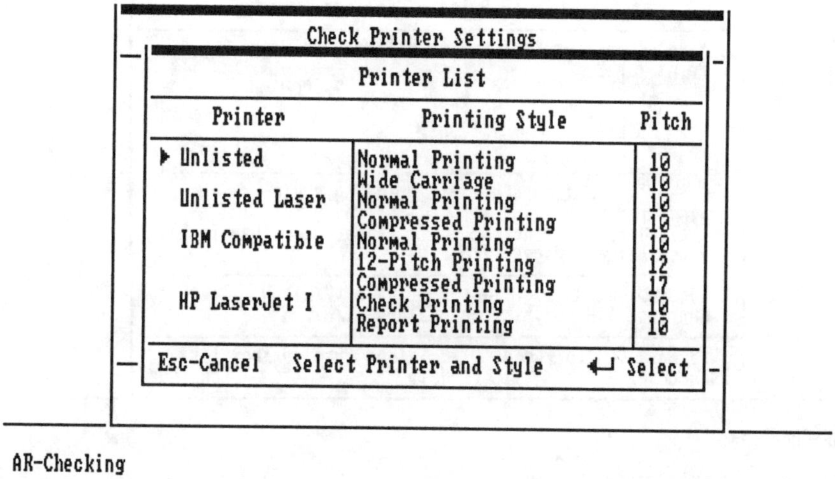

Figure 13.7. The Printer List.

To make a selection, highlight the option and press Enter. The Printer Settings screen appears. In most cases you will not need to change these settings unless you have a serial printer. If you do not want to make changes, press Ctrl-Enter to record your selection and return to the Change Settings Menu. The following section describes the options on the Printer Settings screen.

The Printer Settings Screen

The Printer Settings screen allows you to adapt Quicken to your printer if you have a serial printer or an unlisted printer, or if you want to take advantage of other printer features. You may need to consult your printer manual for the correct settings for your printer.

Figure 13.8 shows the Check Printer Settings screen. The Report Printer Settings and Alternate Report Printer Settings screens are identical except for the heading. (Press F9 to return to the Printer List to make a different selection.) The Printer Settings screen consists of three boxes. The first identifies your printer and the port to which it is connected. The second allows you to tell Quicken how your printer will print reports and checks. The third allows you to choose between page oriented printers (which use sheet paper) others (which use continuous forms) and to indicate whether your printer can recognize IBM graphics characters.

```
                     Check Printer Settings

  Name of printer (optional): Unlisted Printer
  Print to: 2
       1. PRN:          4. LPT3:         7. COM2:
       2. LPT1:         5. AUX:
       3. LPT2:         6. COM1:
  Indent: 0

            Settings for this printing style
  Lines per page: 66              Print pitch: 10
  Characters per line: 80         (characters per inch)
  Pause between pages (Y/N): N

  Page-oriented (e.g. laser) printer (Y/N): N
  Supports IBM graphics characters (Y/N): N

  F8-Edit Control Codes   F9-Select Printer From List
Esc-Cancel              F1-Help                ↵ Continue

AR-Checking
```

Figure 13.8. The Printer Settings screen.

At the bottom of the screen, you will see an option labelel F8-Edit Control Codes. Control codes govern such things as type size and quality (letter quality or draft, for example). You can edit these by pressing F8. Control codes are somewhat technical, but your printer manual should provide the information you need.

If you have a serial printer or enter control codes, you will need to complete an additional window to complete your printer settings.

Basic Printer Settings

The preset printer settings are for parallel printers that are connected to a standard printer port (LPT1:) and use standard 8.5 by 11-inch paper. To change a setting, type a new entry and press Enter. Tab and Shift-Tab move you forward and backward from blank to blank as usual. Press Ctrl-Enter to record your changes when you have finished. Descriptions of each setting follow.

Name of printer: Merely identifies your printer.

Print to: Identifies the port to which your printer is connected. PRN, LPT1:LPT2:, and LPT3: are parallel ports. AUX, COM1:, and COM2: are serial ports. Parallel printers are most commonly connected to LPT1:. Serial printers ar most commonly connected to COM1:. If you are not certain which port your printer is using, you can check your setting by using the Print Screen command after you have saved your settings. If you select a serial port, the Serial Port Settings window appears after you complete this screen.

Indent: The number of spaces Quicken indents when you print reports. The default is 0, meaning that the margin is at the left edge of the paper. Unless you encounter a problem, do not indent for checks. If you elect to indent, be sure to adjust Characters per line.

Lines per page: The number of lines per page on Quicken reports. This is simply the height of your paper times the number of lines your computer prints per inch. Since most computer paper is 11 inches high and most printers print 6 lines per inch, the correct entry is usually 66 (6 x 11 inches).

Print Pitch: This entry tells Quicken what how many characters per inch your computer will print when you write checks. This entry does *not* change your printer's pitch. To do that, you must enter control codes or make another selection from the Printer List.

Characters per line: The number of characters per line is your printer's pitch times the width of the paper. If your printer prints 10 characters per inch and use 8-inch-wide paper, for example, the correct setting is 80 (10 x 8 inches). If you use wide paper or elect to indent, adjust the calculation accordingly.

Pause between pages (Y/N): This entry should be set to N(o) if you use continuous computer paper or your printer is equipped with a sheet feeder. If you insert each page in your printer manually, change the setting to Y(es).

Page-oriented (e.g. laser) printer (Y/N): If you have a laser printer, this setting should be Y(es); otherwise, it should be N(o). This setting affects only check printing.

Supports IBM graphics characters (Y/N): If your printer can print IBM graph ics characters, Quicken will use them in report headings. Otherwise, headings will be separated by hyphens or equal signs. If you're not sure, set the heading to Y(es) and try printing a report. If odd symbols appear on the report, change the setting to N(o).

Serial Printer Settings

If you select a serial port (COM1: or COM2:) the Serial Port Settings window (Figure 13.9) appears when you complete the Printer Settings screen. This is technical information about how your computer communicates with your printer. You can get this information only from your printer manual.

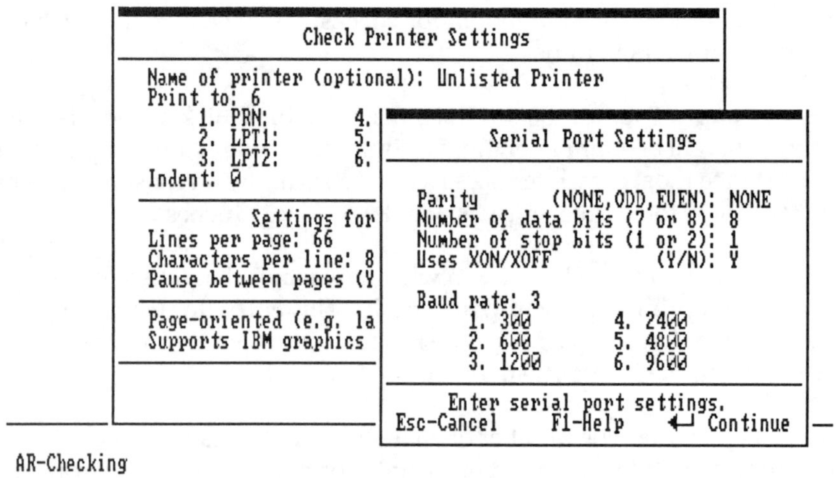

Figure 13.9. The Serial Port Settings window.

Setting Control Codes

If you select one of the printers listed on the Printer List, you don't have to enter control codes; they've already been set. However, if your printer isn't listed, you can use control codes to change type size and to take advantage of other special features, such as bold type.

Control codes are different for different printers, so you'll have to look them up in your printer manual. To set printer codes from the Printer Settings screen, press F9 to call up the Printer Control Codes window (Figure 13.10). The settings are described below. For Epson FX and similar printers, for example, the code for compressed mode (17 pitch) is \15, and the code for standard 10 pitch is \18. To print in condensed type, then, you would enter \15 for Before printing and \18 for After printing to return the printer to its normal setting.

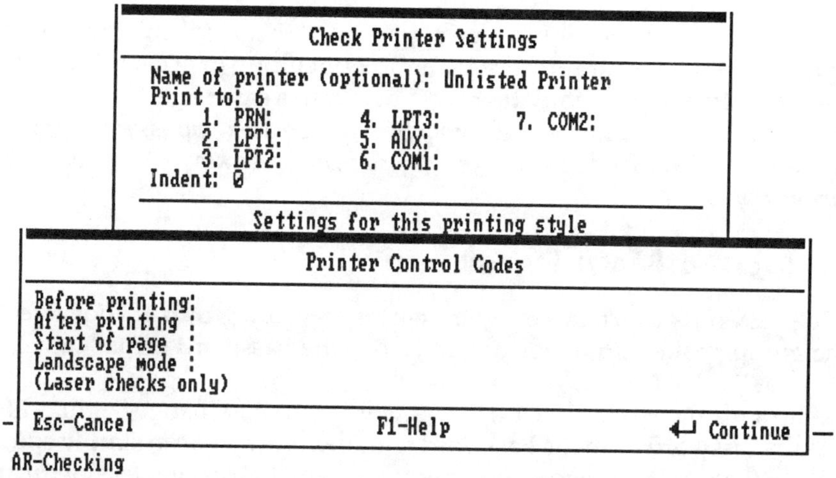

Figure 13.10. The Printer Control Codes window.

Before printing: Code sent before printing to determine type size or other characteristics.

After printing: Resets the printer to its normal mode. (The printer will continue to be governed by the first code until it receives another.)

Start of page: Some printers require a code at the beginning of each page, to activate a sheet feeder, for example. Most do not.

Landscape mode: For inserting checks sideways into laser printers. Otherwise, ignore.

PASSWORD

Quicken allows you to set up two kinds of password for controlling access to your financial records. The main password controls access to the current account group. If you have more than one account group, you can set up different passwords for each. A transaction password limits access to transactions recorded before a certain date. This will prevent unauthorized people from changing transactions for "closed" accounting periods, or those for which you have already printed permanent records. (In fact, it will prevent you from inadvertently changing such transactions yourself.)

NOTE: Once you set up either type of password there is absolutely no way to display it, even if you are already in the account group or accounting period it protects. Write the password down and save it in a safe place—and be doubly careful to avoid typographical errors when you create the password. *If you lose your password or record it incorrectly, you may be locked out of your records permanently.*

Setting Up a Main Password

The main password governs access to the current account group. If you have more than one group, make certain you are in the one the password is for.

To set up a main password, select 5. Password from the Change Settings Menu, then 1. Main Password from the Password window. Now you can simply enter the password on the Set Up Password window. It can be up to 16 characters long; capital and lowercase letters are treated the same. Double check the spelling, then press Enter to record the password.

Quicken will now ask you for the password any time you open this account group. Losing your password will mean that you cannot get back into your own records.

Setting Up a Transaction Password

Transaction passwords are designed to protect transactions in periods for which you have already created permanent records. If you have already printed a quarterly report, for example, you will need to print an updated version it if you change transactions during the period.

In addition to a password, you will set the last date for which a password is required to make changes. For example, if you want to protect transactions through the first quarter of 1989, you would enter 3/31/89. You will still be able to review transactions before the password date, but Quicken will ask for the password when you record a revised transaction.

To set up a transaction password, select 5. Password from the Change Settings Menu, then 2. Transaction Password from the Password window. When the Set Up Password window appears, type the password (up to 16 characters, with no distinction between upper and lowercase). Double check the spelling, then press Enter. On the next line, enter a date (or press Enter to confirm the current date). Quicken records the password.

From now on, Quicken will ask for the transaction password whenever you record changes in a transaction recorded before the cutoff date. Be sure to write down the password and put it in a safe place. If you lose it, you will not be able to change the transactions it covers.

Removing and Changing Passwords

To change or remove a main password or a transaction password, you basically repeat the process of setting it up. You can update the cutoff date for a transaction password the same way.

To change a password, select 5. Password from the Change Settings Menu, then 1. Main Password or 2. Transaction Password from the next window. In the designated blank of the Change Password window, type in the old password and press Enter. The next blank asks for New Password. To change the password, type the new password and press Enter. To remove it, leave New Password blank and press Enter. Finally, for a transaction password only, you can enter a new date. When the Change Settings Menu reappears, your changes are in place.

Other Settings

Other Settings, the last option on the Change Settings Menu, allows you to change the way Quicken responds in certain situations. You may want to experiment with the program before changing these settings. You can readjust them at any time.

When you select this option, an Other Settings window appears (Figure 13.11.) Most of the options are a matter of personal preference. Use Tab to move forward and Shift-Tab to move back. You can change any setting by typing a new entry. The settings are described below.

```
                     Other Settings

  1.  Beep when recording and memorizing (Y/N): Y
  2.  Request confirmation (for example,
           when changing the Register) (Y/N)  : Y
  3.  Require Category on transactions (Y/N)  : N
  4.  Extra message line on check (printed
           on check but not recorded) (Y/N)   : N
  5.  Days in advance to remind of postdated
           checks and scheduled groups (0-30) : 3
  6.  Change date of checks to today's date
      when printed (Y/N)                      : N
  7.  MM/DD/YY or DD/MM/YY date format (M/D)  : M
  8.  Billminder active (Y/N)                 : Y
  9.  Print categories on voucher checks (Y/N): Y
  10. 43 line register/reports (EGA,VGA) (Y/N): N
  11. Show Memo/Category/Both    (M/C/B)      : B
  12. In reports, use category Description/
           Name/Both (D/N/B)                  : D

 Esc-Cancel              F1-Help           ↵ Continue
AR-Checking
```

Figure 13.11. The Other Settings window.

1. **Beep when recording and memorizing (Y/N):** When this option is set to Y(es), Quicken makes a beeping sound whenever you record data.

2. **Require confirmation (for example, when changing the Register) (Y/N):** When set to Y(es), Quicken will ask "OK to record?" whenever you record new information. Setting this option to No saves keystrokes, especially when you are entering information in the Check Register. The disadvantage is that the program will not remind you to check your information for errors before recording it.

3. **Require Category on transactions (Y/N):** When this option is set to N(o) (the default), you can freely record transactions without assigning them to categories (or transfer accounts). This may be the best choice if you use Quicken mainly to print checks and balance your checkbook, with relatively few categorized transactions (tax-related expenses, for example).

For business records, or more advanced personal financial management, you will probably want to categorize all or most of your transactions. If you change the setting to Y(es), Quicken will warn you if you try to record a transaction without assigning a category or transfer account. This helps keep you from leaving a transaction uncategorized inadvertently. You still have the option of recording the transaction without a category.

4. **Extra message line on check (printed on check but not recorded) (Y/N)** : When set to Y(es), this option allows you to write an extra message (in addition to a memo) on your Quicken checks. The extra message will be printed to the right of the address box on the check. You can include an extra message in a memorized transaction, but it will not be recorded in the Register.

5. **Days in advance to remind of postdated checks and scheduled groups (0-30):** If you use Quicken's Billminder feature, the program will remind you of up coming bills you have recorded as postdated checks and of transaction groups you have designated to recall at certain intervals.

   This option sets the number of days in advance that the program gives you a reminder. It should be set so that you are reminded of all checks to print before the next time you use your computer. Thus, if you use your computer every day (except weekends), you can set days in advance to 0; you will be reminded only of bills currently due. However, you will want to see all of the bills due within the next six days if you use your computer only once a week, or for the next 30 days if you use your computer only once a month. The default setting is 3.

6. **Change date of checks to today's date when printed (Y/N):**You should leave this option set to N(o) if you sometimes print a batch of postdated checks to be mailed over several days. If you change the setting to Y(es), the date on all checks will be changed to the current date.

7. **MM/DD/YY or DD/MM/YY date format (M/D):** The default setting, M(onth), displays June 16, 1989 as 6/16/89. If you change the setting to D(ate), Quicken switches to the European style 16/6/89.

8. **Billminder active (Y/N):**This setting is applicable only to computers with hard disks. If it is set to Y(es), Quicken reminds you of checks to print at the DOS prompt whenever you boot up your computer, even if you do not use Quicken in the current session. If it is set to N(o), Billminder still reminds you of checks due when you start the program, but not at the DOS prompt. On floppy drive computers, the reminder appears when you start Quicken.

9. **Print categories on voucher checks (Y/N):**This setting applies only to split transactions on voucher checks. When it is set to Y(es), both categories and descriptions entered in the Split Transaction window are printed on the voucher. When it is set to N(o), the description is printed, but not the category.

10. **43 line register/reports (EGA,VGA) (Y/N)**: If you have a high resolution monitor (EGA or VGA), set this option to Y(es) if you want Quicken to display twelve transactions on the Register rather than six. This option also allows you to see more of your reports on the screen at once. You cannot use this feature with other types of monitors.

11. **Show Memo/Category/Both (M/C/B)**: This setting the information displayed on the second line of each transaction in the Register when the transaction is not highlighted. When set to B(oth), the default setting, both the memo and category are displayed. (If they are long, they may be truncated.) You can change the setting to M(emo) to display only the memo or C(ategory) to display only the category.

12. **In reports, use category Description/Name/Both (D/N/B)**:This option determines how categories and classes appear in reports. When it is set to D(escription), the default, Quicken uses the description, if there is one, or the category or class name if there is not. If you select N(ame) reports will include category and class names and leave out descriptions. If you choose B(oth), both will appear.

Conclusion

Unlike many programs, Quicken requires almost no set up other than making a working copy of the program or installing it on your hard disk. However, the Change Settings Menu gives you the tools to tailor the program to your computer, printer, and personal preferences. For the most part, you will not need to change these settings once you are satisfied with the program's operation.

The selection you will use most often is Account Group Activities. If you have more than one account group, you will use it whenever you switch groups. And even if you have only one account group, you should use the back up option regularly to avoid losing valuable data in the event of a computer or disk disaster.

INDEX